IMAGES
of America

HOBE SOUND

On the Cover: Hobe Sound Beach is considered one of the most pristine beaches on the Treasure Coast. The beach has been able to maintain its wild beauty over the centuries, and is a favorite spot for both residents and visitors. This photograph captures the essence of a Sunday afternoon relaxing with friends and family. The image is from a postcard from 1950. (Author's collection.)

IMAGES
of America

HOBE SOUND

Jennifer Gilliland

ARCADIA
PUBLISHING

ISBN 978-1-4671-0888-1

Published by Arcadia Publishing
Charleston, South Carolina

Printed in the United States of America

Library of Congress Control Number: 2022939475

For all general information, please contact Arcadia Publishing:
Telephone 843-853-2070
Fax 843-853-0044
E-mail sales@arcadiapublishing.com
For customer service and orders:
Toll-Free 1-888-313-2665

Visit us on the Internet at www.arcadiapublishing.com

The book is dedicated first and foremost to my husband, Eric, daughter Piper, and Ana, my foreign exchange student who spent the year with us here in Hobe Sound. This project would not have been possible without their support, encouragement, and understanding over the last 10 months. In addition, I would like to thank all of the residents of Hobe Sound who offered encouragement and excitement for the project since its inception.

Contents

Acknowledgments

Special thanks go out to all the research librarians, staff, and volunteers at the University of Florida, Martin County Historical Society, Stuart Heritage Museum, and State Archives of Florida who spent countless hours helping me research our beautiful town. Linda Geary of the Elliott Museum was invaluable and kind with her time and assistance. Local historian Sandra Thurlow was most gracious with her knowledge and collections. Additional thanks to the Apollo School Foundation and Kathy Spurgeon, Whitney Pidot Sr., Annie Pettway, the Town of Jupiter Island, University of Texas, Ford House Museum, Andrew Foster, Theodore Morris, Jacksonville Historical Society, and the University of Wisconsin–Madison.

INTRODUCTION

Florida—the name elicits images of sandy beaches, blowing palm trees, puffy cumulus clouds, and warm ocean breezes. It has enticed and entranced people from all walks of life since the 1500s. This is the story of one of the Treasure Coast's hidden gems. Hobe Sound is a small town between Jupiter and Stuart, both of which are thriving Florida towns frequently listed as top tourist and retirement destinations. Hobe Sound includes Jupiter Island, one of the wealthiest zip codes in America (33455). Jupiter Island has been home to some of the oldest families in America, including Ford, DuPont, Bush, and Firestone, as well as the vacation spot of past presidents, including Harding, Bush, and Cleveland. Today, it is one of the most exclusive beachfront islands in America. Seclusion is a treasured commodity.

One would think that Hobe Sound, given its prime location, would have developed along with its sister cities; however, amongst all the unavoidable development, to some degree it has managed to protect and maintain its quaint "Old Florida" feel. It is a community, both on the island and on the mainland, where neighbors know their neighbors, kids ride their bikes and skateboards to the beach, children walk to school, and families can be seen walking their dogs after dinner each night. The story presented in this publication is merely a highlight of its early years, its transition through different names in the early 1900s, its agricultural history, recreation and leisure activities of residents and visitors, and some newsworthy events that affected the town. Hopefully, this will encourage residents and visitors alike to look around, dig through their photo albums, share stories, and inspire the next generation to capture their family memories before they are lost.

Interestingly, Hobe Sound has a history that includes Native Americans, shipwrecks, development due to Henry Flagler's famous railroad, the winter home of famous American "Titans of Industry," an artist enclave, a producer's vision for a motion picture studio to rival California, and home to Camp Murphy during World War II.

The first chapter highlights the early years of Hobe Sound. References to the sound date to 1669, when it was called Ho-bay Sound. Ho-bay is thought to be a deviation of Jobe, which was the name of the local indigenous people who have lived here for centuries. In 1669, a British merchant ship sailed from Jamaica en route to Philadelphia when it encountered a hurricane and ended up shipwrecked in Hobe Sound. On board were 250 passengers, including Jonathan Dickinson and his family along with beef, molasses, rum, and sugar. Dickinson went on to describe his experience with the local Jobe Indians in his now-famous *Jonathan Dickinson's Journal: A True Story of Shipwreck and Torture on the Florida Coast in 1696*. What was Camp Murphy is now Jonathan Dickinson State Park.

In 1763, all of Florida was acquired by the English after the Ango-Spanish War, then ceded back to Spain after the American Revolution in 1783. In 1790, the Spanish monarch offered land grants as rewards and as encouragement to settle the new colony. One such person was Don Eusebio Gomez, a Spanish merchant involved in the colonization of St. Augustine. As part of his grant, 12,000 acres would become Jupiter Island and an additional 8,000 acres would become mainland Hobe Sound. Gomez is a well-known street that runs along the Intracoastal Waterway and is on the island today.

Over the next 150 years, the land changed hands multiple times. In 1892, a group of Gomez's heirs formed the Indian River Pineapple and Coconut Growers Association. They hoped to form a pineapple plantation. Today, pineapples still flourish in the area. The boom came in 1895 when Henry Flagler brought his railroad through Hobe Sound on its way south to Palm Beach Island and Miami. Over the next several decades, Hobe Sound flourished as an agricultural center with an inn being built, people moving to the area, businesses arising, and investors advertising the beautiful water to their friends back north. Travel was still primarily by boat in the area, through the rivers and tributaries, across the Indian River Lagoon, and along the beaches, but the railroad stop was key to growth. The Trade and Transportation chapter highlights the agricultural background and travel in the 19th and 20th centuries.

By the early 20th century, the area was becoming known as a wonderful vacation spot with great weather and fishing; more people were traveling south to explore Florida. The Olympia Improvement Company was created to entice people to invest in real estate in the area. Due to its close proximity to Palm Beach, the area was rich in opportunity and development. A New York actor, Joseph Jefferson, who had visited family, left with a vision and a desire to create an enclave for creative artists in Hobe Sound. He hoped to rename the area Jeffersonville; however, the community never materialized. In the 1920s, another group wanted to create a "Hollywood of the South" and sought to entice actors, directors, and others to relocate to the area. The Olympia and Picture City chapter traces the rise and fall of both visions from 1900 to 1933.

Recreation and leisure go hand in hand in Florida, and Hobe Sound is no different. It has provided a varied selection of activities since its earliest days—boating, sailing, fishing, golfing, hunting, camping, swimming, snorkeling, and surfing to name a few. The Recreation and Leisure chapter attempts to share the fun-filled days that individuals and families have enjoyed over the centuries in this beautiful place. Finally, all towns have newsworthy events that capture the interest of the residents at the time. The final chapter highlights a few of the more memorable events in the town's history.

Hobe Sound is a special place with its own story among all the other towns along the Treasure Coast. It is a community rich in history and natural beauty, and many who come to visit never leave.

One

The Early Years

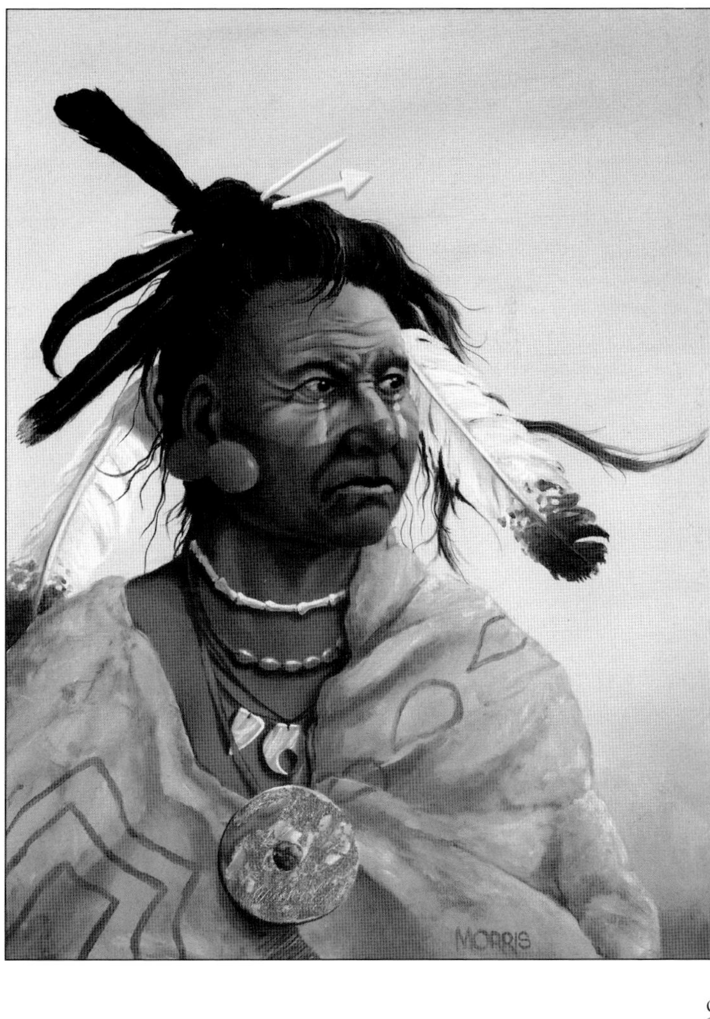

Native residents have been in the Hobe Sound area for centuries, with the first documented encounters in the 1500s with Spanish explorers. While the Jaega had learned to live with Spanish explorers, their lives started to change significantly when Jonathan Dickinson, a Quaker merchant sailing from Jamaica to Philadelphia, found himself shipwrecked here and documented his experiences in a diary. Hobe Sound was a name written in the annals of history—a place rugged and remote but with unsurpassed beauty. (Courtesy of Theodore Morris.)

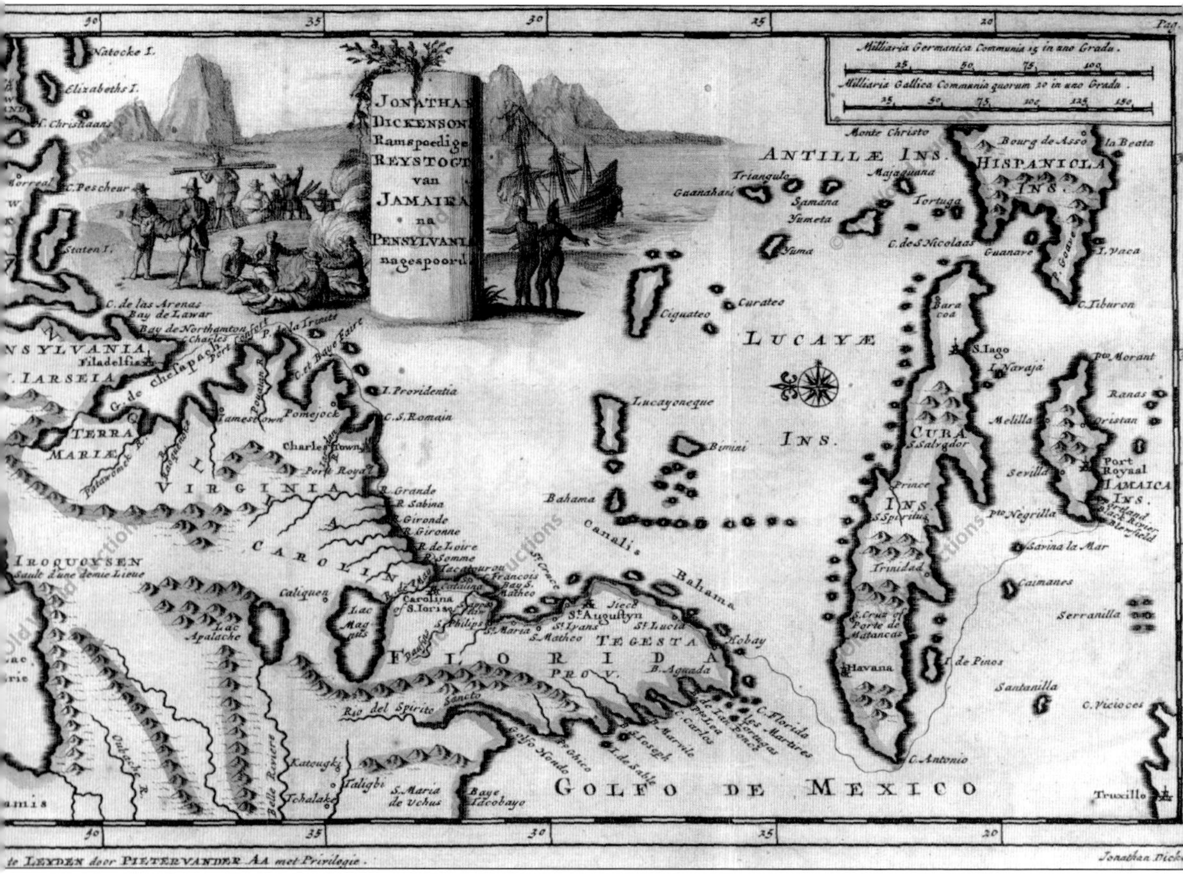

Pictured is the 1706 "Jonathan Dickinson Captivity Narrative and Map of Florida, Carolina, Virginia, and Cuba." "Ho-bay" is the origin of the name Hobe Sound. It was inhabited by the Ais, the most powerful tribe on the Treasure Coast. Their capital at that time is believed to have been a town called Jece near Pelican Island In Indian River County, and their empire included the Jaega Tribe in and around Jupiter Inlet. To most explorers at the time, the Treasure Coast was little more than a shadowy land of danger, a place where unlucky travelers shipwrecked and disappeared forever. Sailing ships were no match for storms with surging waves, and to travel the Gulf Stream was to roll the dice and face a chance of dying on the reefs. (Courtesy of the Martin County Historical Society.)

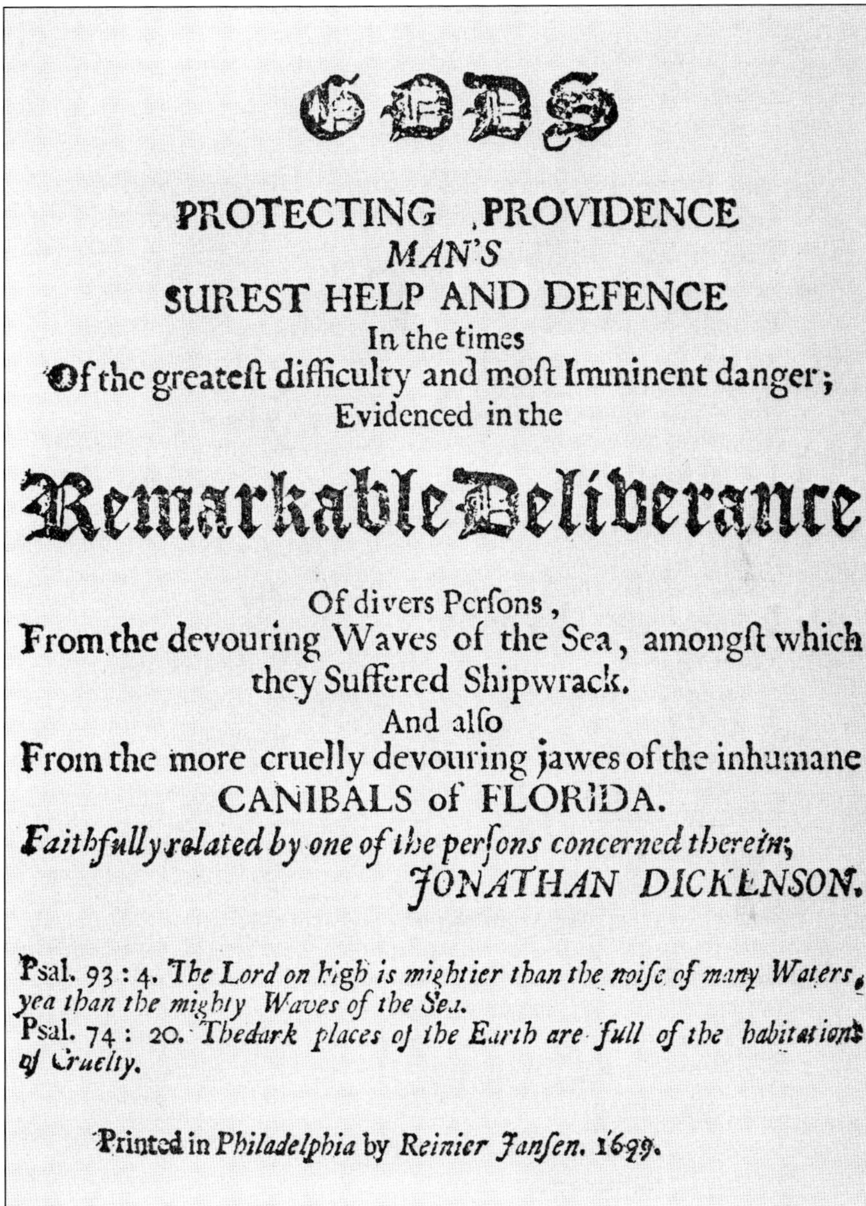

GODS

PROTECTING PROVIDENCE

MAN'S

SUREST HELP AND DEFENCE

In the times

Of the greateſt difficulty and moſt Imminent danger;

Evidenced in the

Remarkable Deliverance

Of divers Perſons,

From the devouring Waves of the Sea, amongſt which they Suffered Shipwrack.

And alſo

From the more cruelly devouring jawes of the inhumane CANIBALS of FLORIDA.

Faithfully related by one of the perſons concerned therein;

JONATHAN DICKENSON.

Psal. 93 : 4. *The Lord on high is mightier than the noiſe of many Waters, yea than the mighty Waves of the Sea.*

Psal. 74 : 20. *The dark places of the Earth are full of the habitations of Cruelty.*

Printed in *Philadelphia* by *Reinier Janſen.* 1699.

On September 3, 1696, the ship *Reformation* wrecked off the coast of Florida near present-day Hobe Sound. Onboard was Quaker merchant Jonathan Dickinson, traveling from Port Royal, Jamaica, to Philadelphia with his family. The shipwrecked survivors were harassed and at times held captive by the Ais and the Jaega. Dickinson and the other survivors traveled north along the undeveloped coast, finally reaching St. Augustine on November 15. The Spanish helped the party travel north to Charleston, South Carolina, and from there to Philadelphia. Dickinson wrote a journal of his ordeal as a castaway and captive, which was first published in 1699 as *God's Protecting Providence*. It is one of the earliest detailed accounts of Native American life in this part of Florida during the late 17th century and continues to be a resource for both historians and anthropologists. The State of Florida named a park near the shipwreck site in Martin County after Dickinson. It opened in 1950. (Courtesy of Florida State Archives.)

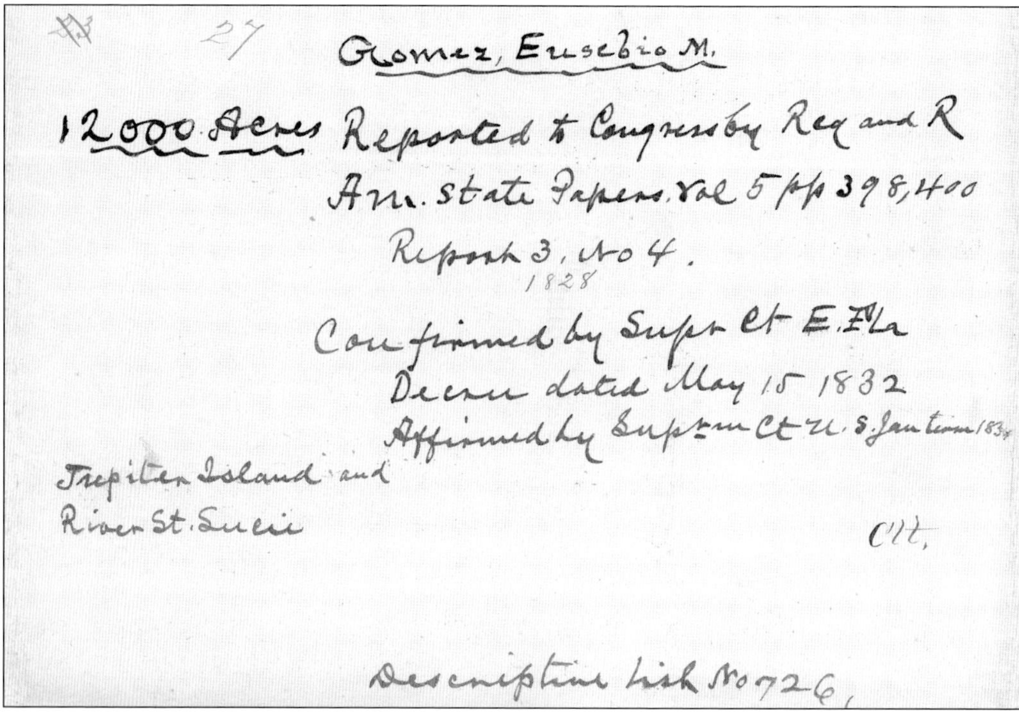

27

Gomez, Eusebio M.

12000 Acres Reported to Congress by Reg and R

Am. State Papers, Vol 5 pp 398, 400

Report 3, No 4.

1828

Confirmed by Supr Ct E. Fla

Decree dated May 15 1832

Affirmed by Supm Ct U.S. Jan term 183[illegible]

Jupiter Island and

River St. Lucie

Ct.

Descriptive List No 726.

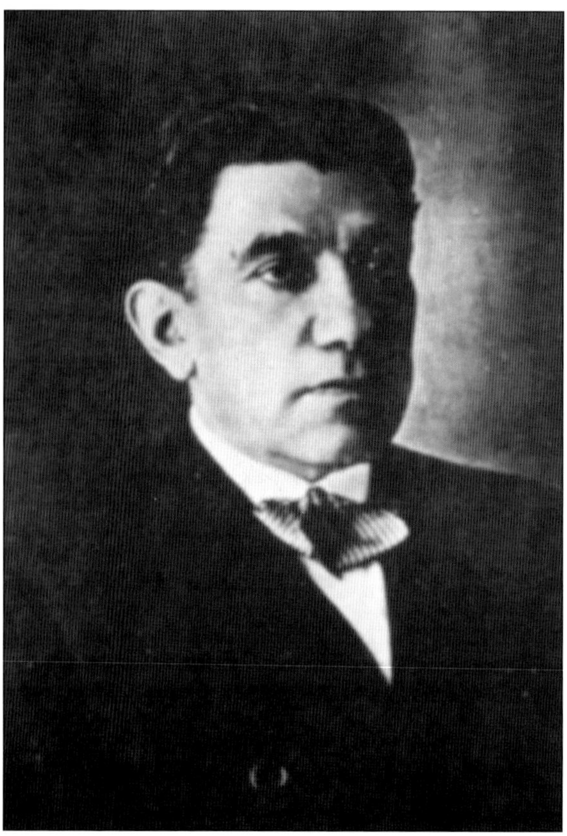

In 1790, Spain offered grants of land to certain individuals as a reward and to encourage settlement in the Florida colony. For services to the crown, Don Eusebio Gomez, a merchant-shipper and defender of St. Augustine, was one such land grantee in 1815. His royal grant of 12,000 acres included what would be Jupiter Island and an 8,000-acre tract of land on the mainland, Hobe Sound. The United States agreed to honor these land grants when it gained control of the territory, provided that they were shown to be valid. However, it took Eusebio Gomez and his family 20 years and a decision by the US Supreme Court to verify his rightful ownership. (Above, courtesy of the P.K. Yonge Library of Florida History, Special and Area Studies Collections, George A. Smathers Libraries, University of Florida; left, courtesy of Library of Congress.)

George Chapin stated, "From the top of the ridge a magnificent view is had of the gorgeous sunrises, which in this section, paint the skies with hues of such brilliancy as are rarely found elsewhere. It is indeed a land of unmatched beauty whose fascinations tempt the lover of nature to linger." Seen here is a view of the Hobe Sound side of Jupiter Island in 1913. (Courtesy of the P.K. Yonge Library of Florida History, Special and Area Studies Collections, George A. Smathers Libraries, University of Florida.)

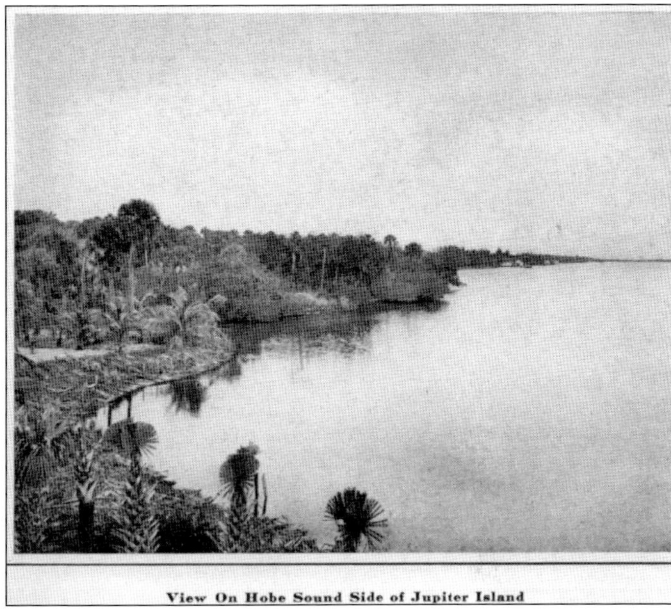

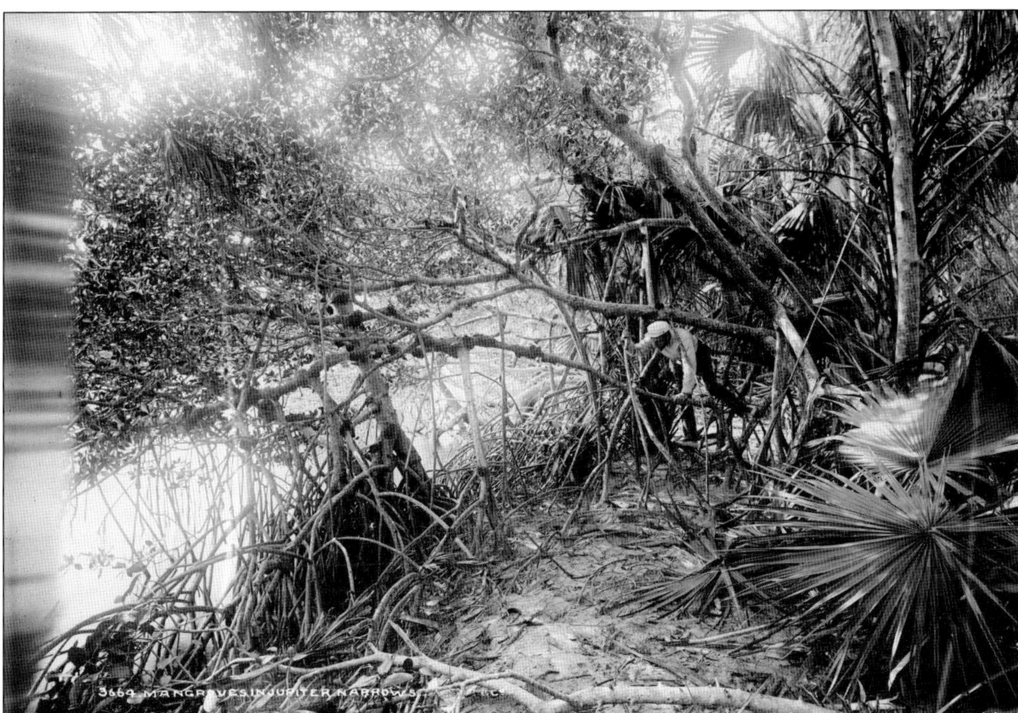

Mangrove forests are important habitats along the shoreline of the Indian River Lagoon. Mangrove trees provide food and shelter for many animals, above the water and below. Their root systems create a great hiding place for fish, crabs, and shrimp. In 1996, the Florida legislature enacted the Mangrove Trimming and Preservation Act to limit mangrove removal by landowners in order to protect Florida's remaining mangrove forests. See here is a photograph by William Henry Jackson of the untouched mangroves in and around Hobe Sound in the late 19th century. (Courtesy of Library of Congress.)

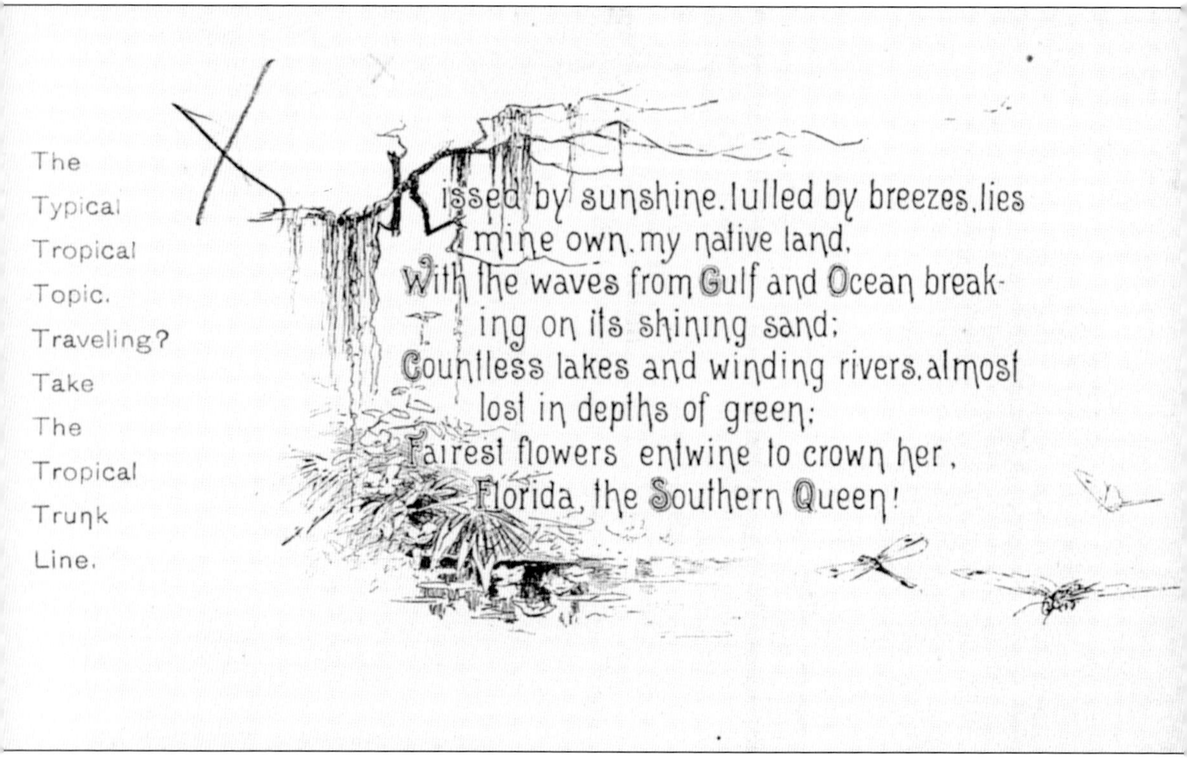

The Indian River Lagoon holds a special place in the hearts of people who have spent time in its waters, grew up along its banks, or who have visited. Local historian Sandra Thurlow stated, "I believe the people coming down to Florida in the late 1800s and early 1900s were looking for a kind of rebirth. They were leaving the cold industrialization of the north for 'paradise.' " Seen here is the booklet *Song of the Indian River Lagoon*, by Ada Stewart Shelton, published in 1890. (Courtesy of the P.K. Yonge Library of Florida History, Special and Area Studies Collections, George A. Smathers Libraries, University of Florida.)

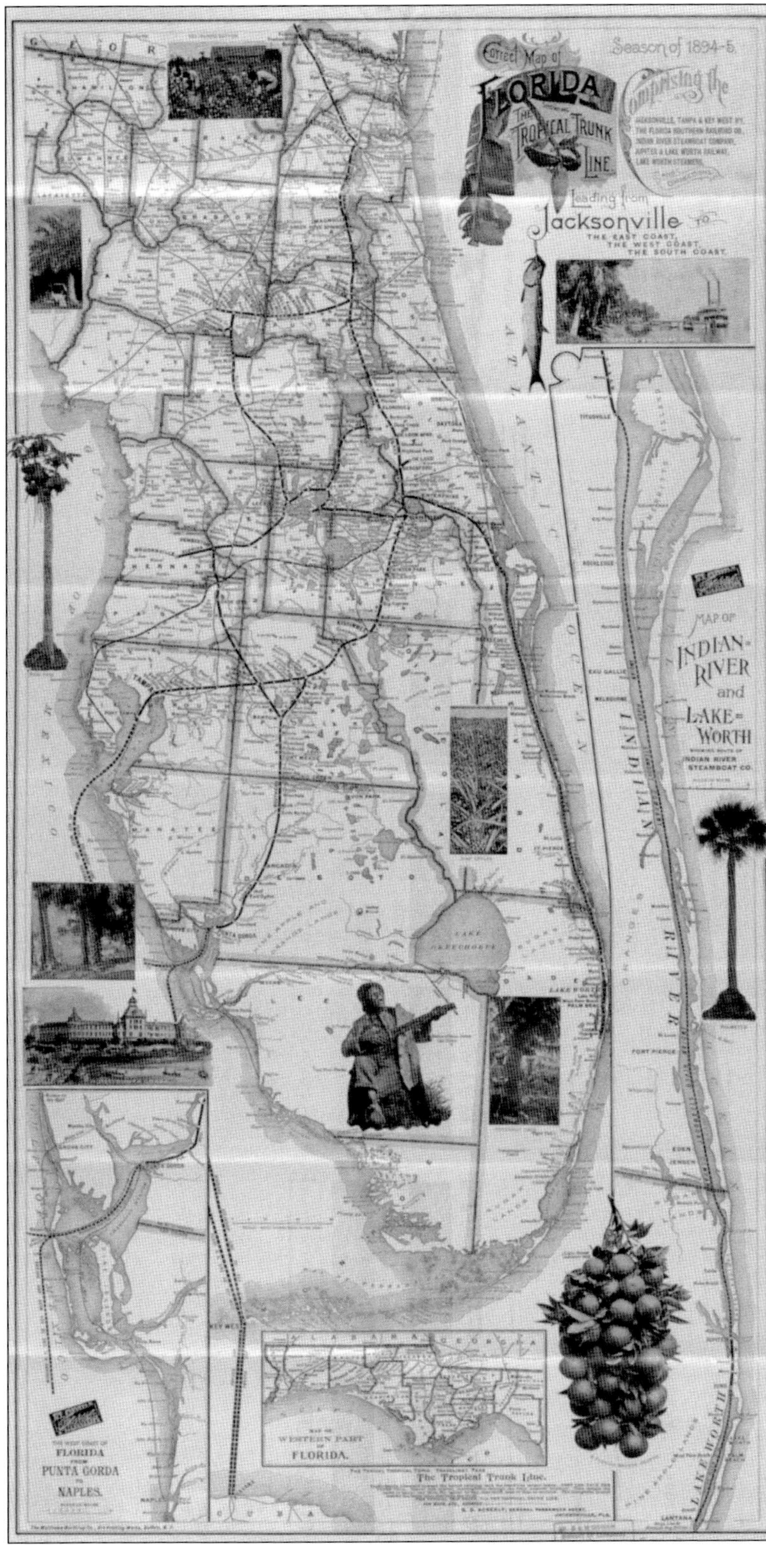

This Tropical Trunk Line advertisement from 1896 highlights the railroad options throughout the state. In addition, it features all the great things about Florida, from its trees to its tropical fruit and many other riches. The hope was to encourage people from the north to visit via railroad. (Courtesy of the P.K. Yonge Library of Florida History, Special and Area Studies Collections, George A. Smathers Libraries, University of Florida.)

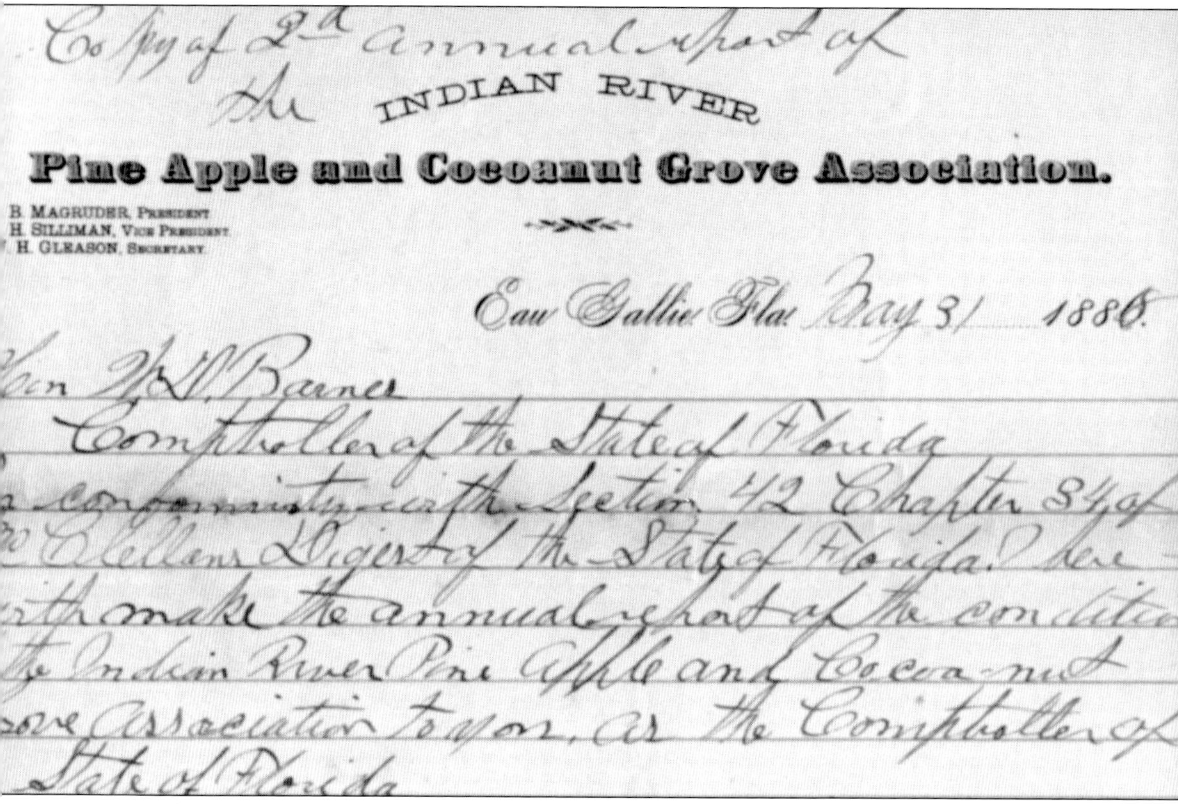
Copy of 2d annual report of the

INDIAN RIVER

Pine Apple and Cocoanut Grove Association.

B. MAGRUDER, PRESIDENT
H. SILLIMAN, VICE PRESIDENT
H. GLEASON, SECRETARY

Eau Gallie Fla. May 31 1886.

Hon W. D. Barnes
Comptroller of the State of Florida
In conformity with Section 42 Chapter 84 of McClellans Digest of the State of Florida I here-with make the annual report of the condition of the Indian River Pine Apple and Cocoanut Grove Association to you, as the Comptroller of State of Florida

It is not known if Don Eusebio Gomez ever visited the land granted to him. He sold 8,000 acres, excluding Jupiter Island, to Joseph Delespine for $1 an acre. The following year, Delespine disposed of half the acreage to Michael Lazarus for $4,000. Two years later, Lazarus sold all interest in his 4,000 undeveloped acres for only $50,000. Gomez left Florida for Cuba with 4,000 granted acres, including Jupiter Island, unsold. In 1892–1893, a group of Englishmen bought land from Don Eusebio Gomez's heirs, intending to develop a pineapple plantation, the Indian River Pineapple and Coconut Growers Association. This was not an easy purchase, as they were forced to establish the validity of the title to the land like many other Spanish land grant assignees. (Courtesy of the P.K. Yonge Library of Florida History, Special and Area Studies Collections, George A. Smathers Libraries, University of Florida.)

In 1892, a second group of English investors, acting through the Land Bank of Yorkshire, bought property in northern Florida as well as 4,000 acres of the Gomez Grant from the pineapple growers. Unfortunately, a hard freeze in 1895 was not good for the pineapple crop and William Angas, a Scotsman, was put in charge of saving the investment. For 10 years, Angas, located in Jacksonville, Florida, oversaw the investment. At right is the original Articles of Incorporation, and below are the initial subscribers. (Both, courtesy of the P.K. Yonge Library of Florida History, Special and Area Studies Collections, George A. Smathers Libraries, University of Florida.)

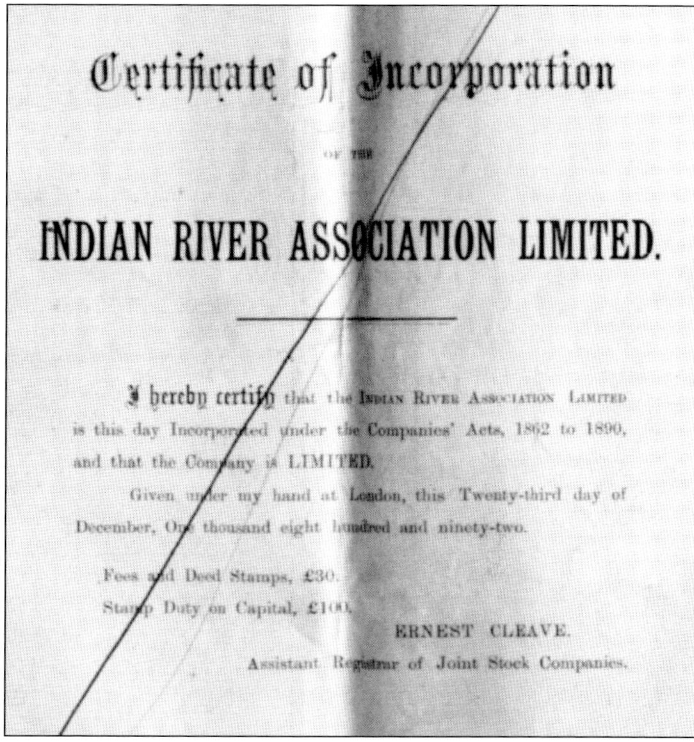

Certificate of Incorporation

OF THE

INDIAN RIVER ASSOCIATION LIMITED.

I hereby certify that the INDIAN RIVER ASSOCIATION LIMITED is this day Incorporated under the Companies' Acts, 1862 to 1890, and that the Company is LIMITED.

Given under my hand at London, this Twenty-third day of December, One thousand eight hundred and ninety-two.

Fees and Deed Stamps, £30.

Stamp Duty on Capital, £100.

ERNEST CLEAVE.

Assistant Registrar of Joint Stock Companies.

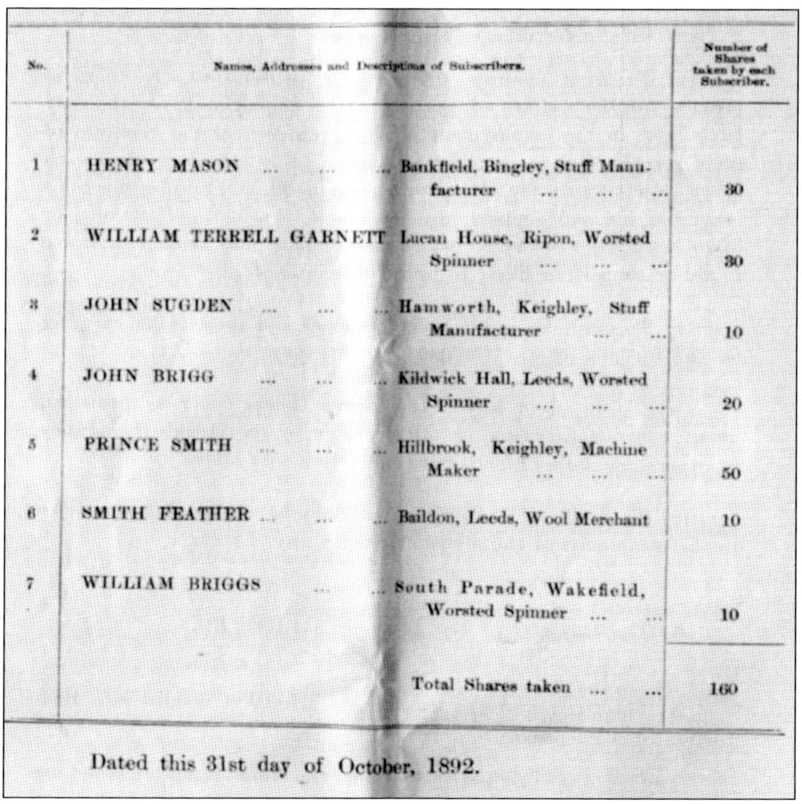

No.	Names, Addresses and Descriptions of Subscribers.		Number of Shares taken by each Subscriber.
1	HENRY MASON	Bankfield, Bingley, Stuff Manufacturer	30
2	WILLIAM TERRELL GARNETT	Lucan House, Ripon, Worsted Spinner	30
3	JOHN SUGDEN	Hamworth, Keighley, Stuff Manufacturer	10
4	JOHN BRIGG	Kildwick Hall, Leeds, Worsted Spinner	20
5	PRINCE SMITH	Hillbrook, Keighley, Machine Maker	50
6	SMITH FEATHER	Baildon, Leeds, Wool Merchant	10
7	WILLIAM BRIGGS	South Parade, Wakefield, Worsted Spinner	10
		Total Shares taken	160

Dated this 31st day of October, 1892.

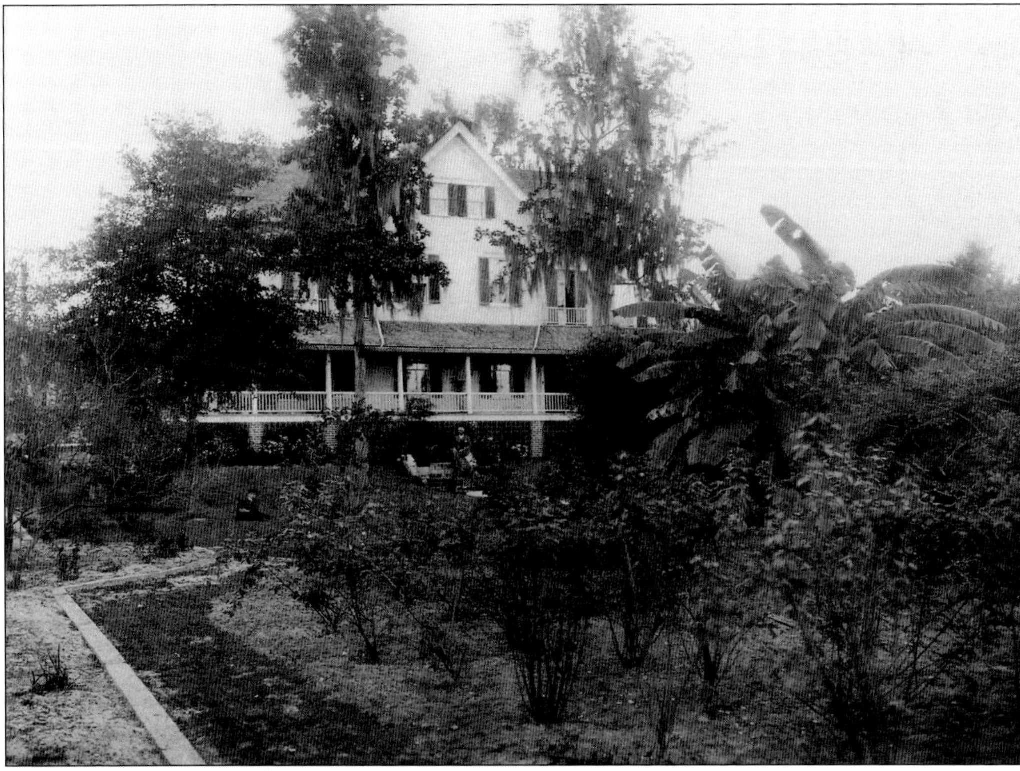

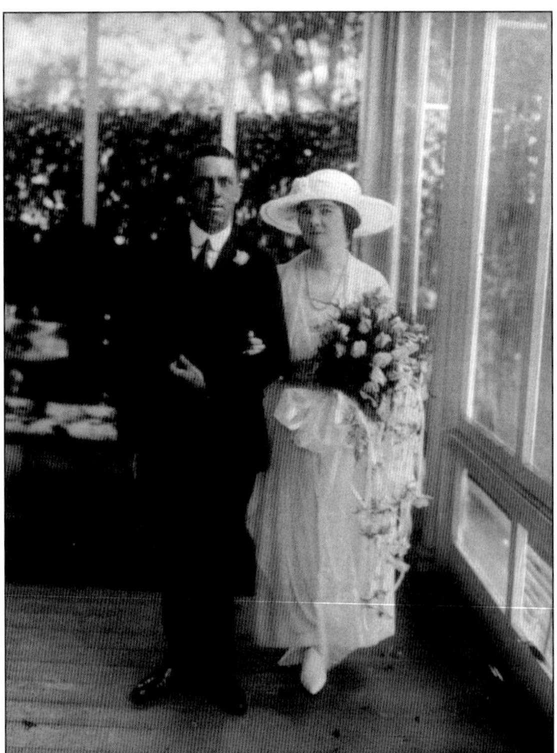

William Moore Angas came to Jacksonville in 1895 as a resident agent and manager for a group of British-owned companies interested in Florida real estate development, including the Indian River Association in Hobe Sound. For more than 50 years, he and his son Robert represented these companies along with smaller real estate and finance companies that backed brick production, citrus farming, forestry, and phosphate mining. Seen above is Angas's primary home in Jacksonville around 1905. The home still exists today as the Inn at Oak Street. At left is Robert Angas on April 14, 1919, when he married Inez Carson of Kissimmee, Florida. Inez was at one time the manager of the Jacksonville Beach Golf Links around 1930. (Both, courtesy of the Jacksonville Historical Society.)

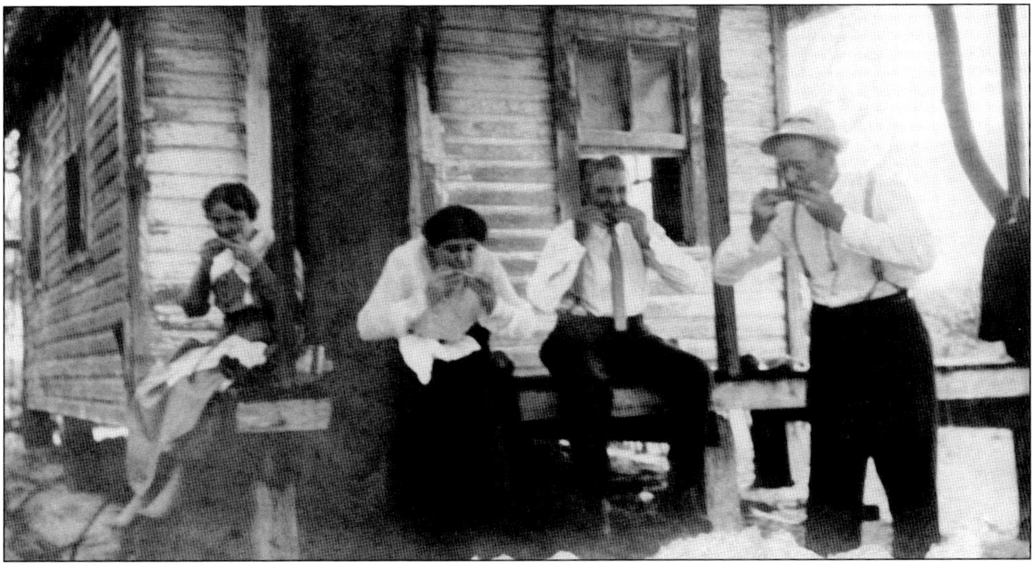

In the early 1900s, the United States was mostly agricultural and many families lived off the land, cultivating their own vegetable and herb gardens and raising their own livestock and poultry. Hunting and fishing provided wild game and other food sources. Meat was a mainstay of the 1908 American diet. Seen above is an unidentified Hobe Sound family enjoying a noon-day meal, most likely on a Sunday after church, based on their dress. Below is a 1920 home on Nassau Street that was originally built by the Indian River Association. (Both, courtesy of the Martin County Historical Society.)

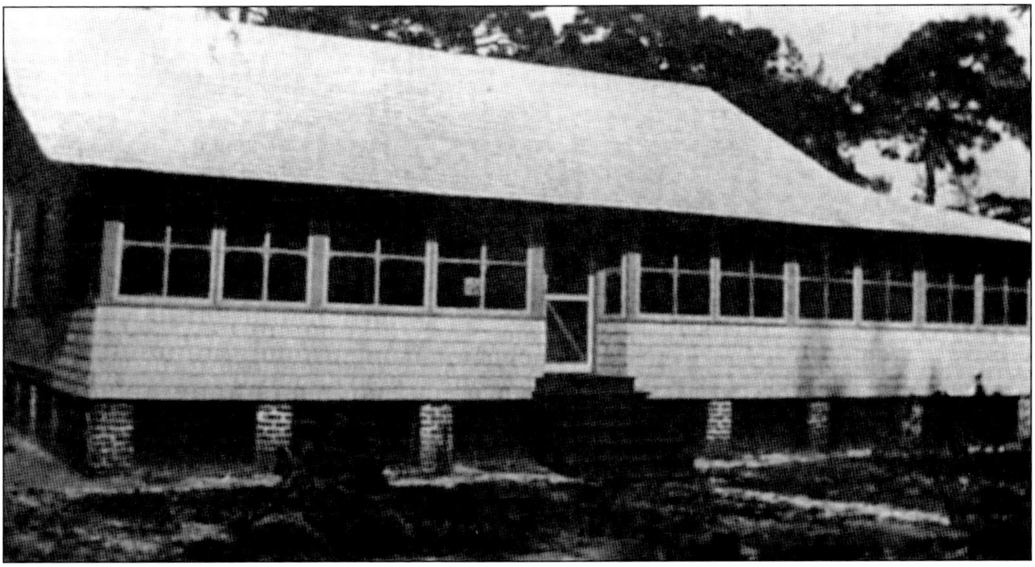

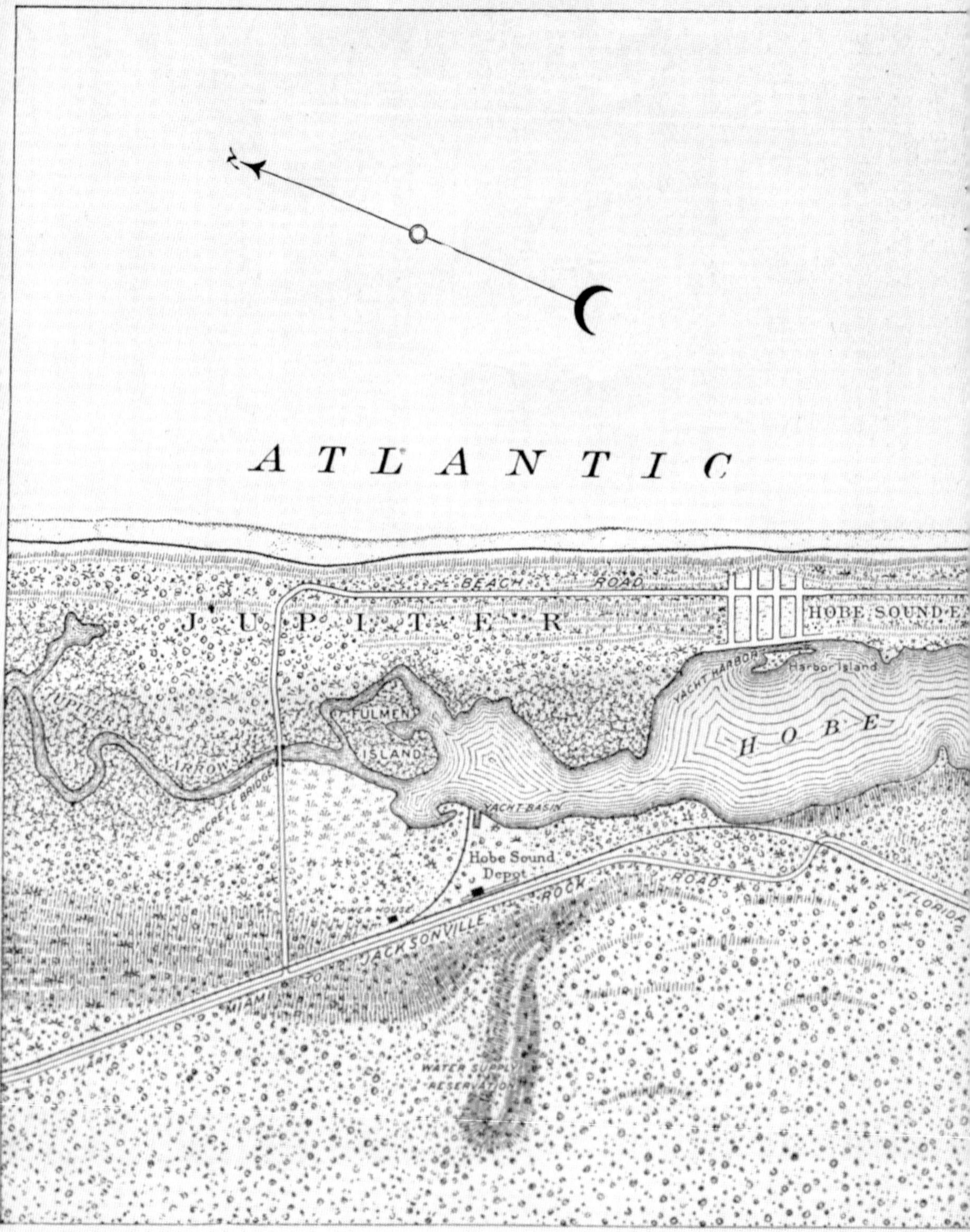
ATLANTIC
BEACH ROAD
JUPITER
HOBE SOUND E
YACHT HARBOR
Harbor Island
HOBE
FULMEN ISLAND
JUPITER
ARROWS
CONCRETE BRIDGE
YACHT BASIN
Hobe Sound Depot
POWER HOUSE
ROCK ROAD
FLORIDA
MIAMI TO JACKSONVILLE
TO STUART
WATER SUPPLY RESERVATION

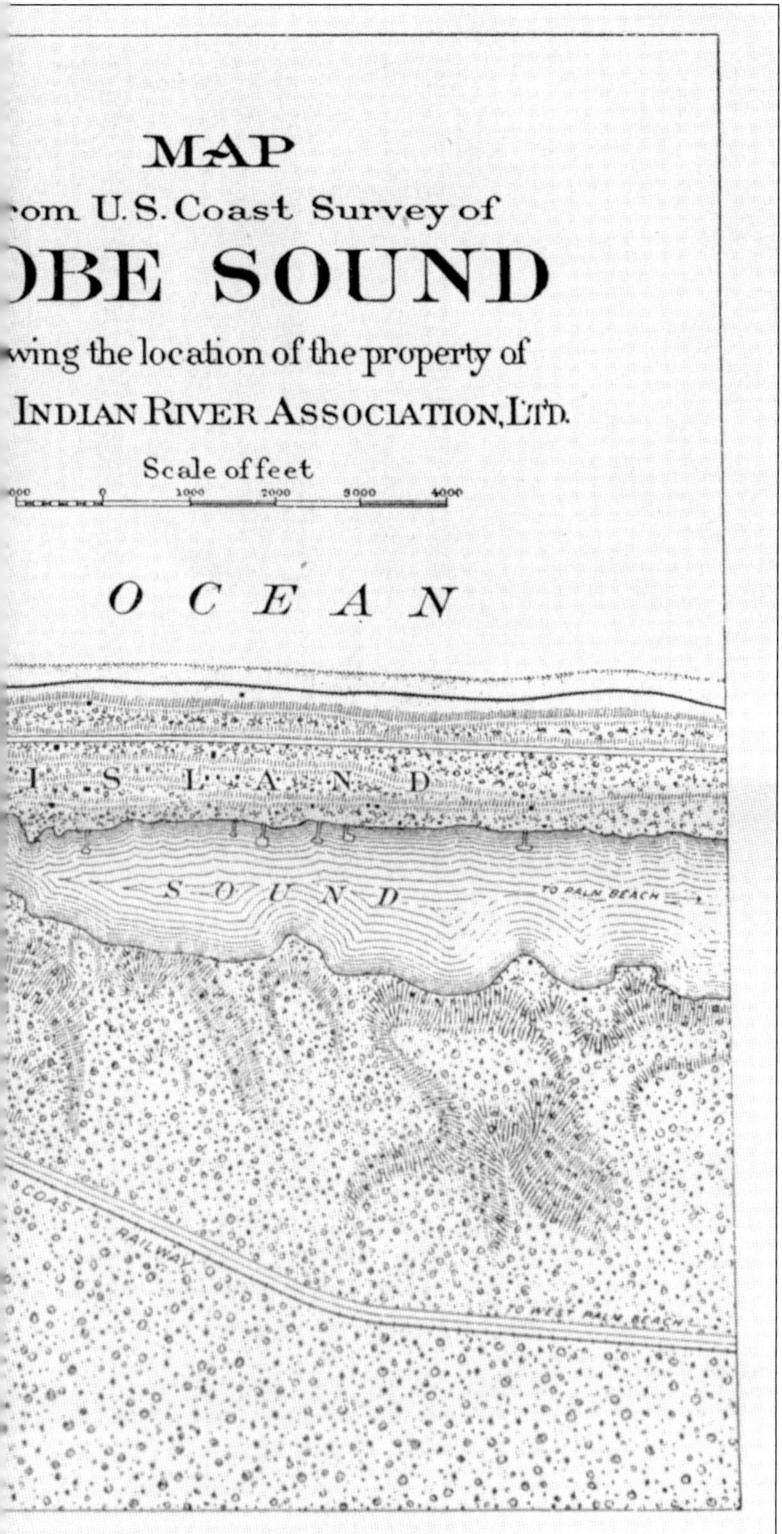

As shown on this coast survey map, the little town of Hobe Sound was at the north end of the sound and just south of Jupiter Narrows. Hobe Sound is 275 miles south of Jacksonville and 25 miles north of Palm Beach, centrally located between Jacksonville and Key West. Hobe Sound East is across the sound on Jupiter Island and about one mile south of the town of Hobe Sound. This map also shows the land owned by the Indian River Association and the outline of the small town in the late 1800s and early 1900s. (Courtesy of the P.K. Yonge Library of Florida History, Special and Area Studies Collections, George A. Smathers Libraries, University of Florida.)

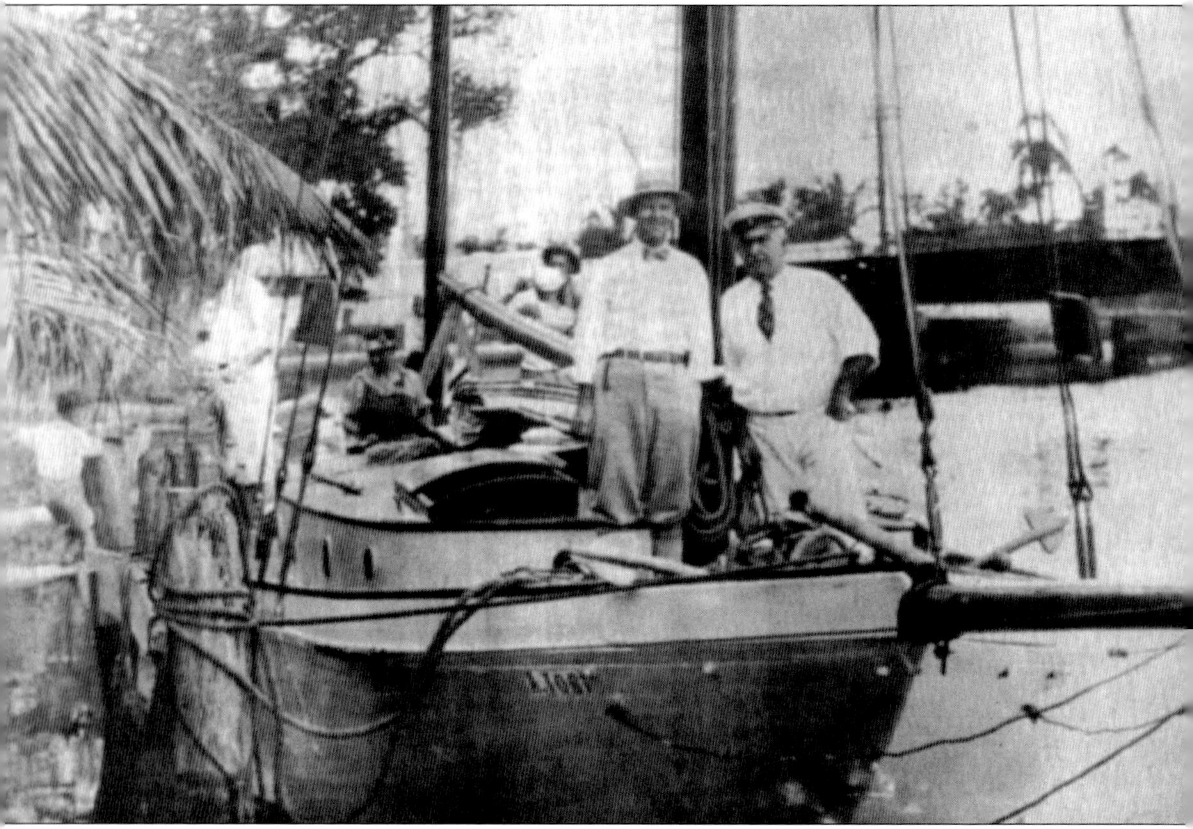

"Skipper" John Harvey Grant was born in London, England, in 1862. The family immigrated to America when John was 19, landing first in Boston. Seeking a better climate, they came to Jacksonville, where they settled. One holiday, Grant and two young friends decided to sail down the east coast of Florida in a small sailboat. Upon reaching Jupiter, they camped out and encountered "Ma Carlin," who fed the boys beans and bread. They decided to stay. Grant joined the lifesaving crew, bought land in Jupiter, and started homesteading at Sugden (now Hobe Sound). He was a county commissioner and even commodore of the Jupiter Yacht Club. Hobe Sound had one of the earliest yacht clubs on the east coast of Florida. Seen here on the right is Skipper Grant in a casual pose on the Sea Scout boat *Companion*. Later, motor launches replaced the picturesque, but slow, sailboats. (Courtesy of the Broward County Historical Commission.)

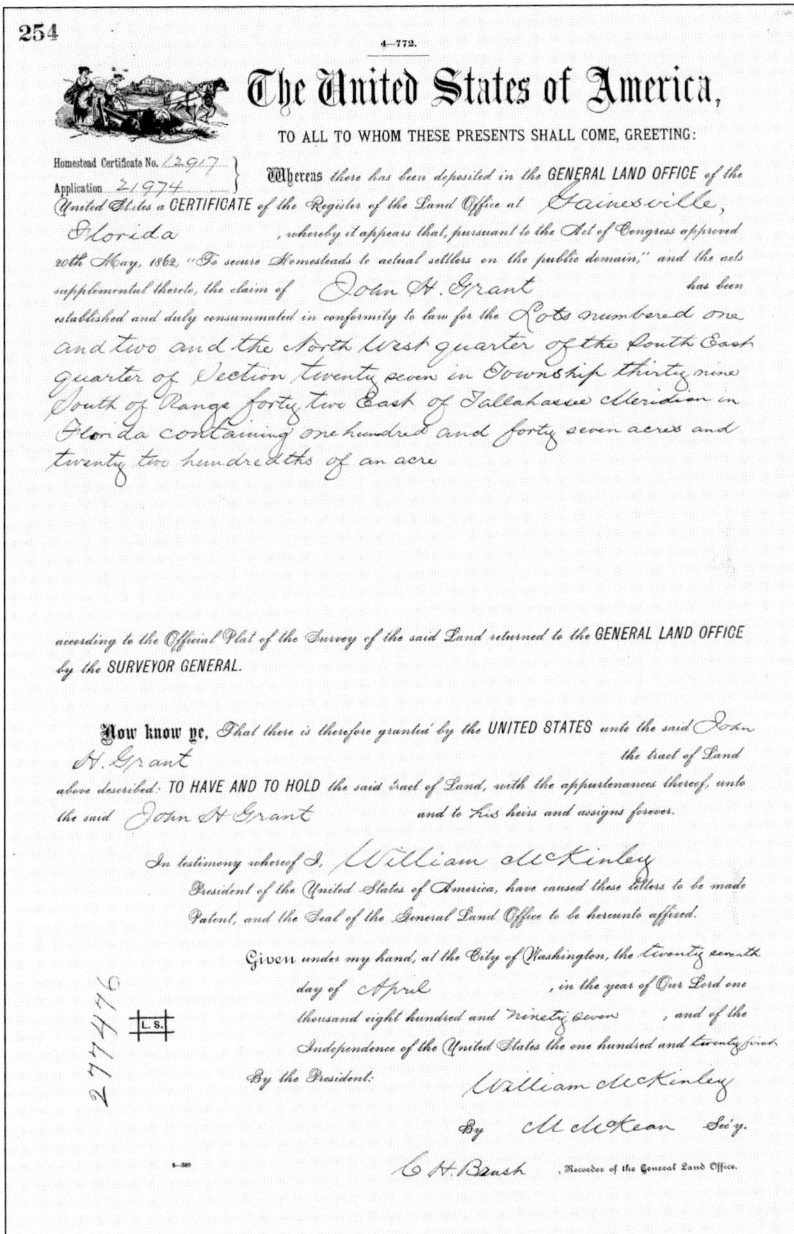

254

4—772.

The United States of America,

TO ALL TO WHOM THESE PRESENTS SHALL COME, GREETING:

Homestead Certificate No. 12917
Application 21974

Whereas there has been deposited in the GENERAL LAND OFFICE of the United States a CERTIFICATE of the Register of the Land Office at Gainesville, Florida, whereby it appears that, pursuant to the Act of Congress approved 20th May, 1862, "To secure Homesteads to actual settlers on the public domain," and the acts supplemental thereto, the claim of John H. Grant has been established and duly consummated in conformity to law for the Lots numbered one and two and the North West quarter of the South East quarter of Section twenty seven in Township thirty nine South of Range forty two East of Tallahassee Meridian in Florida containing one hundred and forty seven acres and twenty two hundredths of an acre

according to the Official Plat of the Survey of the said Land returned to the GENERAL LAND OFFICE by the SURVEYOR GENERAL.

Now know ye, That there is therefore granted by the UNITED STATES unto the said John H. Grant the tract of Land above described: TO HAVE AND TO HOLD the said tract of Land, with the appurtenances thereof, unto the said John H Grant and to his heirs and assigns forever.

In testimony whereof I, William McKinley President of the United States of America, have caused these letters to be made Patent, and the Seal of the General Land Office to be hereunto affixed.

Given under my hand, at the City of Washington, the twenty seventh day of April, in the year of Our Lord one thousand eight hundred and ninety seven, and of the Independence of the United States the one hundred and twenty first.

277476

L.S.

By the President: William McKinley

By M McKean Sec'y.

C H Brush, Recorder of the General Land Office.

In 1896, John Grant married Ola Kyle, a stepdaughter of Fred Cabot, s a contractor who built roads, canals, and railroad right-of-ways. Pictured is a land title from 1897 for 147 acres. In 1898, the Grant family moved to Jupiter Island, where he had purchased a home. There were no telephones or neighbors, and by 1901, they had moved back to the mainland for better water supply and living quarters. In those days, specialist contractors were rare. People built their own houses and boats. John tried his hand at both. He classified himself on the voting register as a pineapple grower, but had many occupations. He had yearly sharecroppers on his land, ran a small fish and oyster house, and supplied road materials and wood for the railroad. He owned a grocery store, built a few boats, sold real estate, ran survey lines, and became local superintendent for the Indian River Association. (Courtesy of Library of Congress.)

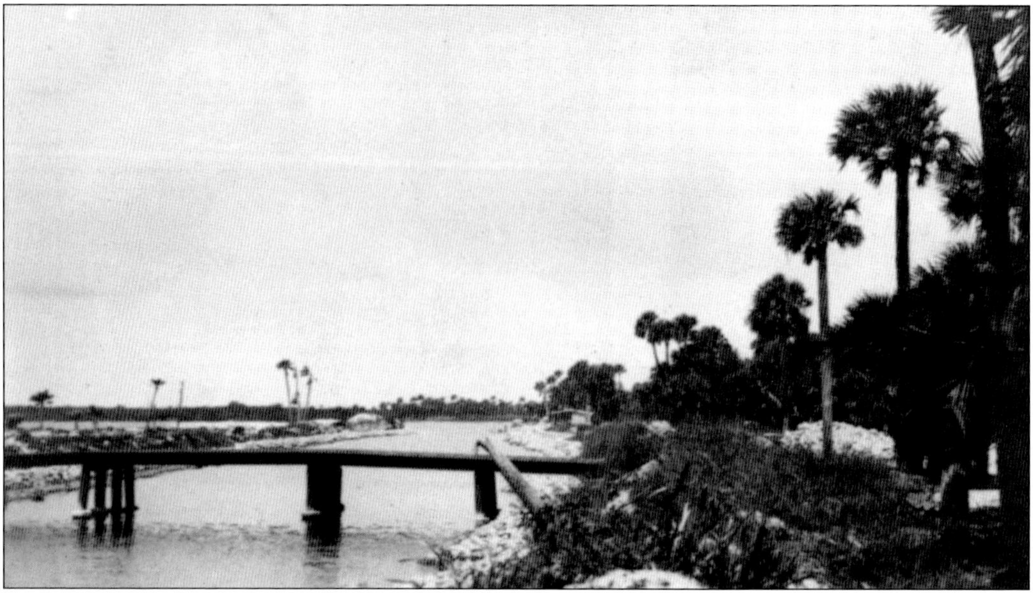

Travel in the area was primarily by boat; however, in 1911, the first bridge (above) was slowly being built by the Indian River Association across the Indian River Lagoon to connect Jupiter Island with Hobe Sound. They also dredged the lagoon near Gleason Street to run a ferry to the island until the bridge was complete. Although steel has been used since the early 19th century, it was not until 1874 that the Keystone Bridge Company completed the Eads Bridge across the Mississippi River. Below is the bridge across Grants Harbor in 1913. (Above, courtesy of State Archives of Florida; below, courtesy of the P.K. Yonge Library of Florida History, Special and Area Studies Collections, George A. Smathers Libraries, University of Florida.)

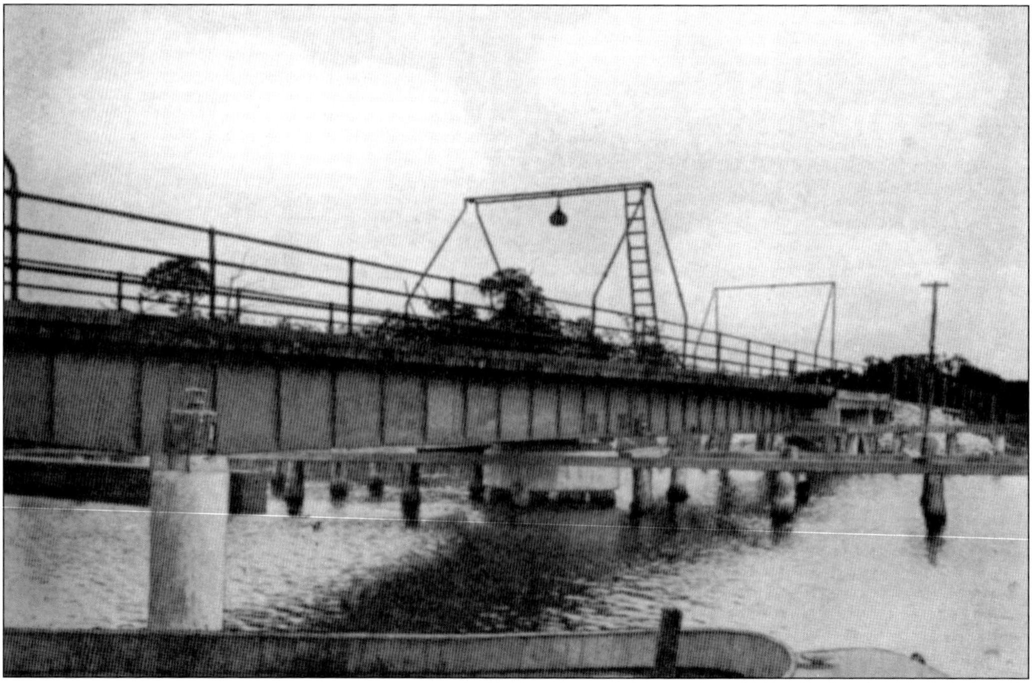

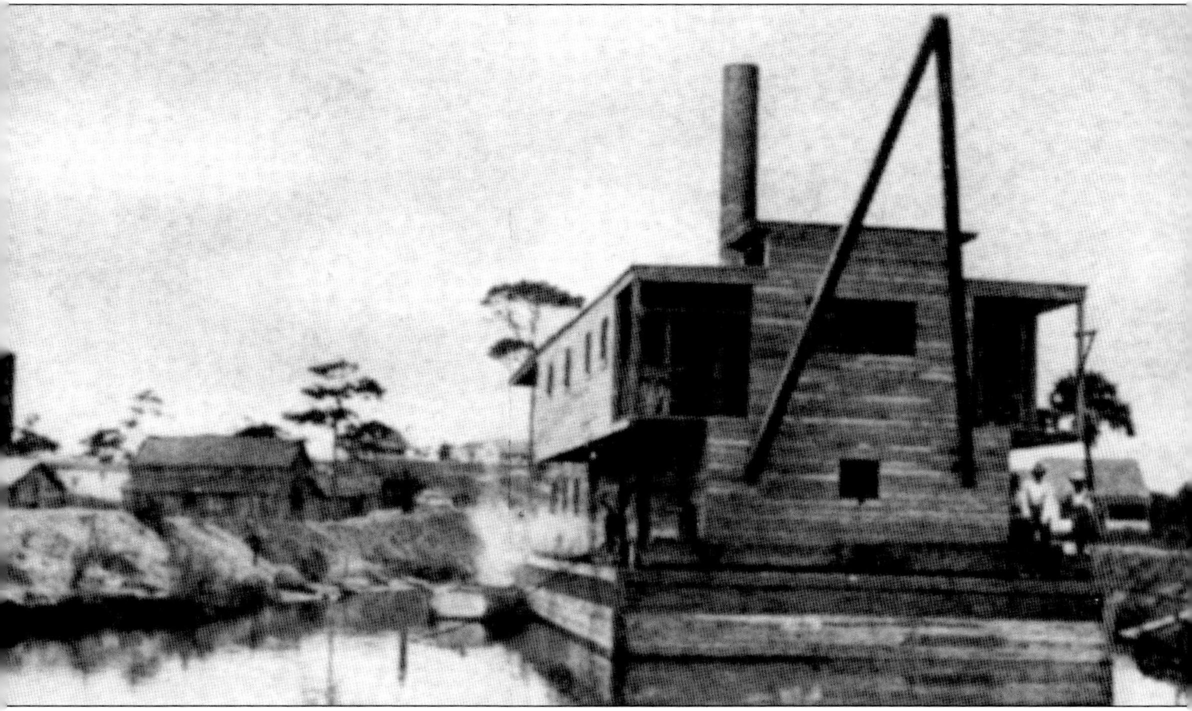

From the beginning of civilization, people, equipment, commodities, and materials have been transported by water. The ability to ship people and goods via inland waterways and oceans was and still is largely dependent on water depth. Since the natural phenomena of siltation and sedimentation threaten the navigational depth of rivers, people constantly fight a battle against silt. For many centuries, this battle was fought by hand, simply digging up the mud. Then in 1575, mud mills arrived. This type of dredging equipment was used for digging inside ports and consisted of a rotating chain with wooden boards to dig up the mud. Then the steam-driven bucket dredger superseded the mud mill. It was not until 1857 that a suction dredger was built in the United States. Seen here is a dredging operation in full swing in Grant's Harbor. (Courtesy of the P.K. Yonge Library of Florida History, Special and Area Studies Collections, George A. Smathers Libraries, University of Florida.)

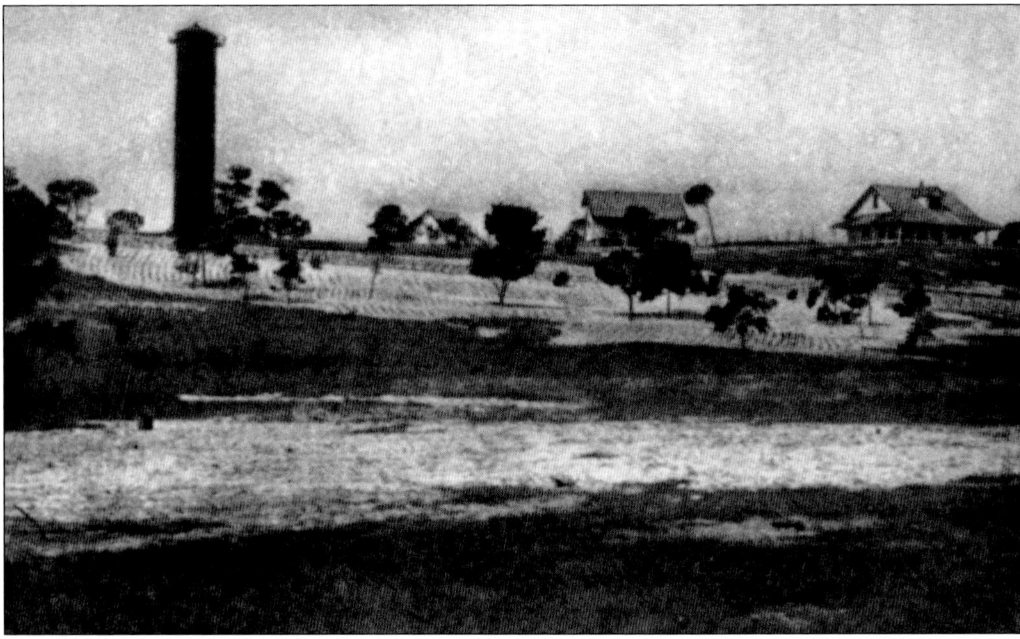

Around 1896, John H. Grant and his wife established the first inn, Highlander, on an elevated section of the mainland, 72 feet above the surrounding landscape, permitting spectacular views. The inn would eventually be called Pine Hill. It was destroyed by fire in 1928. The entire water supply for east Hobe Sound came from the rolling hill country on the mainland west of the high ridge. These hills held water and created a natural reservoir. At this time, there were only a few homes in Hobe Sound. By the early 20th century, there was a post office and an ice plant. Travel was still primarily by boat; however, a train station was erected as part of Henry Flagler's Florida East Coast Railway a few years later. (Both, courtesy of the P.K. Yonge Library of Florida History, Special and Area Studies Collections, George A. Smathers Libraries, University of Florida.)

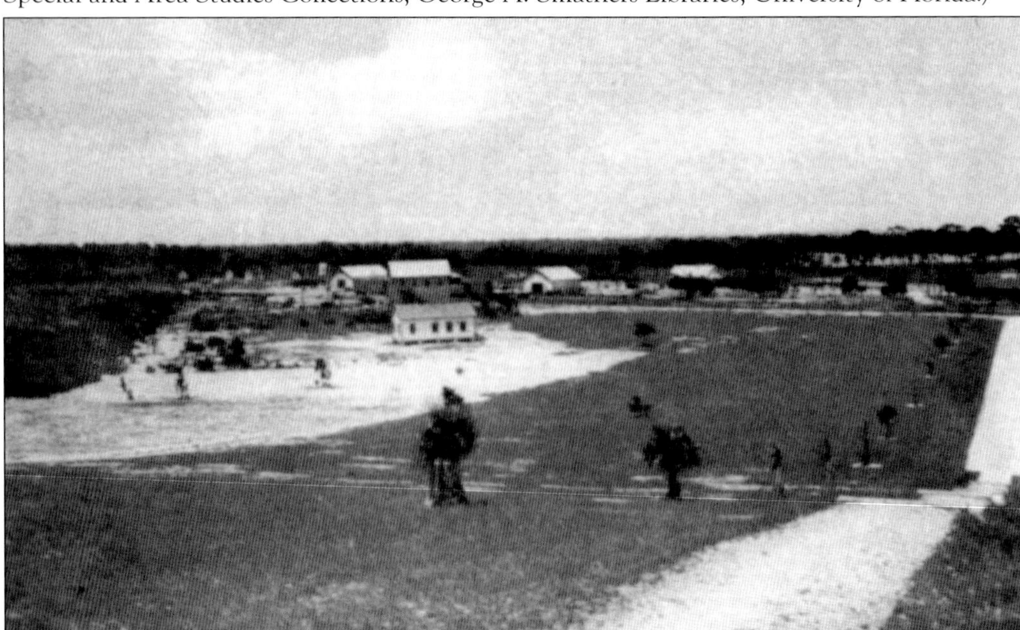

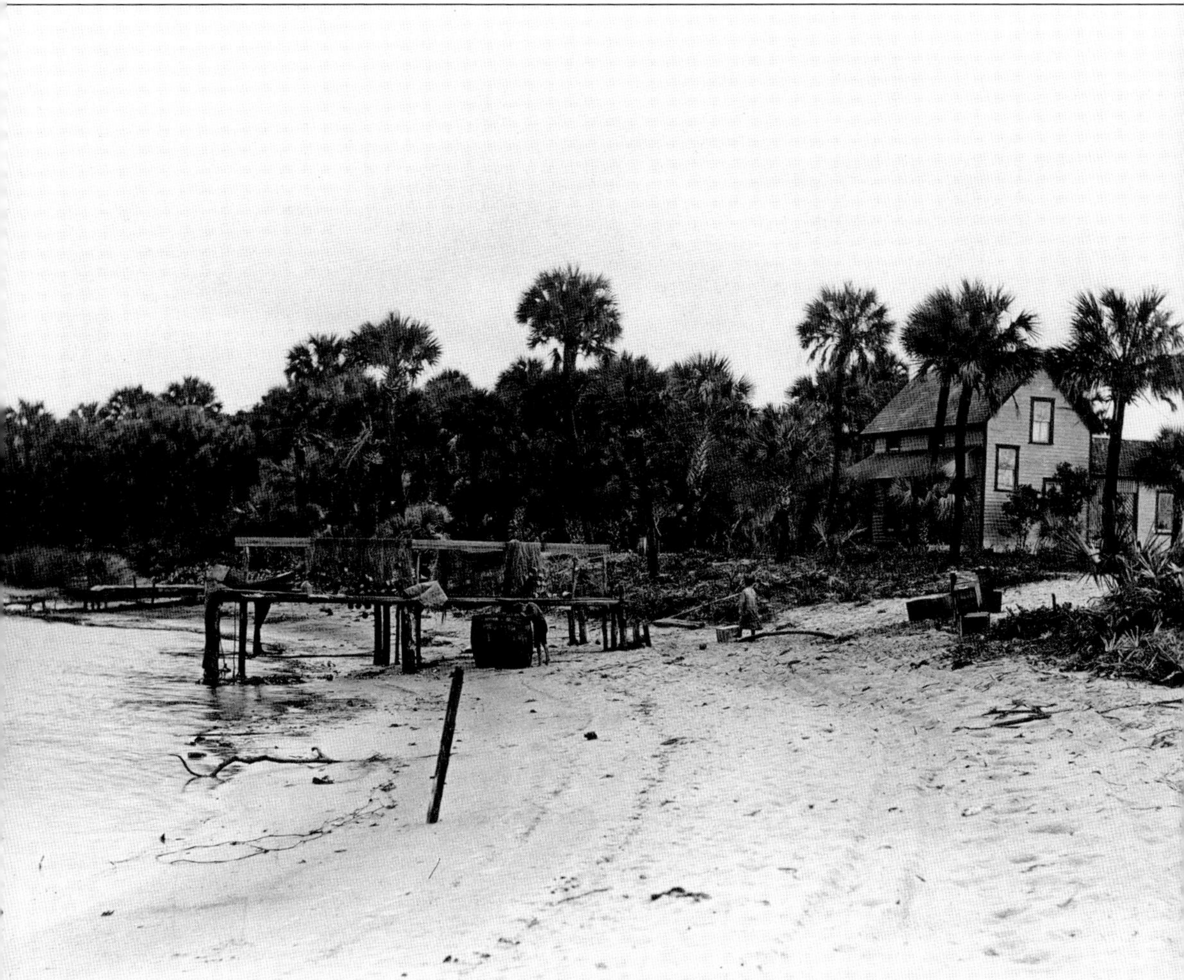

Florida Cracker architecture is a vernacular wood-frame-style home built in the 19th century. Homes typically were oriented to take advantage of the offshore breezes, with raised floors, center hallways, steeply pitched roofs, and porches. Seen here is the Tamquery Boarding House on Jupiter Island around 1890. In the early 1890s, Jupiter Island and Hobe Sound were still relatively unknown. There were few homes or residents. (Courtesy of the State Archives of Florida.)

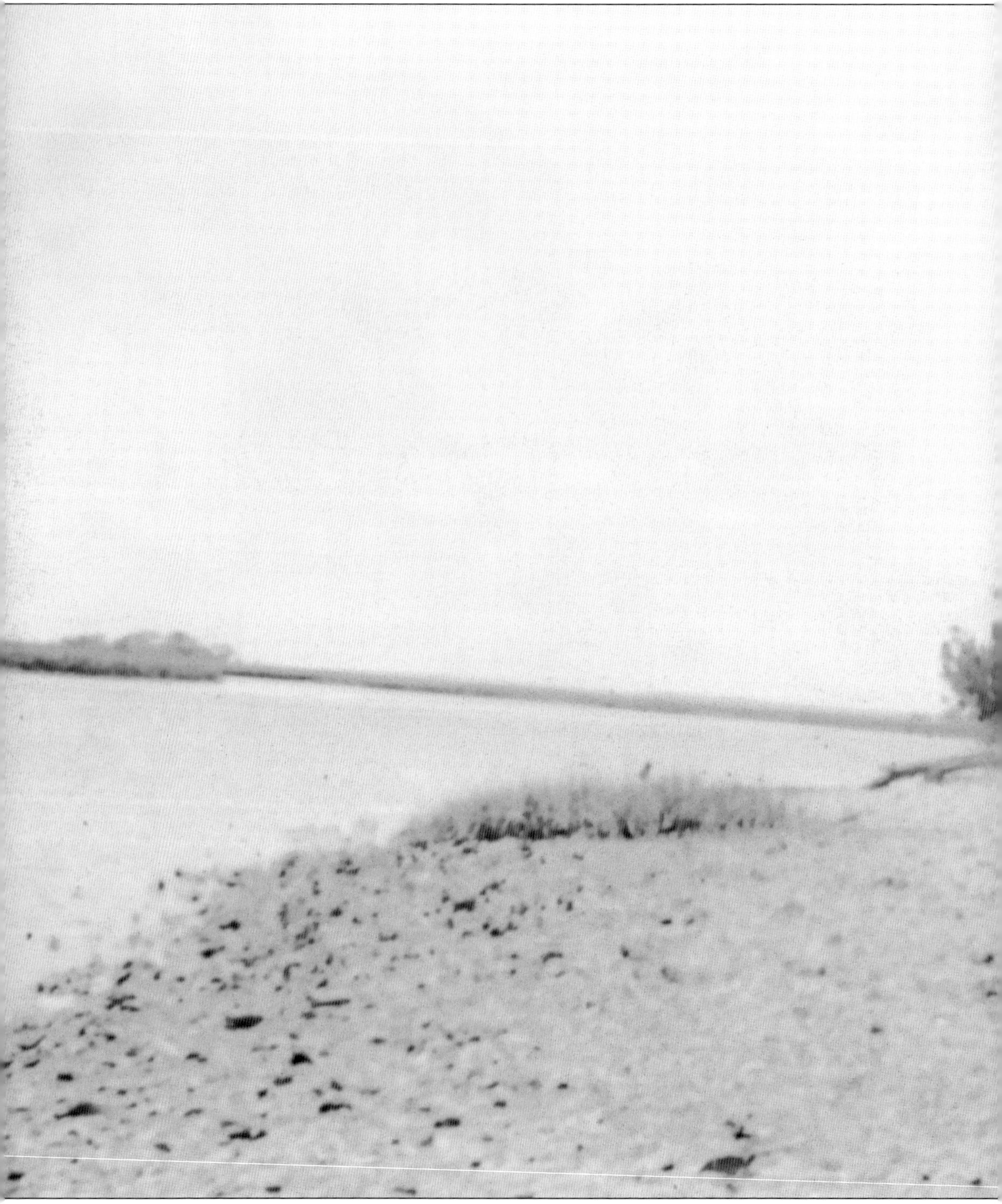

In 1898, Charles Henry Coe published his book *Red Patriots* about the Seminole Indians. It was very unpopular at the time, but is his best-known work. The book dealt with the plight of the Seminoles in Florida. Around 1912, Coe started to travel up and down the Florida coast documenting his travels and his finds. Seen here is Captain Coe at Pecks Lake in Hobe Sound. In 1937 at the age

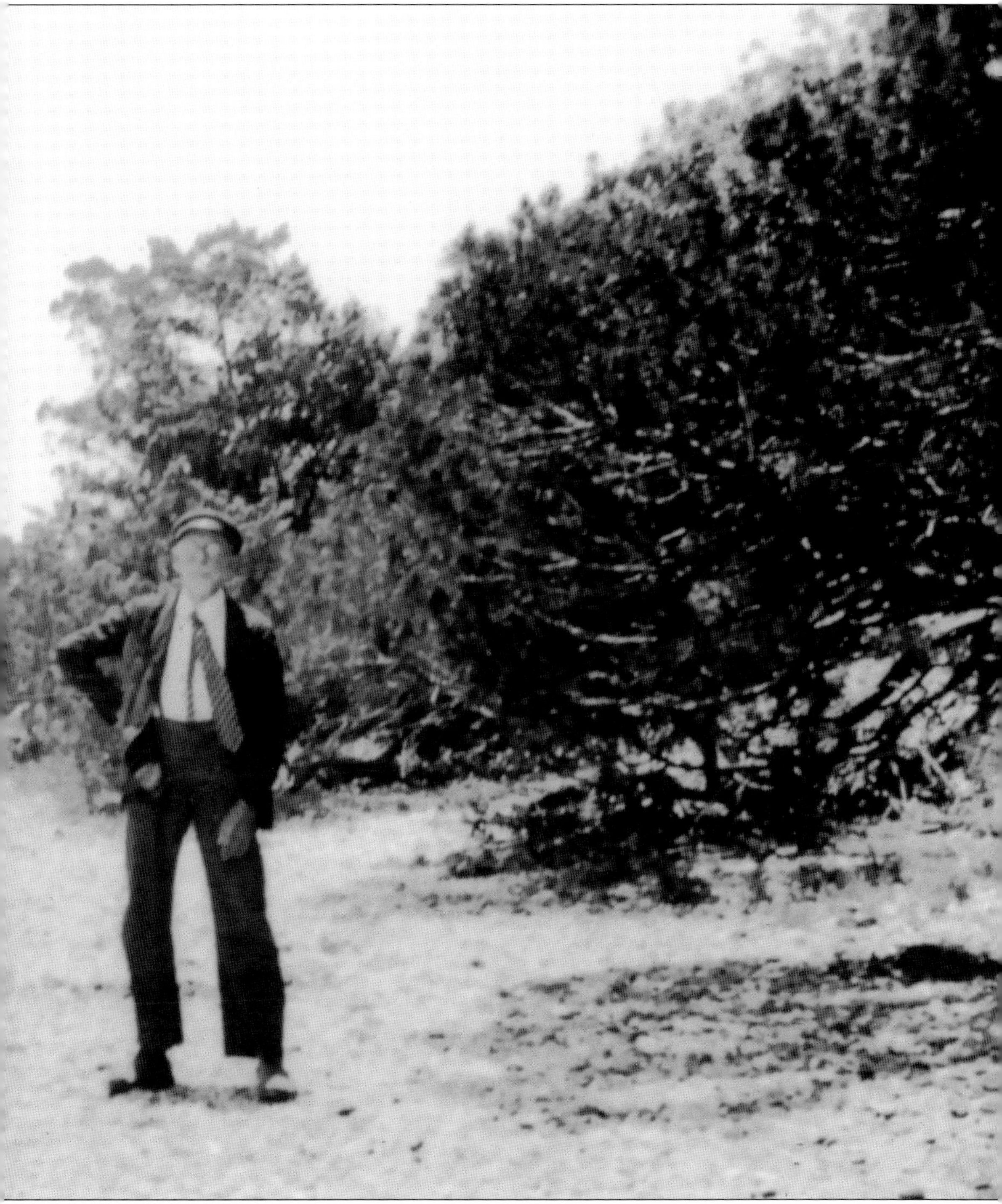

of 81, Coe met Ernest Lyons of the *Stuart News* during a visit to Stuart, Florida. Coe and Lyons went often to Peck's Lake and could be found exploring the Indian mounds there. According to his grandson Andrew, Coe would stay on his boat *Buccaneer* and could often be found sitting on the deck, sipping wine and eating fresh oysters. (Courtesy of Andrew Foster.)

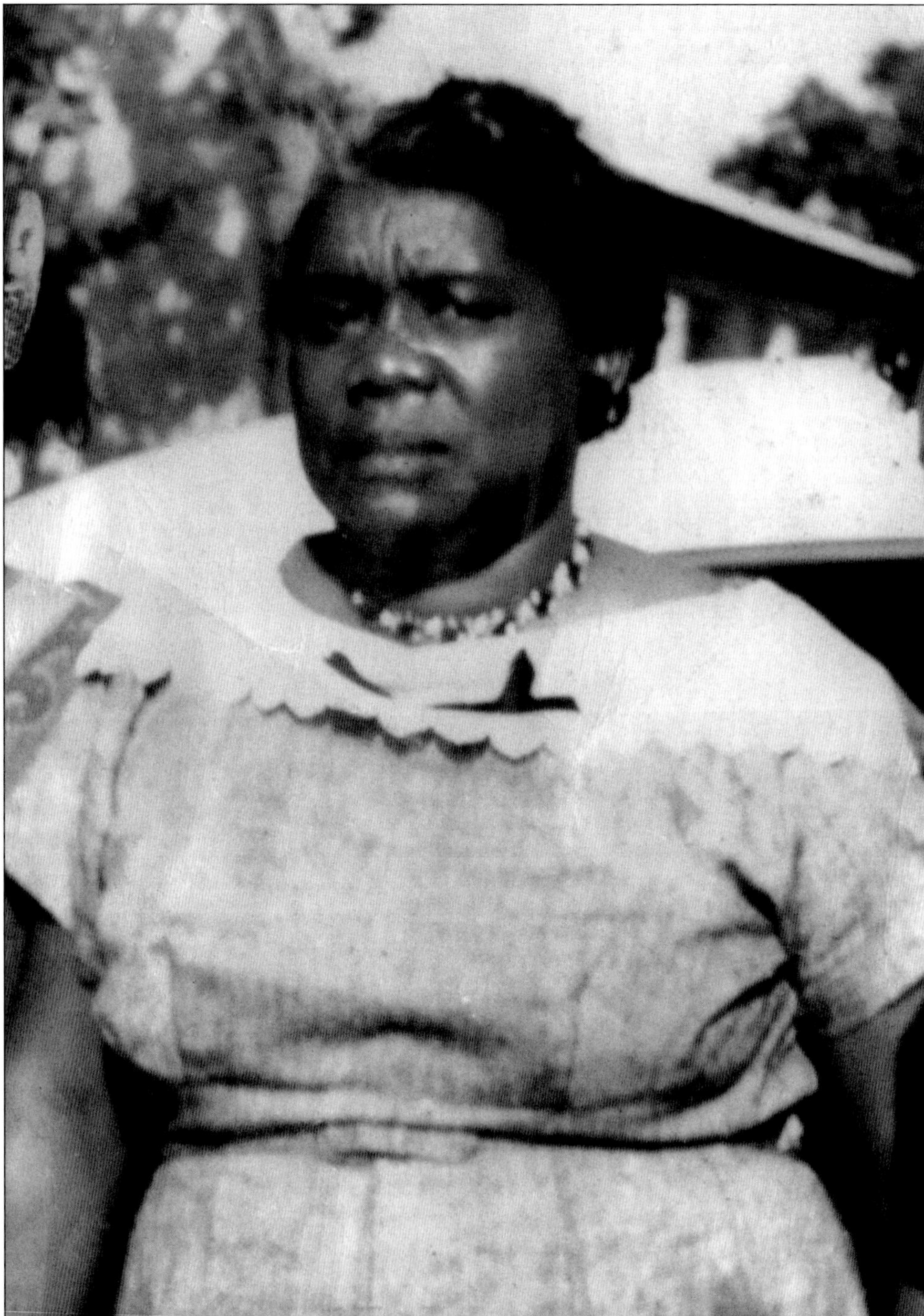

Seen here is Mattie Mae Boykin Pettway. Her husband, Willie Ends Pettway, was a man of many trades during the early days in Hobe Sound. He built many of the roads in Hobe Sound and had a company that hauled items and built driveways. He also owned the sand pit, which is now part of the Soundings neighborhood. He was a porter on the railroad and opened the first black hotel and store in Hobe Sound. (Courtesy of Annie Pettway.)

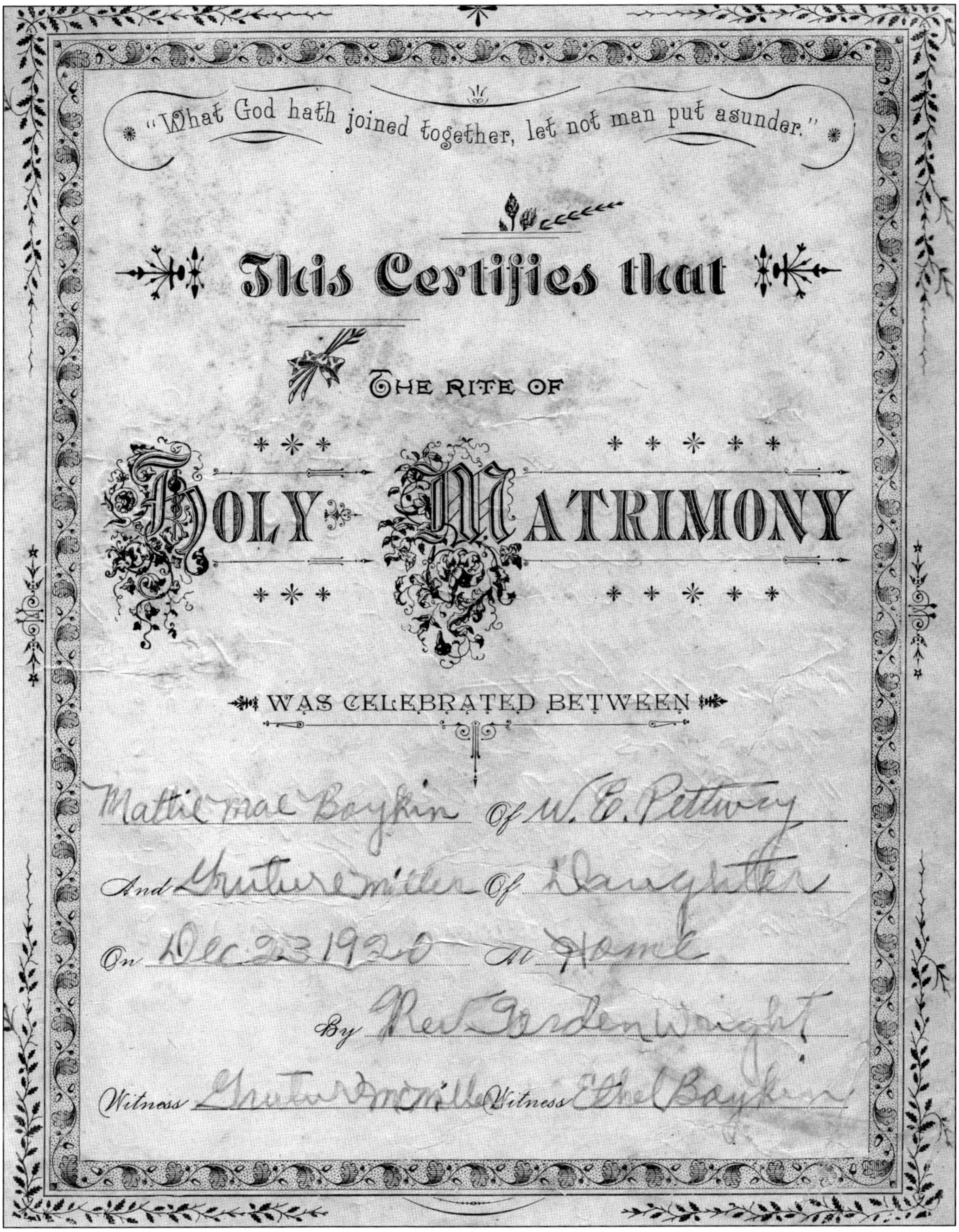

"What God hath joined together, let not man put asunder."

This Certifies that

The Rite of

Holy Matrimony

was celebrated between

Mattie mae Boykin Of W. E. Pettway

And [illegible] Of [illegible]

On Dec 23 1920 At Home

By Rev [illegible]

Witness [illegible] Witness Ethel Boykin

Pictured is the marriage certificate of Mattie Mae Boykin and Willie Ends Pettway. They were married on December 23, 1920. They built a life in Hobe Sound with 14 children, many of whom are still living in the communities of Gomez (the African American community within the Hobe Sound town limits), Hobe Sound, Banner Lake (another African American community in Hobe Sound), and Stuart. (Courtesy of Annie Pettway.)

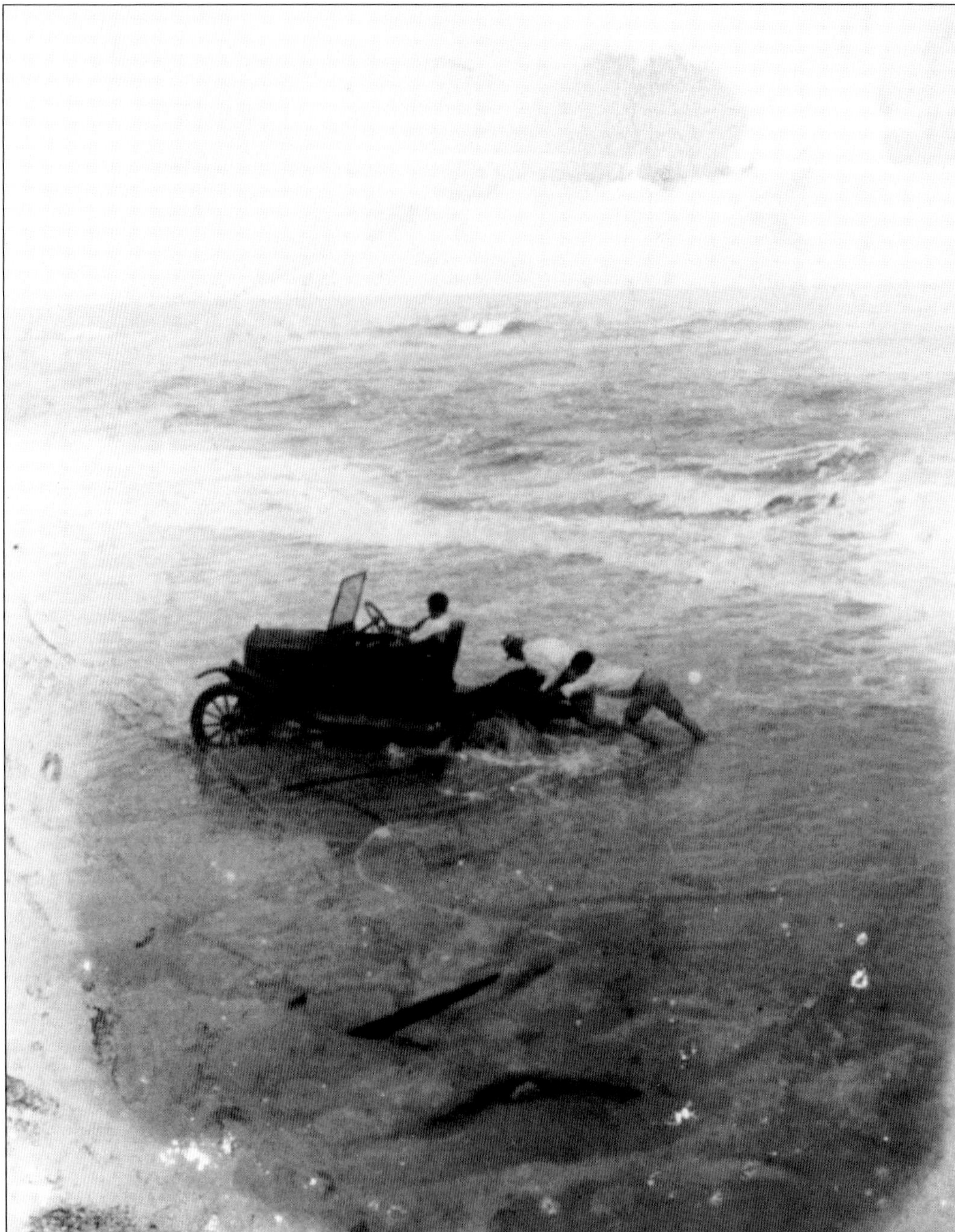

Everyone likes to explore after a storm, particularly on the beach. Seen here are some adventurers stranded on Jupiter Island after a large storm around 1908. The unidentified individuals are trying to push a car out of the sand and water. (Courtesy of the Martin County Historical Society.)

Two

Olympia and Picture City

In 1923, William Angas sold his entire property to an investment group known as the Olympia Improvement Company. The company planned two areas. The first was designated Olympia Beach (at the southern end of the island). The second was Bon Air Beach, which includes what is now North Beach Road, with the town of Olympia on the western shores. By 1925, Olympia sold out to a company called Picture City. Joseph Jefferson, a famous theatrical actor of the 19th century, had a vision of a theatrical enclave in Hobe Sound long before motion pictures. Seen here is a 1926 booklet advertising the planned community of Olympia–Picture City. It describes the planned community, provides maps, and outlines the benefits of settling in the area. The vision, it seemed, was for Olympia to remain the Jupiter Island location, with Picture City added to the western Hobe Sound area. (Courtesy of the Martin County Historical Society.)

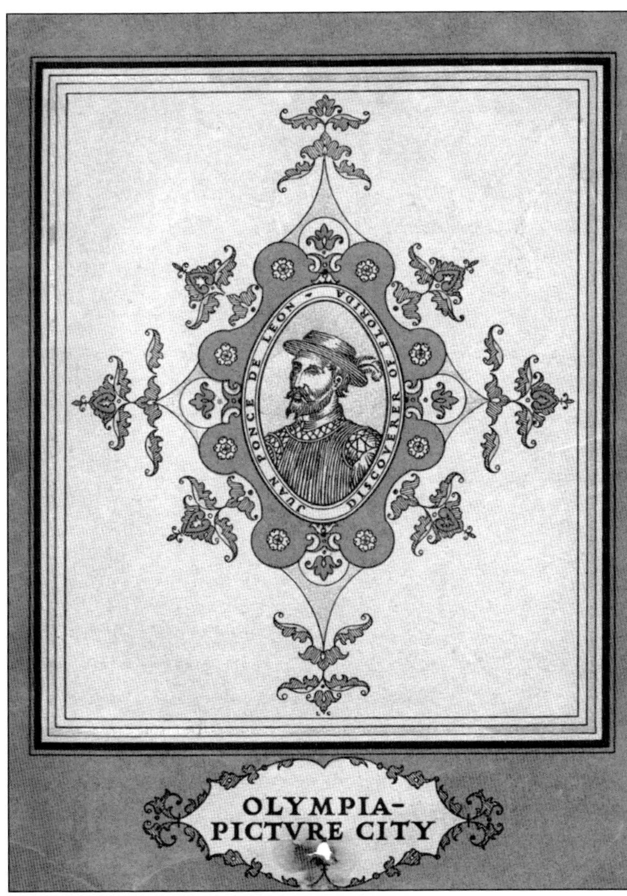

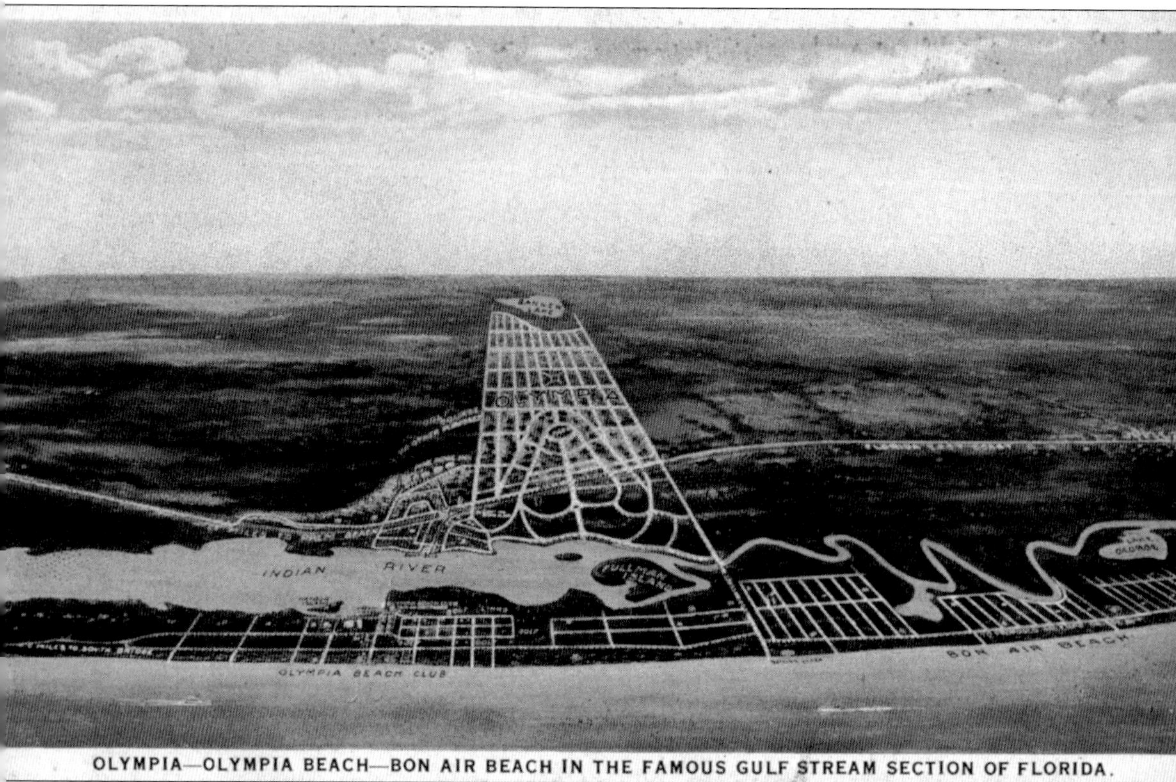

In the early 1920s, Hobe Sound was known as Olympia because much of the 12,000 acres that had been the Gomez Spanish land grant was bought by the Olympia Improvement Company. Developers planned to create a town fashioned on the ancient Olympic athletic grounds. Meacham hired the West Palm Beach engineering firm Carr & McFadden to develop a plan for the Olympia town site, and in early 1924, the Olympia Improvement Company platted Olympia, Olympia Beach, and Bon Air Beach. They went as far as to give streets the Greek and Roman names they still bear today: Athena, Olympus, Mars, Apollo, Adonis, Mercury, and Saturn Streets, all around Zeus Park on the south side of Bridge Road. It was the brainchild of Swiss architect Maurice Fatio of the firm Treanor and Fatio. He relocated in 1925 to Florida for one reason: to design Olympia. (Courtesy of Sandra Thurlow.)

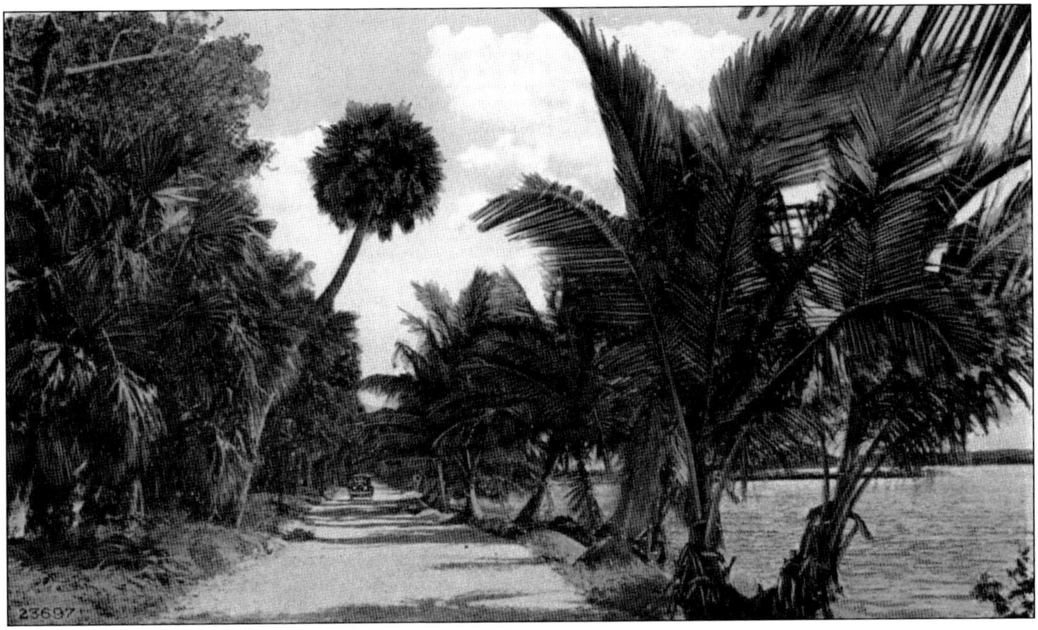

Seen above is a postcard image depicting a motoring road along the Indian River, and below is the Olympia Dock that could accommodate pleasure boating, fishing vessels, and more. Roads were described by George Chapin as being "substantially built, 16 feet wide and thoroughly rolled over a solid foundation." He also described the boat method of reaching the island and mainland: "Water is always available for small launches and every description of small craft." (Both, courtesy of Sandra Thurlow.)

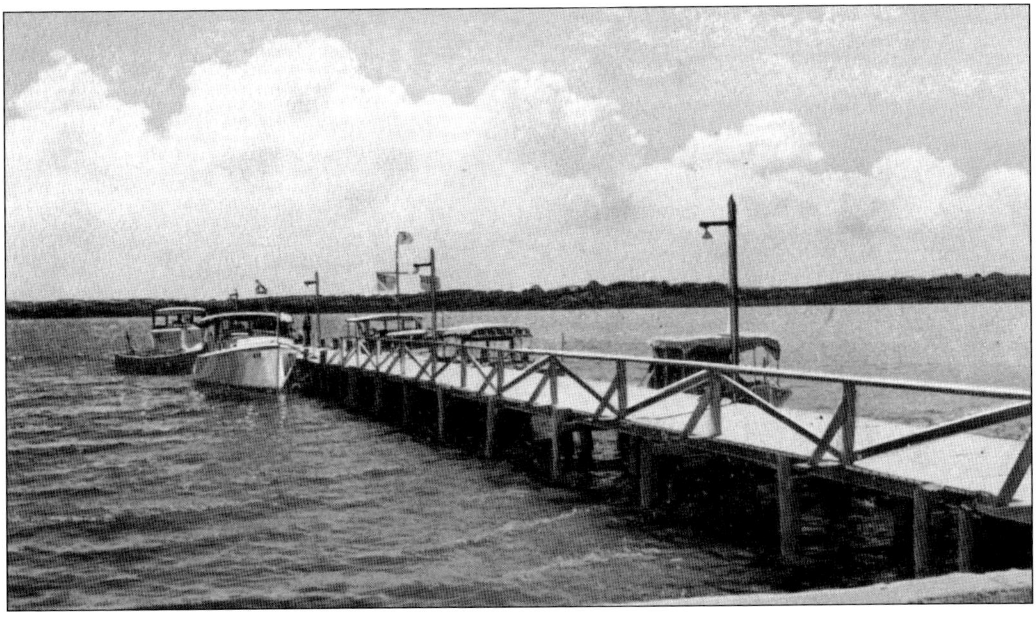

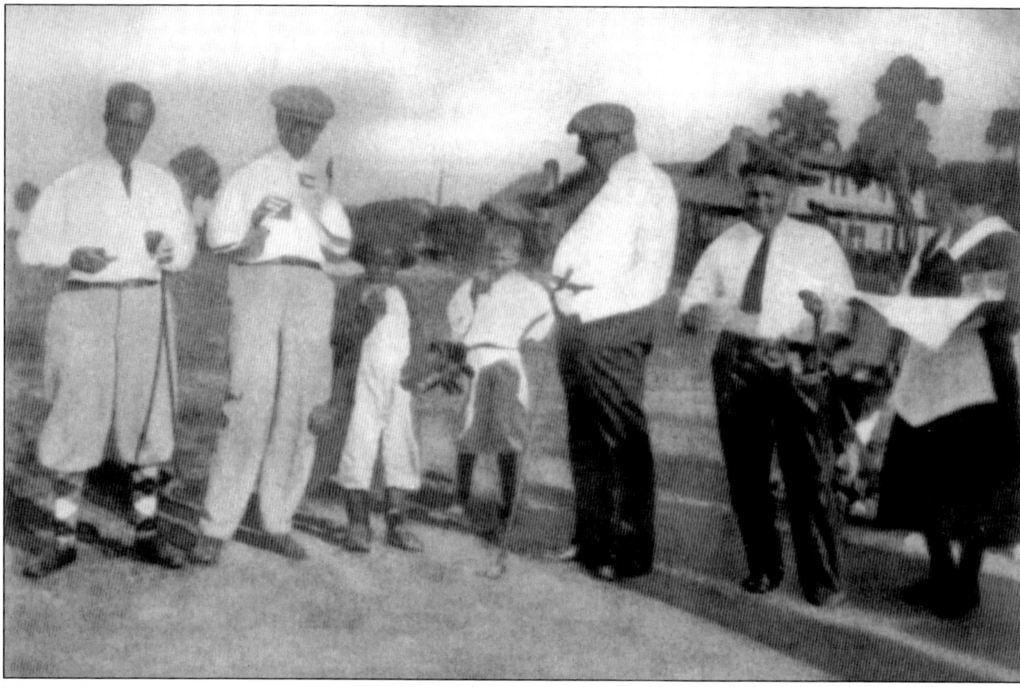

If Pres. Warren Harding visits Olympia, so should everyone else. Pictured above on the Olympia Golf Links is the president, third from right. Harding's administration coincided with a boom in American golf and golf-course construction in the early 1920s, and he was an avid golfer. He is seen below arriving in early 1921 before being sworn in as president. From left to right are First Lady and President Harding with Mr. and Mrs. Edward Beale McLean and their son standing on a pier in Palm Beach. This was not his first trip, as Harding and his wife, Florence, had been visiting Florida since the 1890s. (Above, courtesy of Martin County Historical Society; below, courtesy of the Library of Congress.)

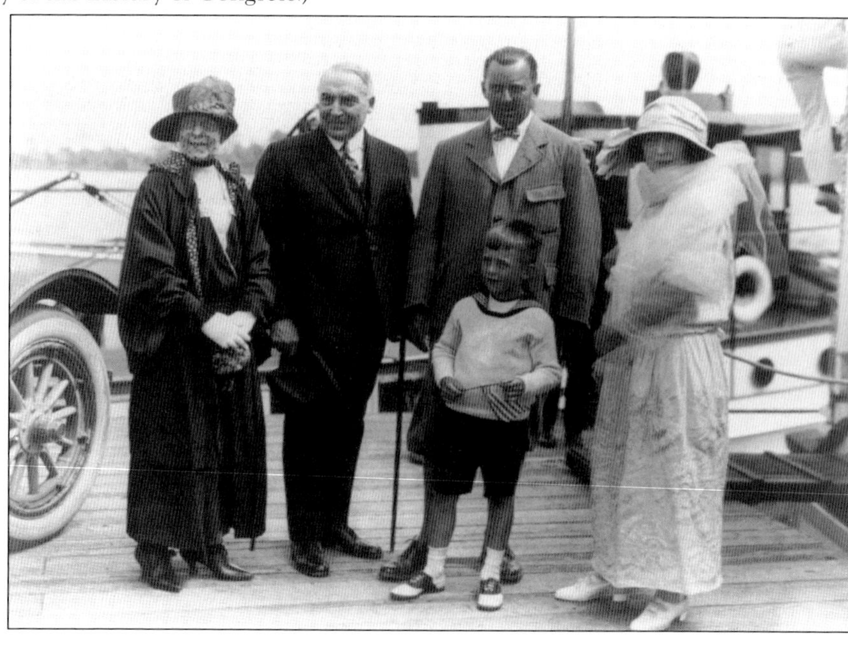

Refrigeration, a necessity for keeping many types of foods fresh, was not available prior to 1917 in Hobe Sound. Instead, ice boxes were used in the early 1900s. Blocks of ice, obtained from an icehouse or manufacturing plant, were stored inside a hollow box lined with tin or zinc and packed with various insulating materials such as cork, sawdust, straw, or seaweed. In 1924, the Andrew Lester family moved to Hobe Sound and soon became prominent members of the community. Lester, born March 13, 1870, in Norway, had come to the United States in 1893 and married Iraymotto Autowell on September 26, 1896. They built Hobe Sound's Olympia Ice Company in 1925, close to the railway depot. The icehouse and cold storage plant (seen below) served as a community gathering place for years. (Both, courtesy of Martin County Historical Society.)

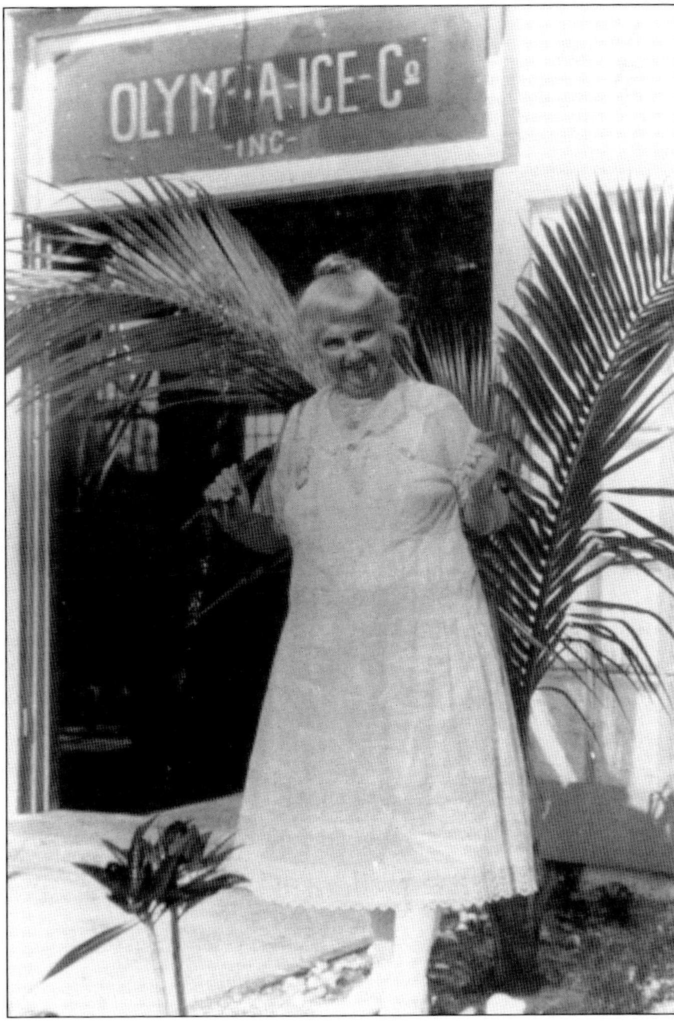

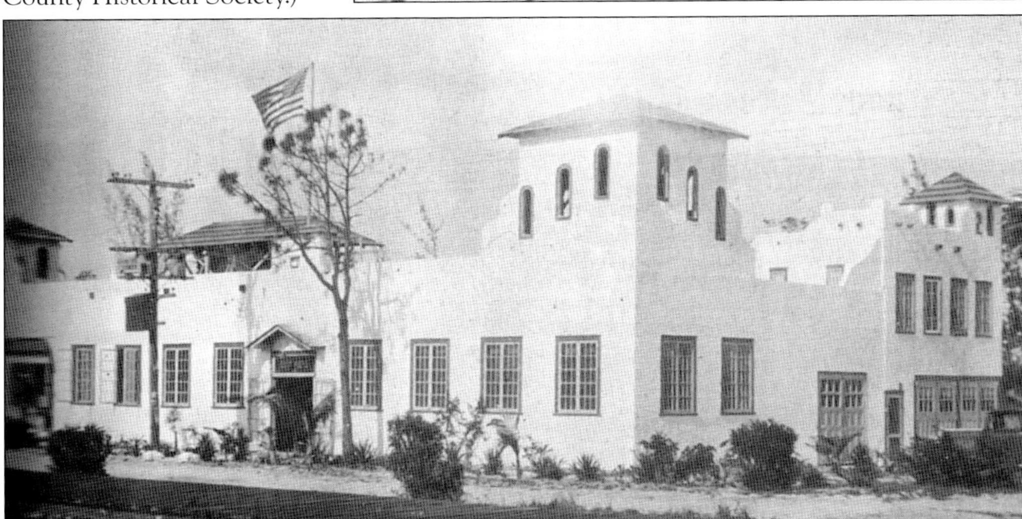

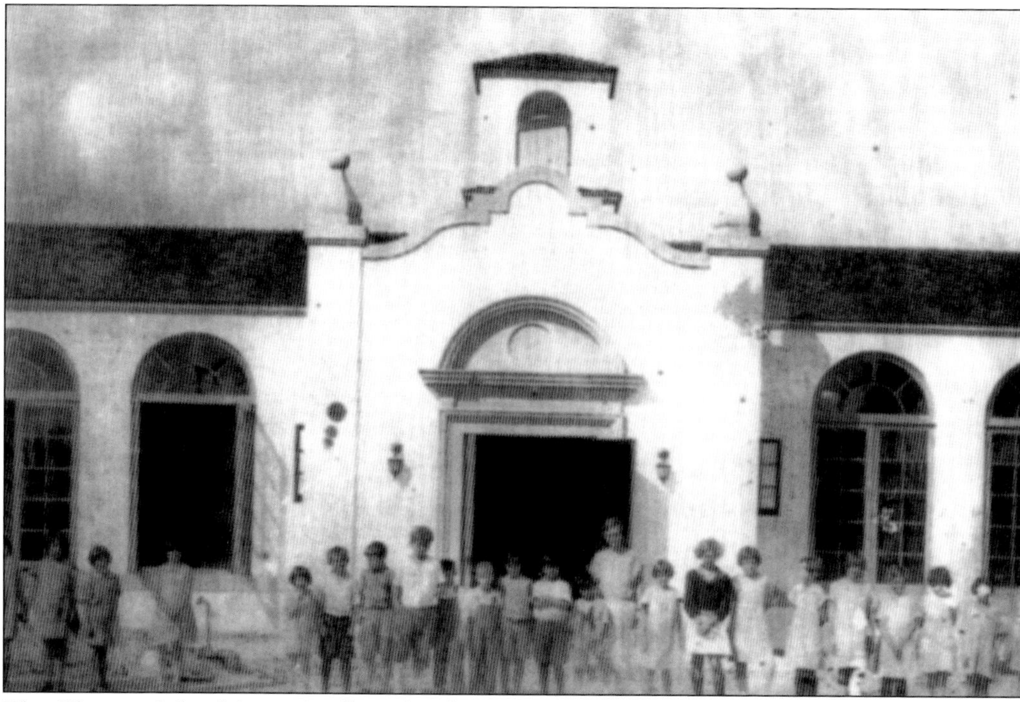

The Olympia School (now Apollo School), was built in 1924. There is a debate as to whether it was built as an office for the Olympia Improvement Company or as a town hall, or maybe even a schoolhouse. The photograph above is dated 1925 and shows children outside. Maurice Fatio designed the Mission-style building, which was used as a school until 1962 when it could no longer support the population of Hobe Sound. It was used briefly as a thrift store and then fell into disrepair. In 2000, the Apollo School Foundation purchased the building. Its goal was to rehabilitate it and open it as a historical museum and cultural arts and educational facility. In 2002, the building was listed in the National Register of Historic Places, the only one in Hobe Sound. Below is the building today. (Both, courtesy of the Apollo School Foundation.)

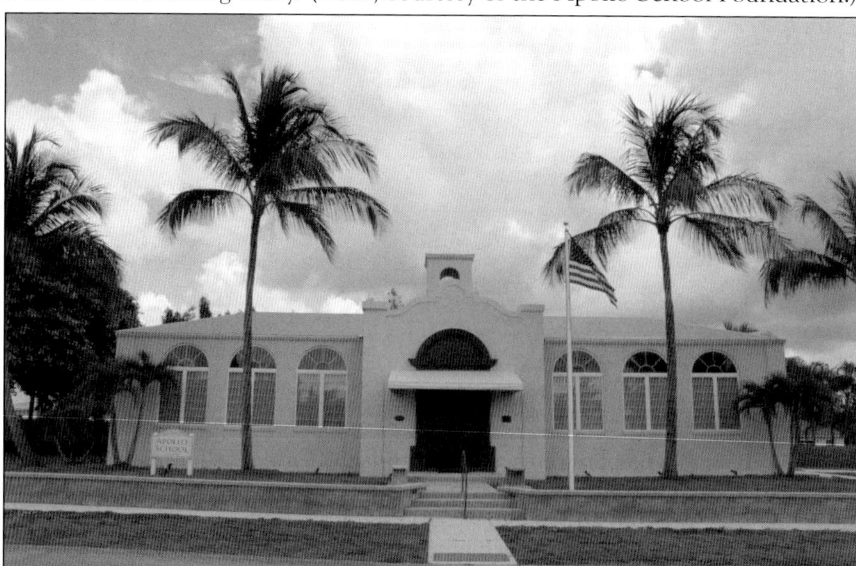

On March 1, 1962, the new Hobe Sound Elementary School opened. At right is the front of the program, and below is a listing of the school officials, board members, faculty, and staff, along with committee members who had organized the ground-breaking ceremony. The school is still open and serving the community of Hobe Sound. (Both, courtesy of Sandra Thurlow.)

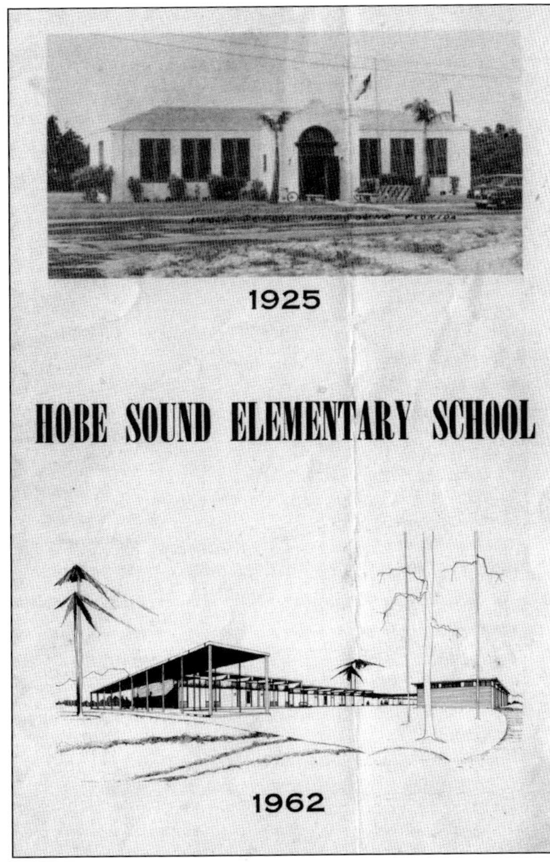

1 9 2 5

School Officials	Formation of Martin County
County Superintendent	J. B. McDonald
Board Members	Chairman - F. W. Baker, Palm City
	J. J. Pitchford, Jensen
	R. G. Eason, Indiantown
	Attorney - A. O. Kenner
Trustees	H. L. Snyder, A. R. Wallace

1 9 6 2

School Officials	
County Superintendent	Thomas L. Crook
Board Members	Chairman - O. D. Hataway
	Frank DeStefano
	Mrs. T. R. Chambers
	T. R. Hellier
	H. G. Kindred
	Attorney - M. G. Littman
Trustees	Albert Walker, George Osborn, Jeanette Odom

Hobe Sound School Faculty 1961 - 1962
Principal Earl Cathcart
June Edwards, Alice Frey, Gisela Leckeband
Martha Martin, Carol Schwarz

Ground Breaking Committee
Coordinator Mrs. T. R. Chambers
Mrs. Carl Dykes, Mrs. James Graham,
Mrs. John B. McArthur, Mrs. Edward C. Shepard

G R O U N D B R E A K I N G C E R E M O N Y
Hobe Sound Elementary School
May 1, 1962 - 2:00 P.M.
First Avenue - Hobe Sound, Florida

P R O G R A M

Invocation	The Rev. Floyd B. Hager
Salute to Flag	All
Welcome	Mr. Thomas L. Crook Superintendent of Schools
Response	Mrs. Edward C. Shepard Secretary P.T.A.
Introduction of Guests	Mrs. T. R. Chambers School Board Member

GROUND BREAKING CEREMONIES
"Pioneer School Officials"

Mrs. Walter R. Moore	P.T.A. President 1931
Mrs. Pearl Bryan	School Custodian 1934
Mr. Samuel B. Thayer	Board Member 1932
Mr. George Blagg	Trustee 1929

"America the Beautiful"	First Stanza
Benediction	

Pupils will assemble at 1:30 P.M. in front of the school for press pictures, then march to the new school site for the ground breaking ceremony

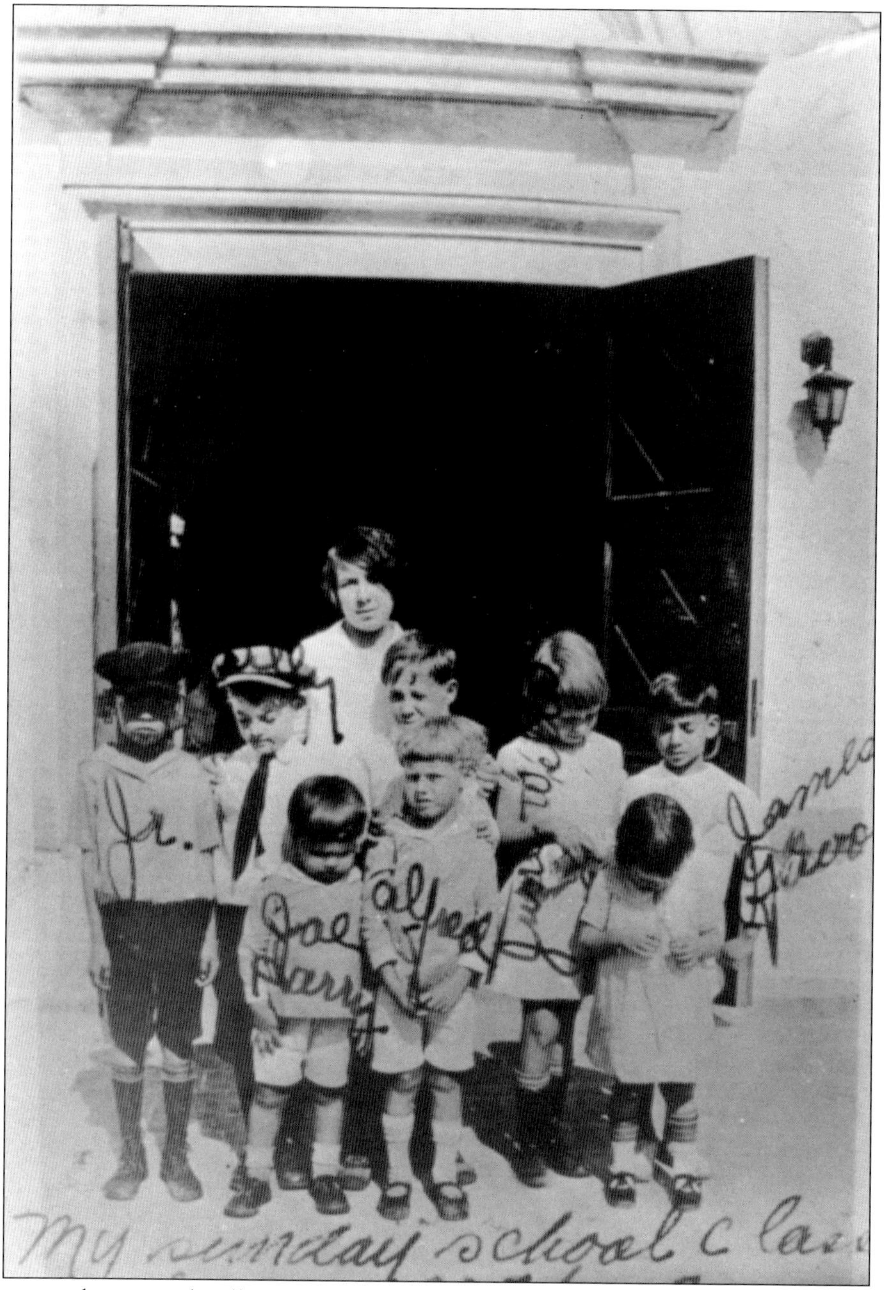

In addition to being a schoolhouse, the Olympia School building was used by the community for many functions and events. When the school was completed in 1925, there was no church building in Olympia. By 1926, members of the community had organized a small congregation and held their first formal church service in the Olympia School. The building was provided free of charge, but the church was asked to pay for its electricity, water, and half of the janitor expenses. The church continued using the school building until the mid-1930s, when the congregation built their own church. Seen here is a photograph from 1925 labeled "My Sunday School Class." Some of the children have been identified with first names only: John, Joe, and Alfred. The ages appear to be mixed. (Courtesy of the Stuart Heritage Museum.)

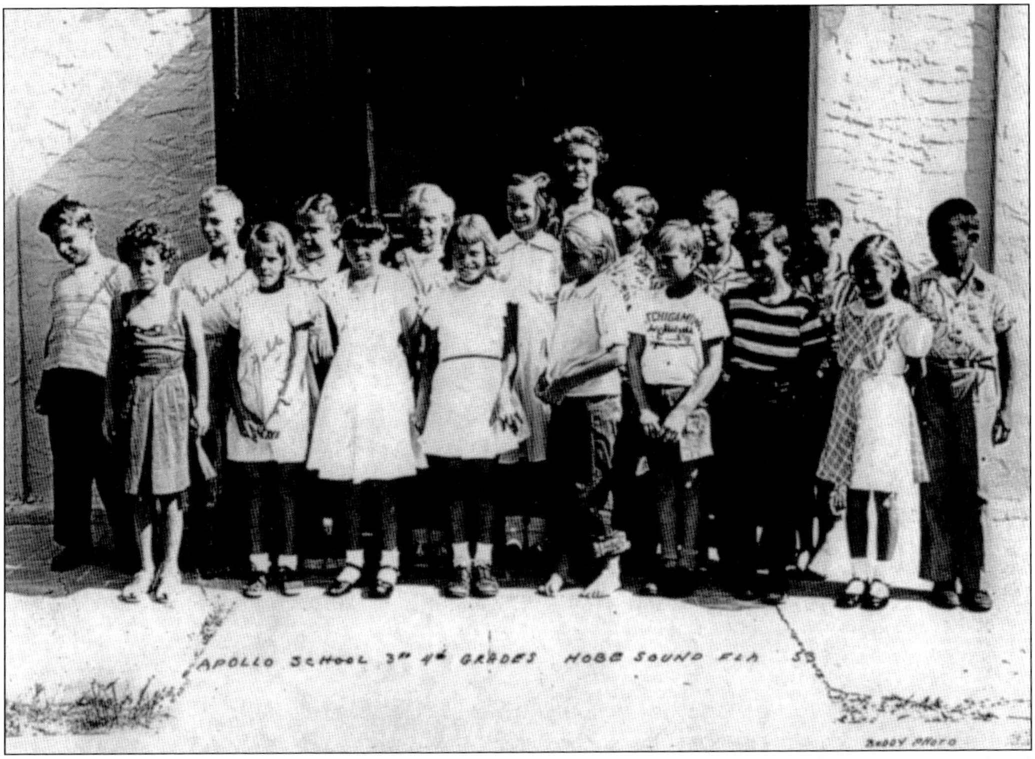

Pictured above are the Apollo School third- and fourth-grade classes during the 1952–1953 school year. Below are the names of all the children and teachers. The Olympia School building was built as a two-room schoolhouse. Prior to the opening of the Olympia School, the elementary students in the area had been bused to Jupiter, while the high school students attended school in Stuart. In May 1925, Martin County was formed, and all schools in the newly formed county came under the jurisdiction of the Martin County Board of Public Instruction). The county was divided into separate school districts, with each district having a representative on the school board. Olympia and Olympia Beach were in District No. 3. (Both, courtesy of the Stuart Heritage Museum.)

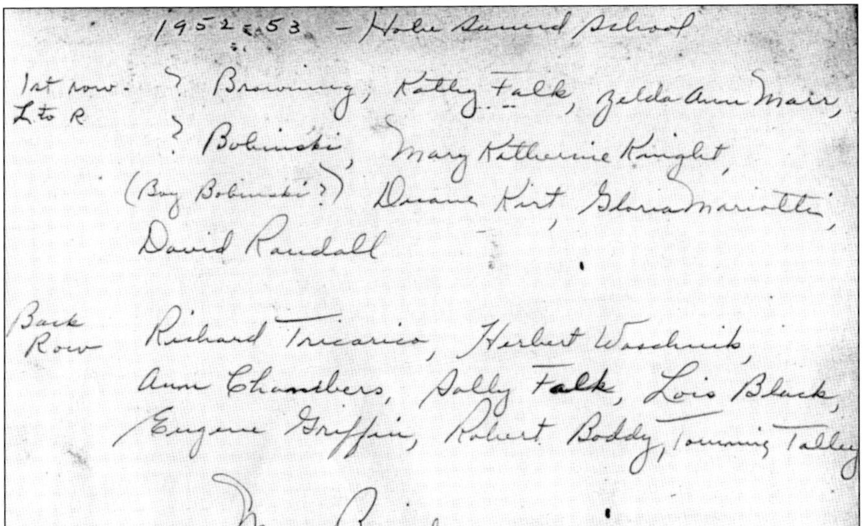
1952-53 – Hobe Sound School

1st row – L to R ? Browning, Kathy Falk, Zelda Ann Mair, ? Bobinski, Mary Katherine Knight, (Boy Bobinski?) Duane Kirt, Gloria Mariotti, David Randall

Back Row Richard Tricarico, Herbert Waschnik, Ann Chambers, Sally Falk, Lois Black, Eugene Griffin, Robert Boddy, Tommie Talley

Mrs. Baisden

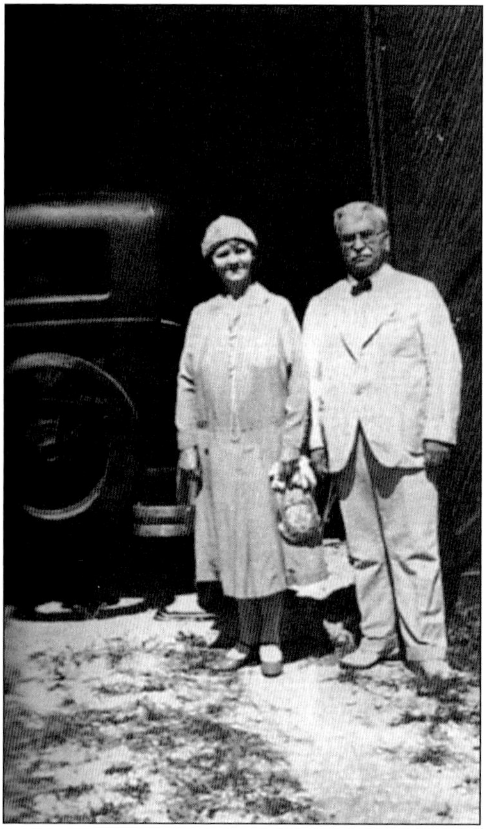

At left is Dr. G.W. Reese, the pastor of the Hobe Sound Community Church, in 1932, with his wife. The Hobe Sound Community Church began in 1925. Below is the Olympia Bible class after meeting in 1925 in the new Olympia Town Hall on Apollo Avenue. Pastor J. McCampbell (far right) was the first regular minister in the community. (Both, courtesy of the Martin County Historical Society.)

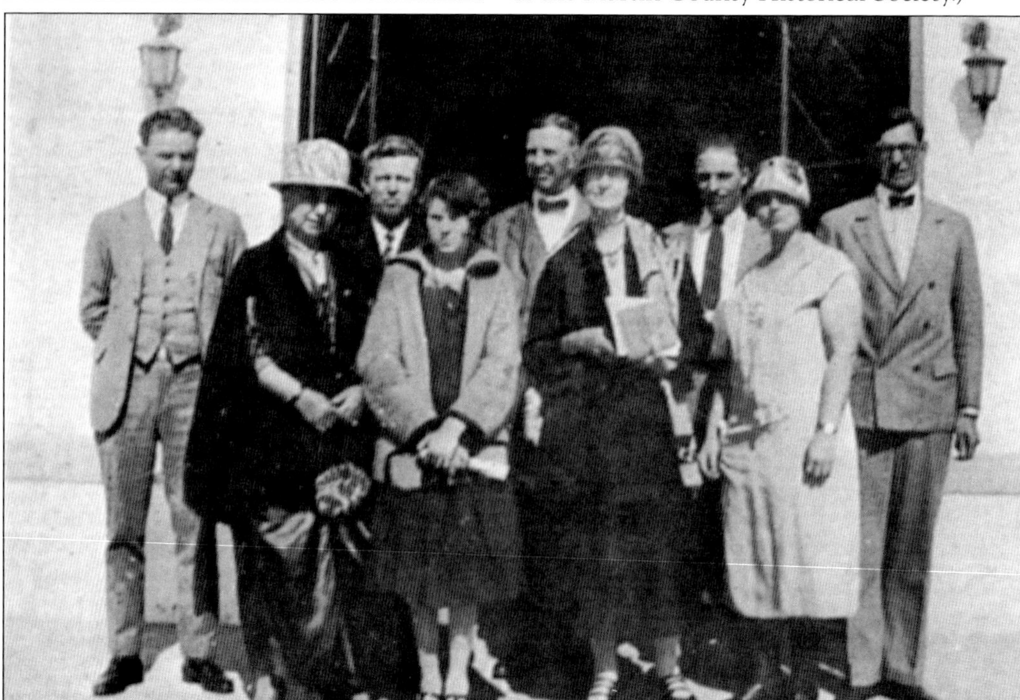

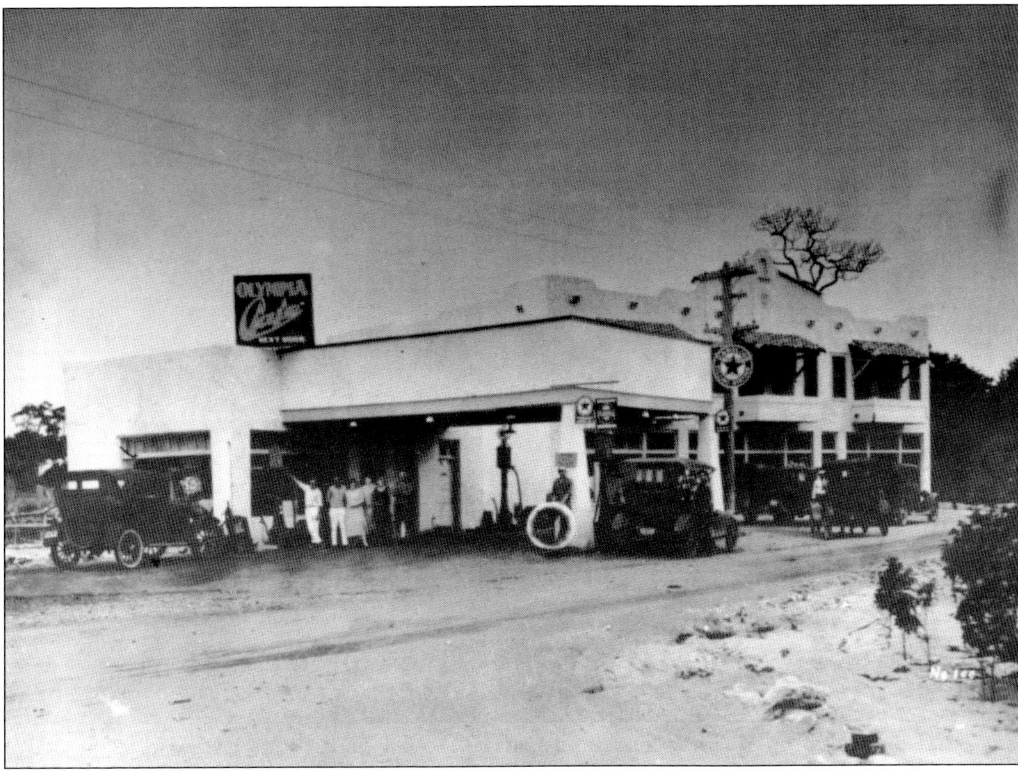

Before Harry and the Natives, a famous eatery in Hobe Sound, there was the Olympia Café. It was in the heart of historic Olympia, near the Olympia Celestial Stop, and close to the bridge to Jupiter Island. It was a perfect location for people to gather, eat, and hear the latest news in town. Below is the Olympia Post Office in 1927. The addition is now gone from the present-day building. (Both, courtesy of the Stuart Heritage Museum.)

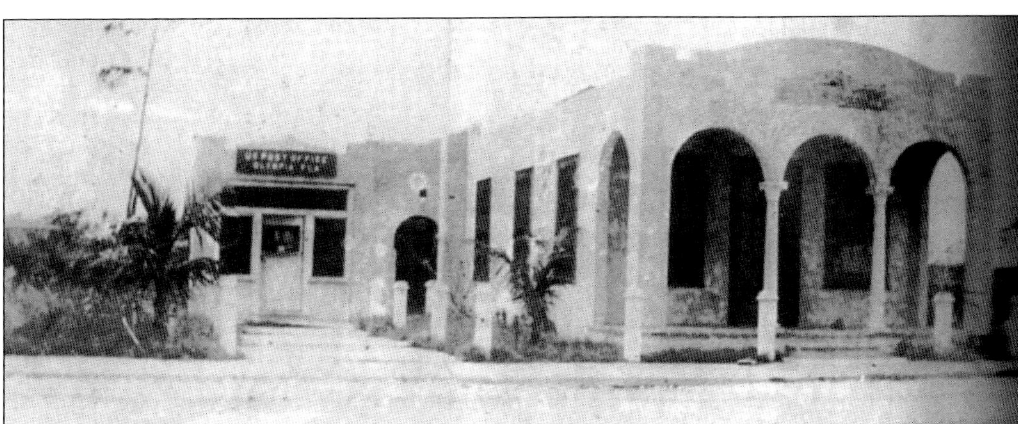

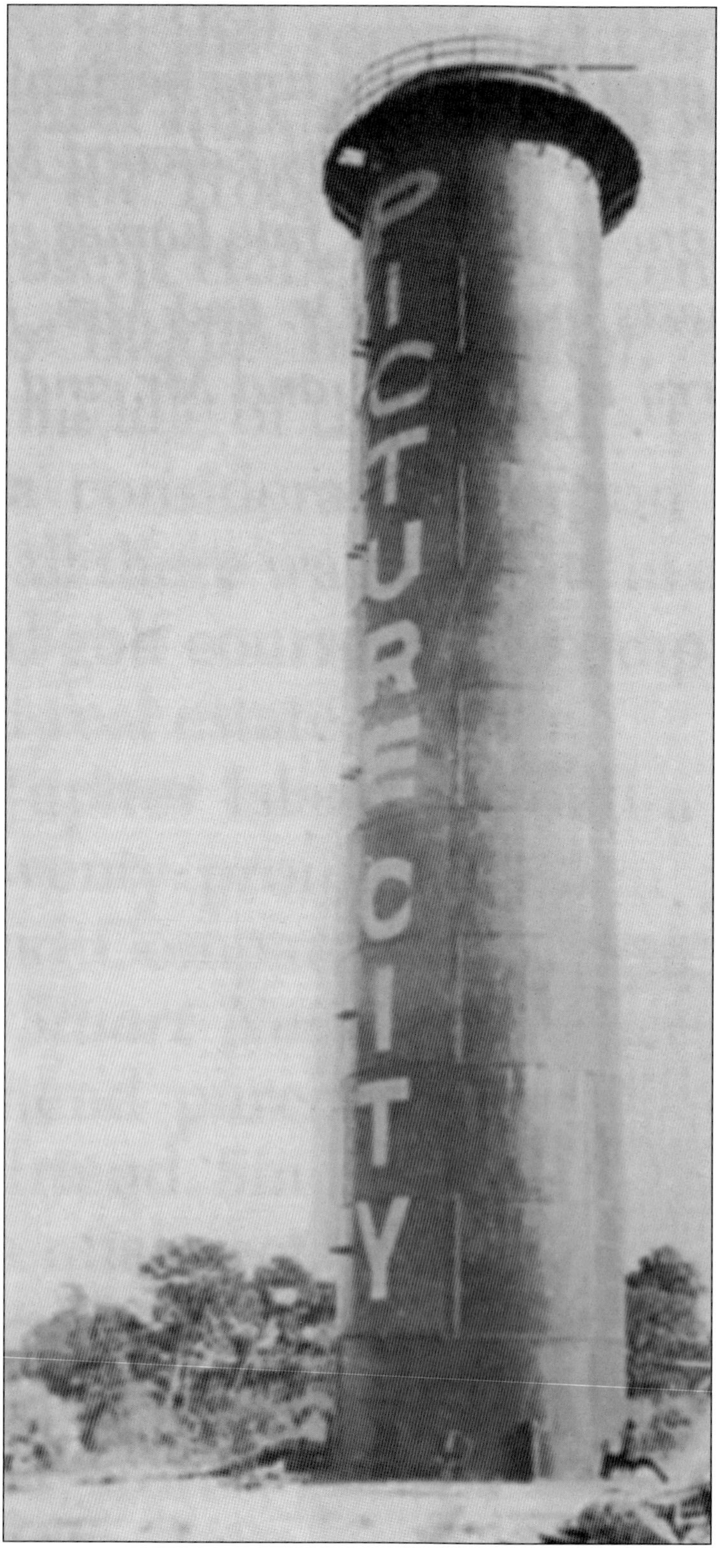

In the early 1920s, Hobe Sound was known as Olympia because of the Olympia Improvement Company. However, change was coming, and it caught several in the community by surprise. On August 30, 1925, *the Stuart Messenger* (predecessor to the *Stuart News*) ran a banner headline across the front page reading "Olympia-Gomez to be Picture City." The water tower (pictured) had been built prior to the Olympia Improvement Company's purchase of the land; however, the name "Picture City" was painted on the side around this time to announce the formal arrival of the motion picture studio. (Courtesy of the Martin County Historical Society.)

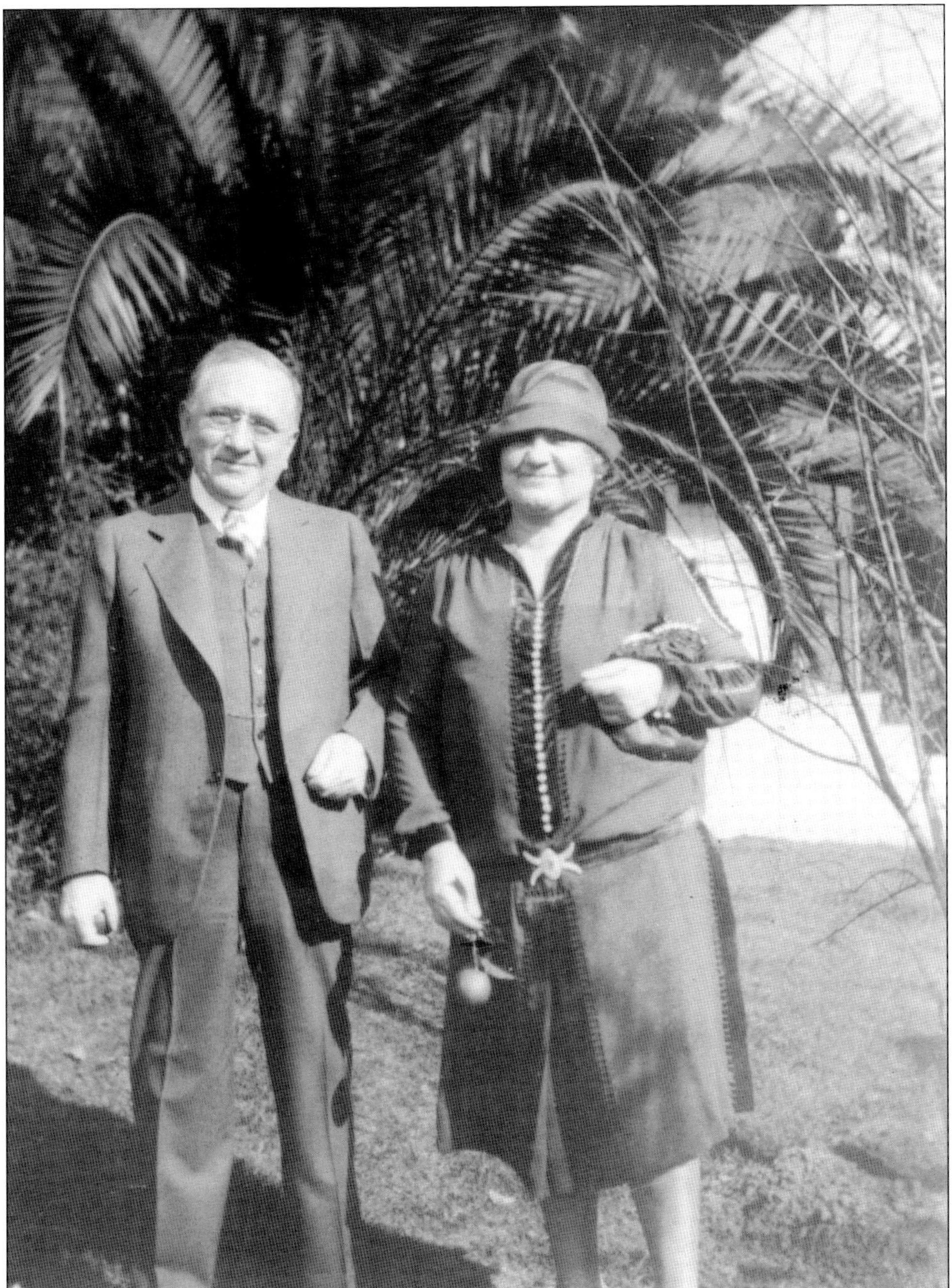

The *Messenger* article stated, "New York picture men buy big tracks for huge development . . . Selznick announces moving picture center that will rival California's best; states studio construction will be rushed." The Selznick referred to was Lewis J. Selznick, a pioneer of silent film production and an independent producer not affiliated with any studio. His sons Myron and David, the latter of whom would become famous for producing *Gone with the Wind* years later, also were involved. Seen here are Lewis J. Selznick and his wife, Florence Sachs Selznick. (Courtesy of the Harry Ransom Center, the University of Texas at Austin.)

56 VARIETY Wednesday, September 2, 1925

PICTURE CITY

OLYMPIA GOMEZ

(Named Because of Its Picturesqueness)

On the Atlantic Ocean, Indian River and the Dixie Highway
Between Palm Beach and Stuart

Site Selected by Felix Isman

CHARLES L. APFEL

Announces

The purchase of the entire CITY OF OLYMPIA together with its Public Utilities of every description, which will hereafter be known as PICTURE CITY—OLYMPIA SECTION.

IN ADDITION THERETO—the purchase of the entire GOMEZ GRANT of 8,000 acres, which will hereafter be known as PICTURE CITY—GOMEZ SECTION.

OLYMPIA and GOMEZ SECTIONS—PICTURE CITY—are united and form a CITY COMPLETE.

The late Henry M. Flagler was said to have been deeply disappointed at his inability to procure the GOMEZ GRANT upon which he desired, by reason of its manifold advantages, to locate Palm Beach.

NOWHERE IN THE ENTIRE STATE OF FLORIDA OR ELSEWHERE CAN BE FOUND BEAUTY SUCH AS THIS WONDERFUL CITY POSSESSES.

No place on the Continent, or in this U. S. A., vies with it in point of beauty, natural advantages, conveniences of access or any of the appurtenances of a modern city.

It is rolling ground—is closest to the Gulf Stream and is the highest point on the Atlantic Coast between Jacksonville and Key West.

It extends four miles along the Atlantic Ocean.

It has a frontage of fourteen miles along the Indian River—the most beautiful of all of Florida's inland waters.

The Dixie Highway extends the entire length of the properties.

Royal Palm Avenue extends through the heart of the entire properties. It has the most beautiful beach of any coast. Hobe Sound is here located with its wonderful islands.

IT HAS THREE RAILROAD STATIONS NOW—IS IN CLOSE PROXIMITY TO A FOURTH—A FIFTH IS TO BE ERECTED

OLYMPIA GOMEZ PICTURE CITY FRUITA SALERNO

Picture City Has Every Improvement

PICTURE CITY now has in course of construction PICTURE CITY HOTEL, the finest on the East Coast.

PINE RIDGE INN and TANGERINE GROVE INN—also located there—have long been famous as fashionable resorts.

It has its own public bathing beaches, bath houses and pavilions.

It has its own Electric Light Plant.

It has its own Water Works—the best water in the State of Florida.

It has an Ice Plant.

It has a nine-hole golf course—now being extended to 18 holes—laid out as fine as money can make it.

It has scores of beautiful homes, owned and occupied.

It has located within its domain scores of the wealthiest residents of the United States whose homes are the finest and most luxurious in the state.

It has five newly constructed homes on sale now—finished in the most modern fashion and furnished by Baumgarten of Fifth Avenue, New York City.

It has Churches and School Houses now.

It has 32 miles of improved sidewalks, streets and boulevards.

PICTURE CITY STARTS WITH ALL THESE ADVANTAGES. LOCATED THERE IS THE ELITE OF FLORIDA.

A CITY COMPLETE—NOT IN THE MAKING

Charles L. Apfel

SELLING AGENTS:

FELIX ISMAN, 501 Fifth Avenue, New York City	WILLIAM H. LINDSAY and ROBERT D. CLOW, 223 Northeast Second Avenue, Miami, Florida; Kettler Theatre Bldg., West Palm Beach, Florida	FERDINAND D. FLEMING, 1516 Chestnut Street, Philadelphia, Pa.

Seen here is a real estate advertisement in *Variety* magazine from September 2, 1925, touting all that Picture City had to offer. It highlights Picture City as one of the most beautiful places, with private beaches, a nine-hole golf course (soon to be 18), and modern amenities including ice, electricity, and some of the nation's best water. It was a complete city (not still being built) with everything needed for investment or a second home. People at the time were familiar with Jacksonville and Palm Beach, but not this area. To get some of the wealthier northern families to take a chance on any area other than Palm Beach, a strategic marketing campaign was key and was undertaken with no cost spared. (Courtesy of Media History Digital Library, University of Wisconsin–Madison Department of Communication Arts.)

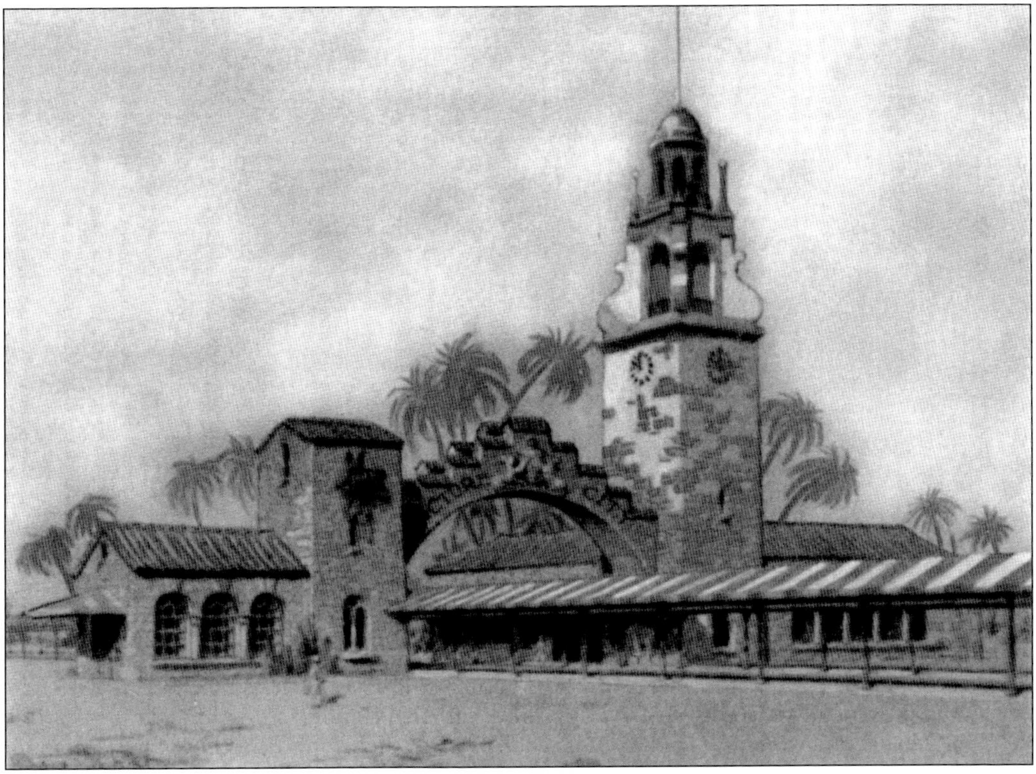

Above is the proposed Picture City Center Station, found in the Olympia advertisement booklet. It was never constructed. Joseph Jefferson (right) from Buzzard's Bay, New York, was a famous actor in the late 19th century and an early proponent of Picture City. He is best know for his role as Rip Van Winkle on Broadway. He was an avid fisherman and had spent a great deal of time in Florida, with a home in Palm Beach. His son Charles had a house in Olympia facing the Indian River. Pres. Grover Cleveland, an avid fisherman and regular visitor to Stuart, was friends with Jefferson and visited him in Hobe Sound often. (Above, courtesy of Martin County Historical Society; right, courtesy of the Brady-Handy photograph collection, Prints and Photographs Division, Library of Congress.)

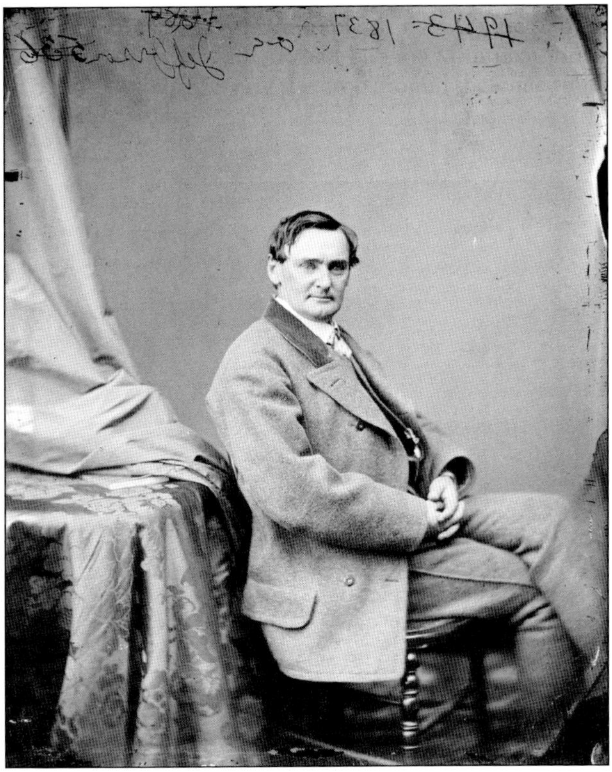

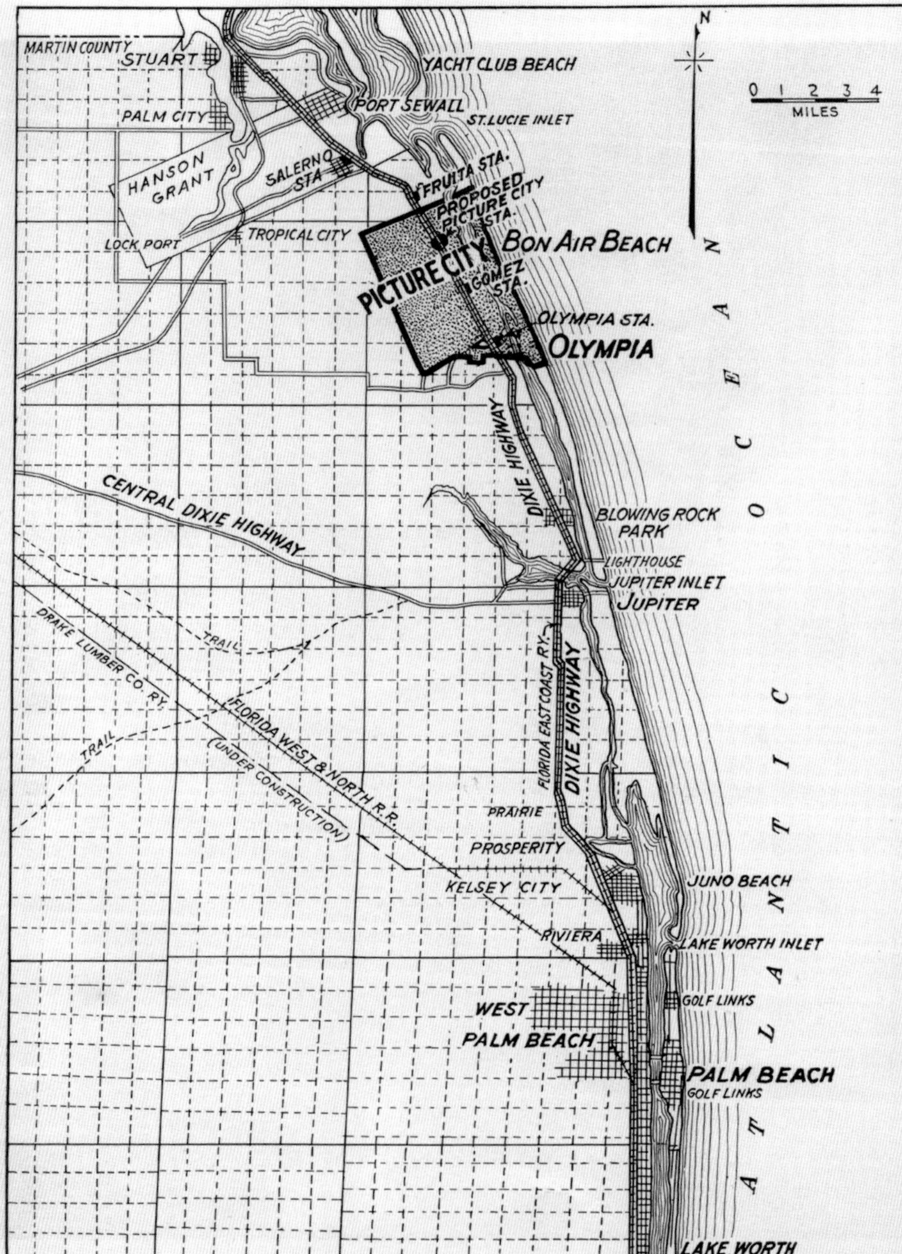

Detail Map Stuart to Palm Beach

Part of the advertising strategy in the Olympia booklet of 1924 was to showcase the location of Olympia–Picture City in relation to Palm Beach. Picture City was envisioned as a metropolis that would rise from the mangroves along the Intracoastal Waterway, where Hobe Sound stands today. Planners envisioned Hollywood-like movie studios and 40,000 residents strolling wide boulevards and verdant parks under bowlers and parasols. (Courtesy of the Martin County Historical Society.)

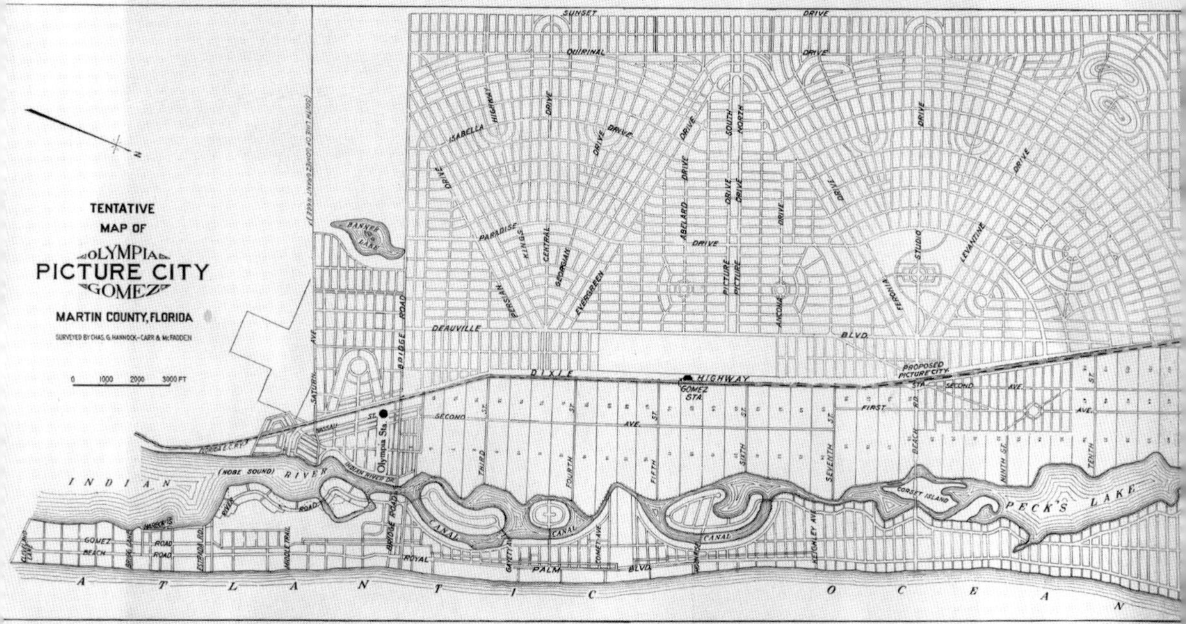

Owing to the fact that Olympia—Picture City embraces many thousands of acres of land, it is impossible to present to the public, in a booklet, other than the above map—which shows only in very small detail, the size and magnitude of the property

With an initial purchase of 2,000 acres and options to acquire 6,000 more, Picture City stretched north from Bridge Road to the northern boundary of the Gomez land grant, and west from the Intracoastal Waterway to the wetlands west of what is now US Route 1. According to "Once There Was Picture City," a 1987 article for the Martin County Historical Society by Walter R. Beales III, "The vast development would include business and residential areas, as well as a movie colony of stars and moguls." Unfortunately, not one house nor studio was built. The studio was supposed to be built from lot sales. Supposedly, many lots were sold, but no one knows where the money went. In March 1926, developers failed to make a loan payment, and six months later, the Farmers Bank and Trust of West Palm Beach foreclosed. A line of concrete light poles along Old Dixie Highway just north of Bridge Road is all that remains of Picture City. Some of the poles are outside the Florida Classic Library. (Courtesy of Martin County Historical Society.)

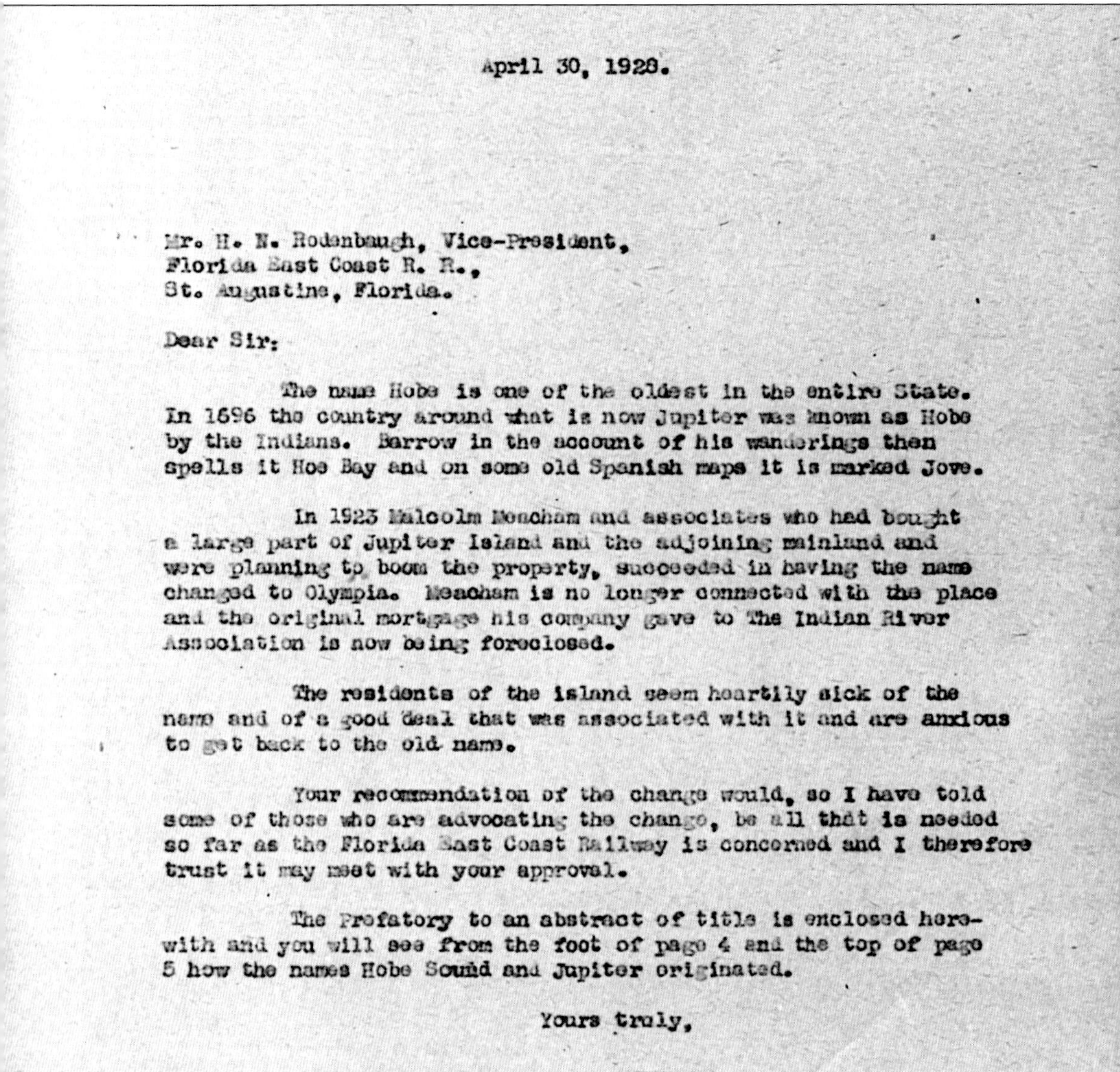

April 30, 1928.

Mr. H. N. Rodenbaugh, Vice-President,
Florida East Coast R. R.,
St. Augustine, Florida.

Dear Sir:

The name Hobe is one of the oldest in the entire State. In 1696 the country around what is now Jupiter was known as Hobe by the Indians. Barrow in the account of his wanderings then spells it Hoe Bay and on some old Spanish maps it is marked Jove.

In 1925 Malcolm Meacham and associates who had bought a large part of Jupiter Island and the adjoining mainland and were planning to boom the property, succeeded in having the name changed to Olympia. Meacham is no longer connected with the place and the original mortgage his company gave to The Indian River Association is now being foreclosed.

The residents of the island seem heartily sick of the name and of a good deal that was associated with it and are anxious to get back to the old name.

Your recommendation of the change would, so I have told some of those who are advocating the change, be all that is needed so far as the Florida East Coast Railway is concerned and I therefore trust it may meet with your approval.

The Prefatory to an abstract of title is enclosed herewith and you will see from the foot of page 4 and the top of page 5 how the names Hobe Sound and Jupiter originated.

Yours truly,

After the collapse of Picture City, followed by the 1926 hurricane that hit Miami, movement to Florida essentially stopped as people's confidence went out the window. Starting in the spring of 1928, there was an effort to replace the name Olympia and return it to the original name of Hobe Sound. This was a somewhat complicated endeavor, as both the post office and the railroad station were named Olympia. In addition, there were different opinions on the name change, and a battle that lasted for months ensued. Pictured is one of the letters describing the argument over the name change. (Courtesy of the P.K. Yonge Library of Florida History, Special and Area Studies Collections, George A. Smathers Libraries, University of Florida.)

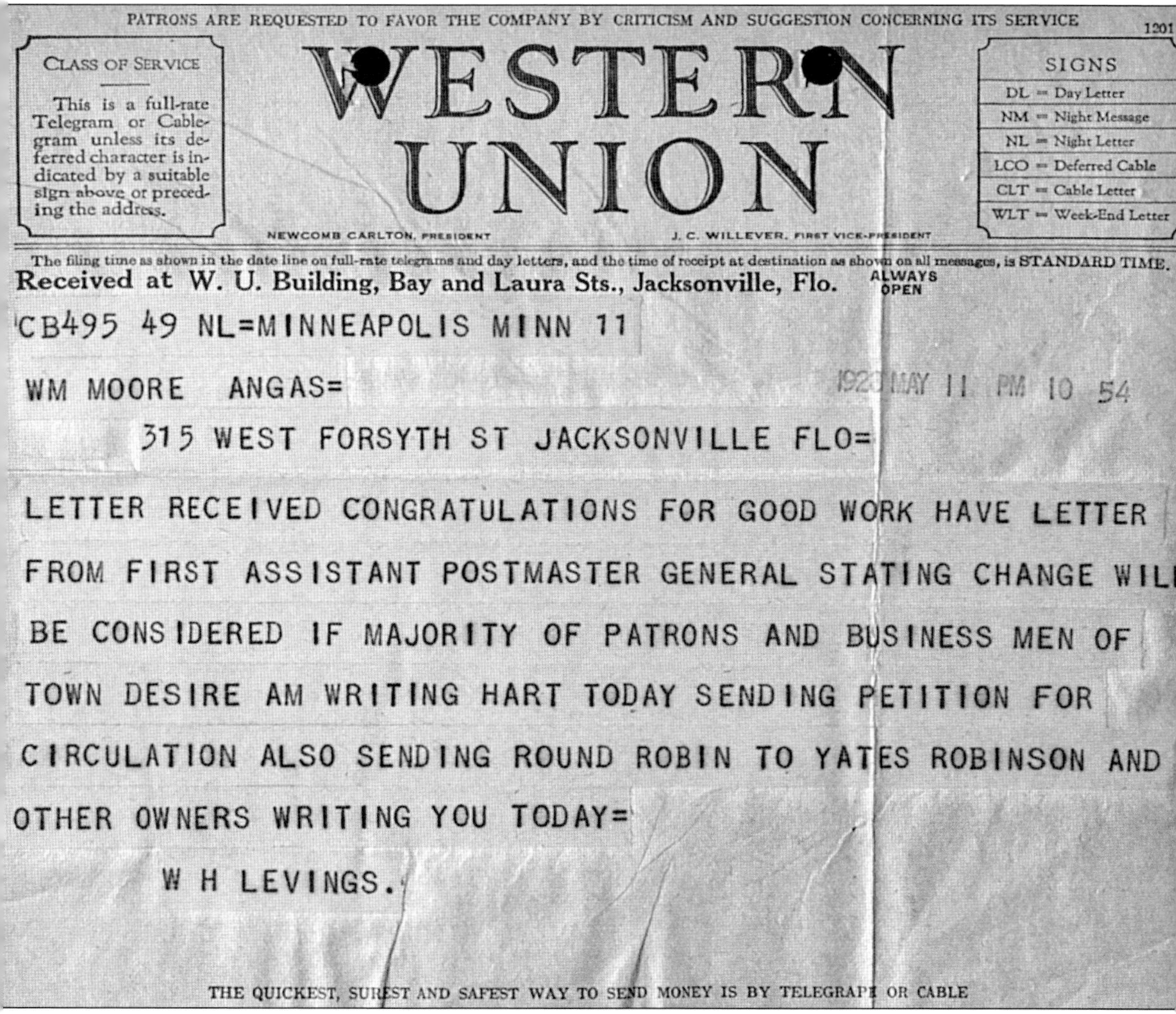

PATRONS ARE REQUESTED TO FAVOR THE COMPANY BY CRITICISM AND SUGGESTION CONCERNING ITS SERVICE 1201

CLASS OF SERVICE

This is a full-rate Telegram or Cablegram unless its deferred character is indicated by a suitable sign above or preceding the address.

WESTERN UNION

NEWCOMB CARLTON, PRESIDENT J. C. WILLEVER, FIRST VICE-PRESIDENT

SIGNS

DL = Day Letter

NM = Night Message

NL = Night Letter

LCO = Deferred Cable

CLT = Cable Letter

WLT = Week-End Letter

The filing time as shown in the date line on full-rate telegrams and day letters, and the time of receipt at destination as shown on all messages, is STANDARD TIME.

Received at W. U. Building, Bay and Laura Sts., Jacksonville, Flo. ALWAYS OPEN

CB495 49 NL=MINNEAPOLIS MINN 11

WM MOORE ANGAS= 1923 MAY 11 PM 10 54

315 WEST FORSYTH ST JACKSONVILLE FLO=

LETTER RECEIVED CONGRATULATIONS FOR GOOD WORK HAVE LETTER FROM FIRST ASSISTANT POSTMASTER GENERAL STATING CHANGE WILL BE CONSIDERED IF MAJORITY OF PATRONS AND BUSINESS MEN OF TOWN DESIRE AM WRITING HART TODAY SENDING PETITION FOR CIRCULATION ALSO SENDING ROUND ROBIN TO YATES ROBINSON AND OTHER OWNERS WRITING YOU TODAY=

W H LEVINGS.

THE QUICKEST, SUREST AND SAFEST WAY TO SEND MONEY IS BY TELEGRAPH OR CABLE

Seen here is a telegram received by William Angas indicating that the letter to change the name of Olympia back to Hobe Sound had been received. In addition, it acknowledged that the postmaster general would consider changing the name if the majority of people living in Olympia supported the change. (Courtesy of the P.K. Yonge Library of Florida History, Special and Area Studies Collections, George A. Smathers Libraries, University of Florida.)

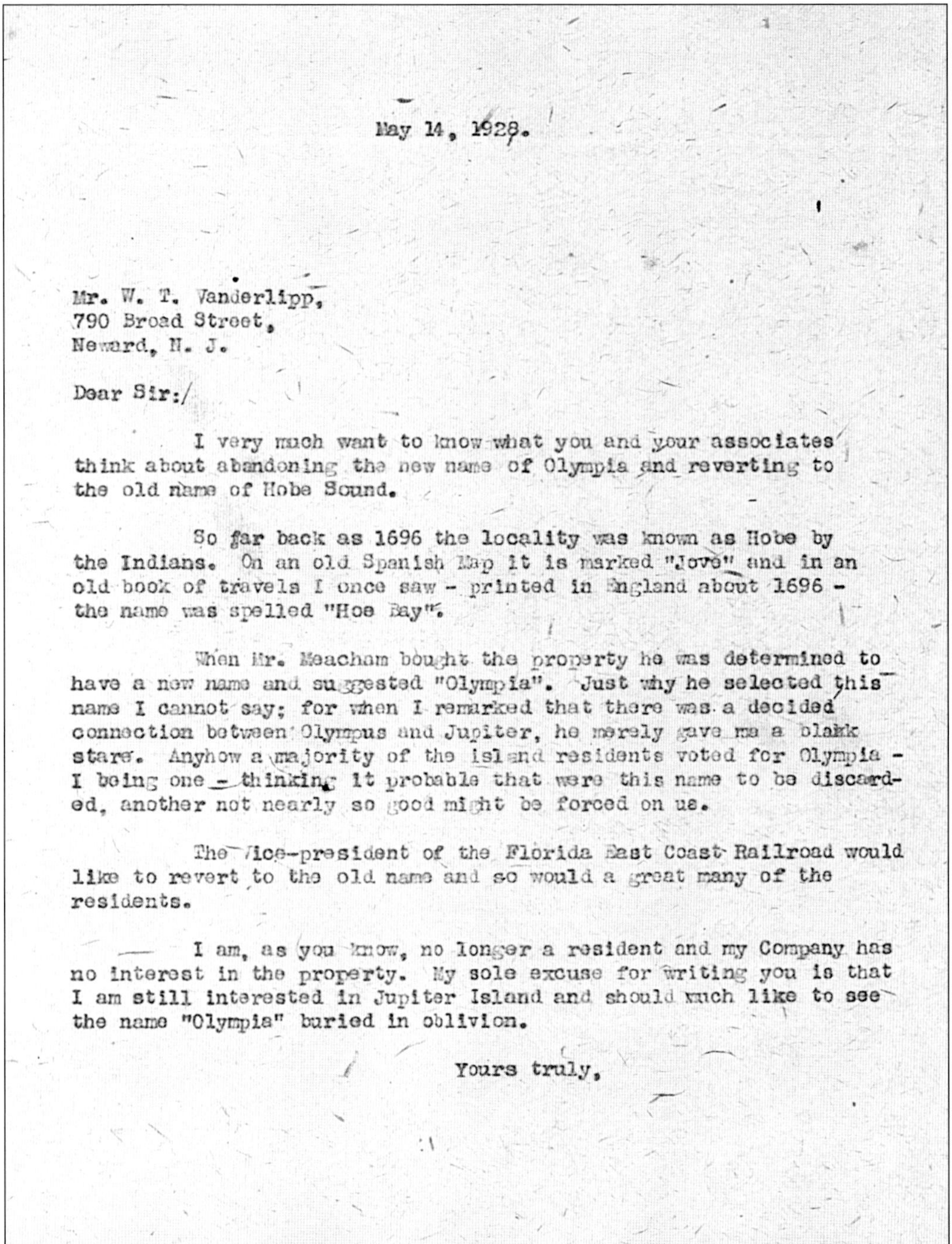

May 14, 1928.

Mr. W. T. Vanderlipp,
790 Broad Street,
Newark, N. J.

Dear Sir:/

I very much want to know what you and your associates think about abandoning the new name of Olympia and reverting to the old name of Hobe Sound.

So far back as 1696 the locality was known as Hobe by the Indians. On an old Spanish Map it is marked "Jove" and in an old book of travels I once saw - printed in England about 1696 - the name was spelled "Hoe Bay".

When Mr. Meacham bought the property he was determined to have a new name and suggested "Olympia". Just why he selected this name I cannot say; for when I remarked that there was a decided connection between Olympus and Jupiter, he merely gave me a blakk stare. Anyhow a majority of the island residents voted for Olympia - I being one - thinking it probable that were this name to be discarded, another not nearly so good might be forced on us.

The Vice-president of the Florida East Coast Railroad would like to revert to the old name and so would a great many of the residents.

I am, as you know, no longer a resident and my Company has no interest in the property. My sole excuse for writing you is that I am still interested in Jupiter Island and should much like to see the name "Olympia" buried in oblivion.

Yours truly,

Pictured is a letter from W.T. Vanderlipp expressing his support for changing the name back to Hobe Sound. He seems to indicate in the letter that the origin of Olympia was unknown and perhaps had a connection to the name of Jupiter, but that it was forced on the Hobe Sound residents. It was his opinion that the name needed to be removed and the old name returned. (Courtesy of the P.K. Yonge Library of Florida History, Special and Area Studies Collections, George A. Smathers Libraries, University of Florida.)

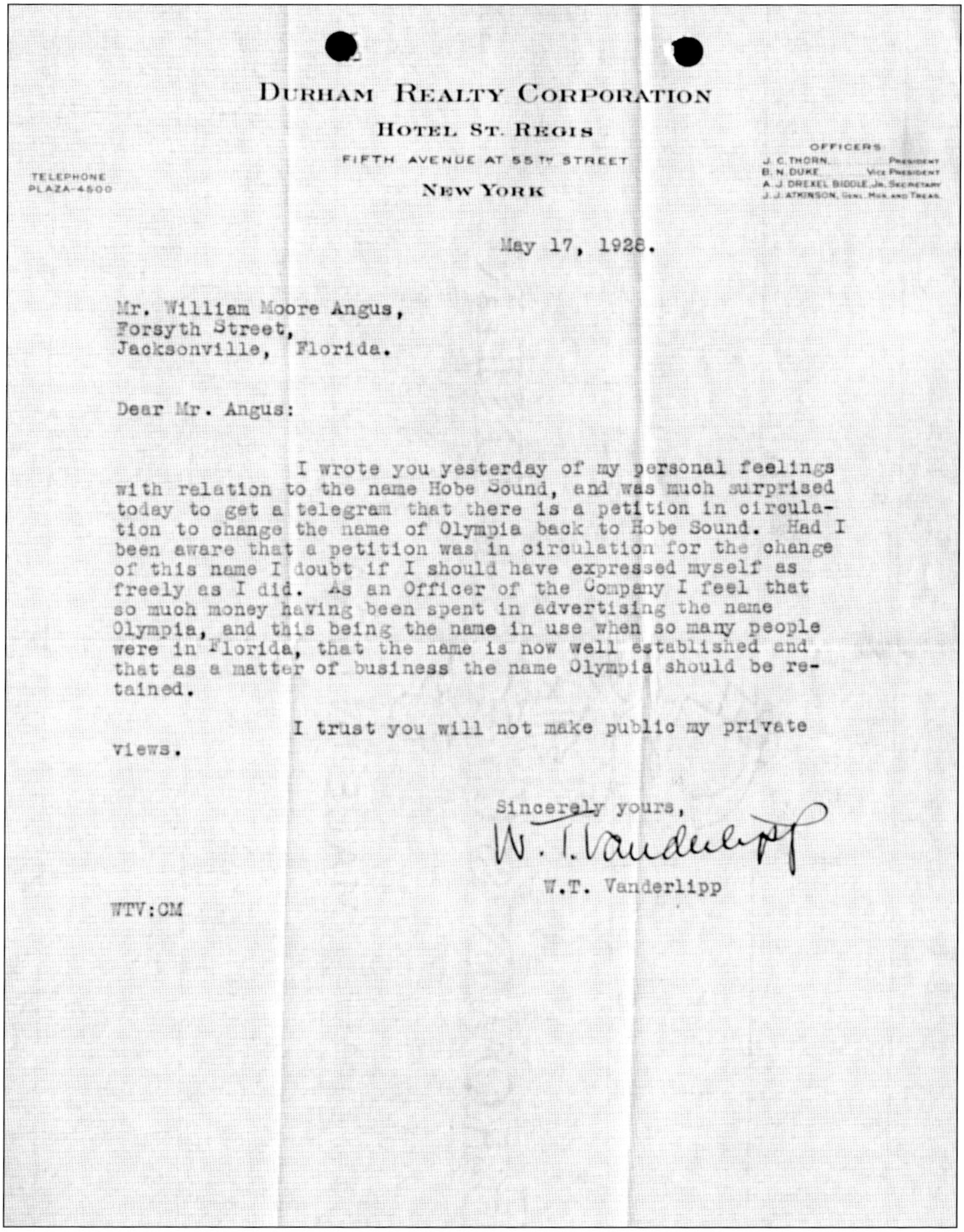

DURHAM REALTY CORPORATION

HOTEL ST. REGIS

FIFTH AVENUE AT 55TH STREET

NEW YORK

TELEPHONE
PLAZA-4500

OFFICERS
J. C. THORN, President
B. N. DUKE, Vice President
A. J. DREXEL BIDDLE, JR., Secretary
J. J. ATKINSON, Genl. Mgr. and Treas.

May 17, 1928.

Mr. William Moore Angus,
Forsyth Street,
Jacksonville, Florida.

Dear Mr. Angus:

I wrote you yesterday of my personal feelings with relation to the name Hobe Sound, and was much surprised today to get a telegram that there is a petition in circulation to change the name of Olympia back to Hobe Sound. Had I been aware that a petition was in circulation for the change of this name I doubt if I should have expressed myself as freely as I did. As an Officer of the Company I feel that so much money having been spent in advertising the name Olympia, and this being the name in use when so many people were in Florida, that the name is now well established and that as a matter of business the name Olympia should be retained.

I trust you will not make public my private views.

Sincerely yours,

W. T. Vanderlipp

W.T. Vanderlipp

WTV:CM

This letter expresses concern about all the money that had been spent to advertise Olympia and the particular business implications of changing the name back to Hobe Sound. At this point, it was only a matter of time until the Olympia Improvement Company suffered the fate of many other American business ventures in the stock market crash of 1929. However, it had a vested financial interest in not changing course. (Courtesy of the P.K. Yonge Library of Florida History, Special and Area Studies Collections, George A. Smathers Libraries, University of Florida.)

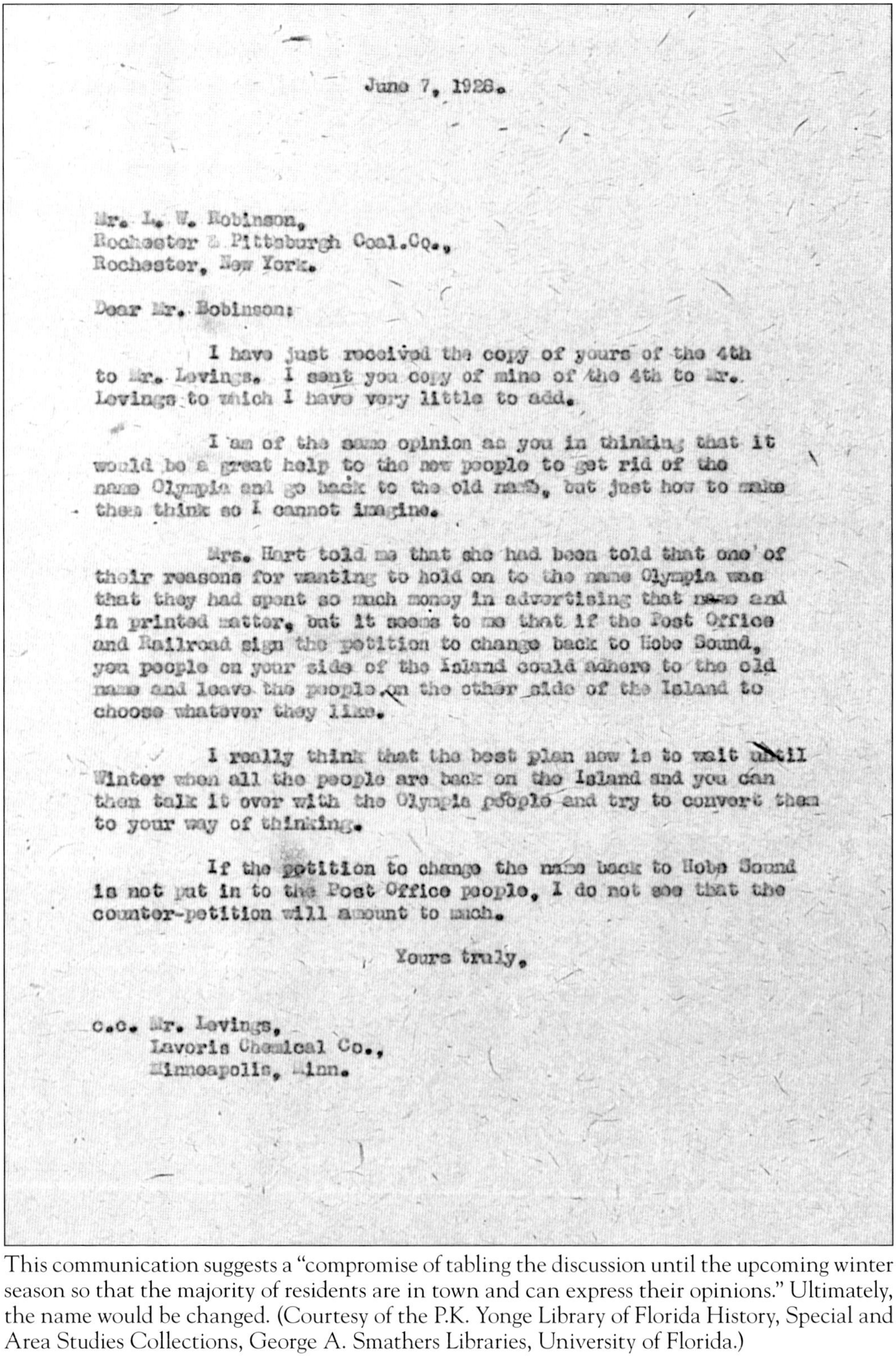

June 7, 1928.

Mr. L. W. Robinson,
Rochester & Pittsburgh Coal.Co.,
Rochester, New York.

Dear Mr. Robinson:

I have just received the copy of yours of the 4th to Mr. Levings. I sent you copy of mine of the 4th to Mr. Levings to which I have very little to add.

I am of the same opinion as you in thinking that it would be a great help to the new people to get rid of the name Olympia and go back to the old name, but just how to make them think so I cannot imagine.

Mrs. Hart told me that she had been told that one of their reasons for wanting to hold on to the name Olympia was that they had spent so much money in advertising that name and in printed matter, but it seems to me that if the Post Office and Railroad sign the petition to change back to Hobe Sound, you people on your side of the Island could adhere to the old name and leave the people on the other side of the Island to choose whatever they like.

I really think that the best plan now is to wait until Winter when all the people are back on the Island and you can then talk it over with the Olympia people and try to convert them to your way of thinking.

If the petition to change the name back to Hobe Sound is not put in to the Post Office people, I do not see that the counter-petition will amount to much.

Yours truly,

c.c. Mr. Levings,
Lavoris Chemical Co.,
Minneapolis, Minn.

This communication suggests a "compromise of tabling the discussion until the upcoming winter season so that the majority of residents are in town and can express their opinions." Ultimately, the name would be changed. (Courtesy of the P.K. Yonge Library of Florida History, Special and Area Studies Collections, George A. Smathers Libraries, University of Florida.)

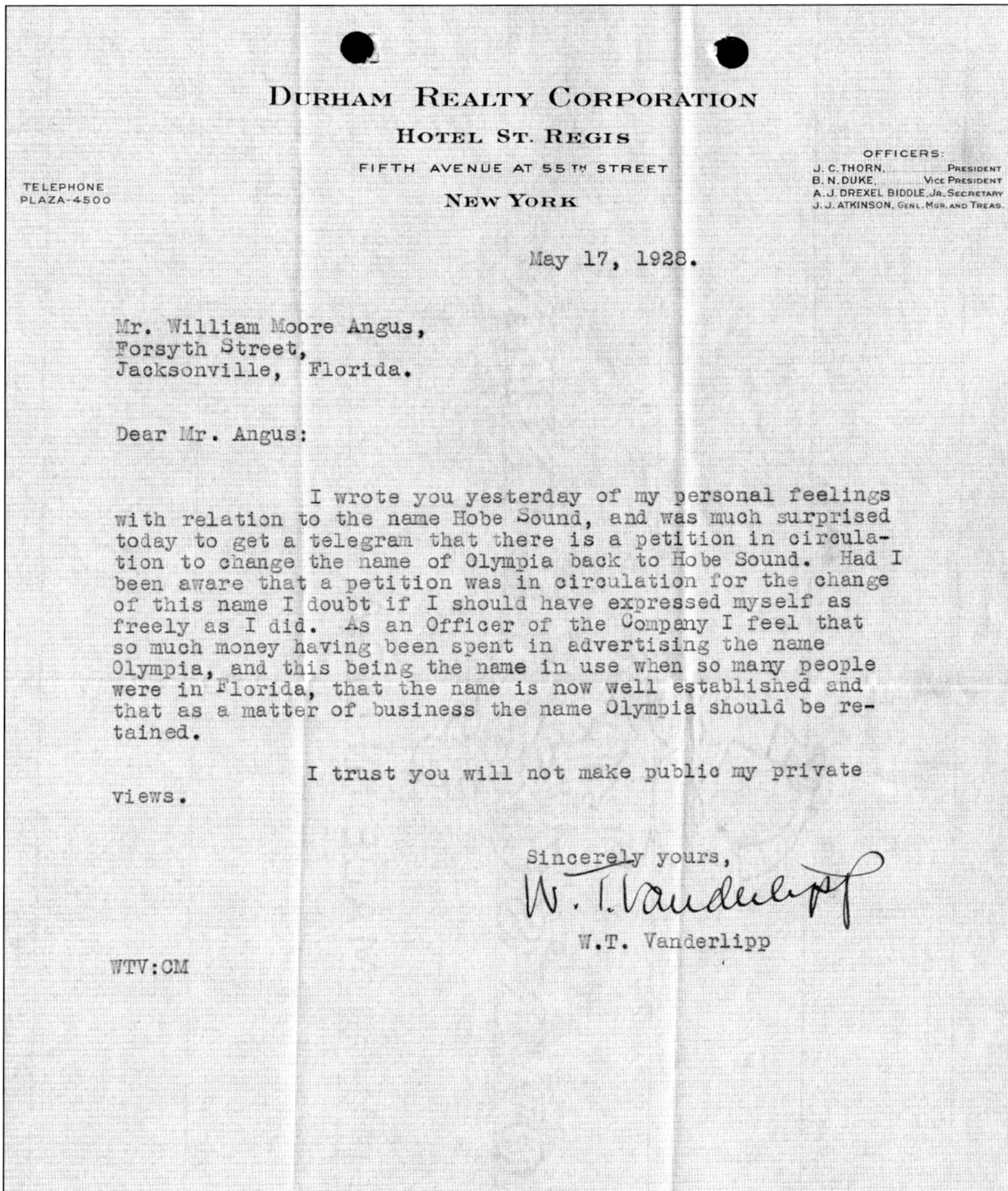

DURHAM REALTY CORPORATION
HOTEL ST. REGIS
FIFTH AVENUE AT 55TH STREET
NEW YORK

TELEPHONE
PLAZA-4500

OFFICERS:
J. C. THORN, PRESIDENT
B. N. DUKE, VICE PRESIDENT
A. J. DREXEL BIDDLE, JR. SECRETARY
J. J. ATKINSON, GENL. MGR. AND TREAS.

May 17, 1928.

Mr. William Moore Angus,
Forsyth Street,
Jacksonville, Florida.

Dear Mr. Angus:

I wrote you yesterday of my personal feelings with relation to the name Hobe Sound, and was much surprised today to get a telegram that there is a petition in circulation to change the name of Olympia back to Hobe Sound. Had I been aware that a petition was in circulation for the change of this name I doubt if I should have expressed myself as freely as I did. As an Officer of the Company I feel that so much money having been spent in advertising the name Olympia, and this being the name in use when so many people were in Florida, that the name is now well established and that as a matter of business the name Olympia should be retained.

I trust you will not make public my private views.

Sincerely yours,

W. T. Vanderlipp

W.T. Vanderlipp

WTV:CM

W.T. Vanderlipp, as an officer in the Olympia Development Corporation, appears to be concerned that his previous letter where he expressed support for the name change could be in conflict with the overall position of the Olympia Improvement Company. Coincidently, there was another major hurricane in the fall of 1928 and then, of course, the stock market crash in 1929. The end of Picture City and Olympia was complete. Luckily, in 1933, a group of island residents including Arthur S. Dwight, Joseph V. Reed, and Samuel Pryor formed the new Hobe Sound Company and purchased for $25,000 the inn, golf course, employee houses, unsold land north of the fork at South Beach Road, and Gomez Avenue, along with other real estate on the mainland. In 1934, Joseph V. Reed purchased the other owners' shares in the Hobe Sound Company where it remained under Reed's leadership until 1996. (Courtesy of the P.K. Yonge Library of Florida History, Special and Area Studies Collections, George A. Smathers Libraries, University of Florida.)

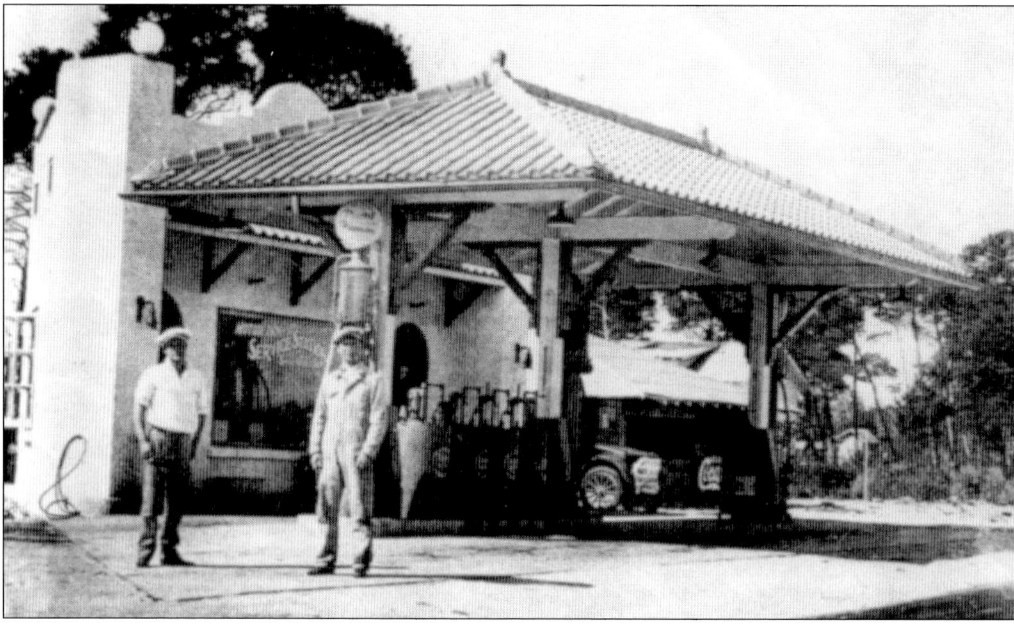

Seen here in the mid- to late 1930s is Diamond's Garage, at the corner of Dixie Highway and Bridge Road. James and Catherine Diamond saw a need for transportation services for seasonal visitors in 1934. They met trains (and later, planes) and provided transportation service that continues today. They became the first car rental business in Martin County starting in the 1940s. Today, Diamond Transfer & Garage is owned by Jim and Catherine's daughter Suzanne and managed by her son Pat Martin, the Diamonds' grandson. (Courtesy of the Stuart Heritage Museum.)

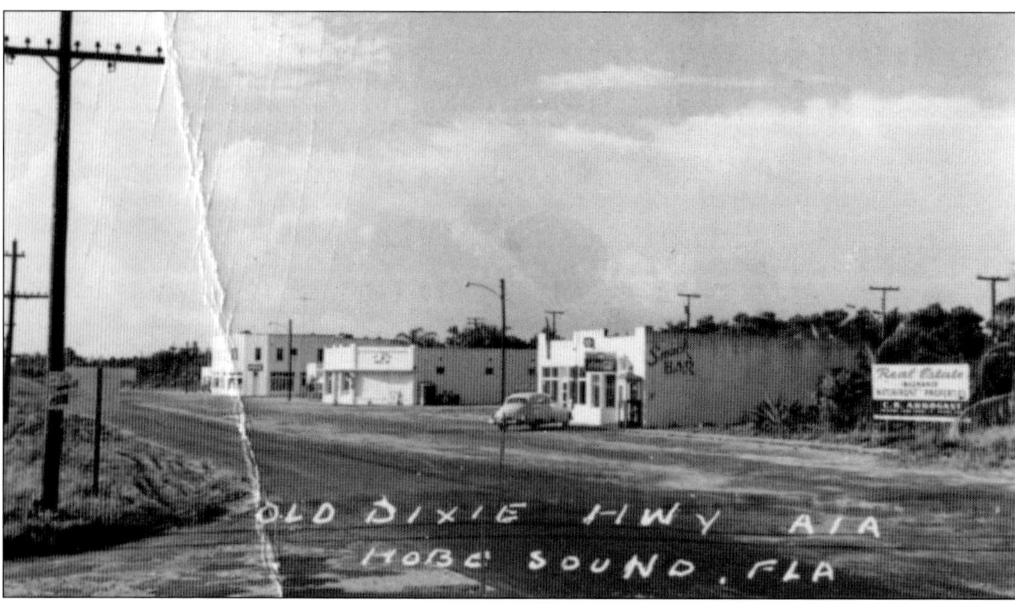

This is a c. 1950 view of Old Dixie Highway. What once was the thriving town of Olympia in the 1920s is a not-so-thriving stretch in the decade after World War II. However, just like in times past, the town would continue to reinvent itself and become a thriving and bustling community once more. (Courtesy of Sandra Thurlow.)

Three

ON THE ISLAND

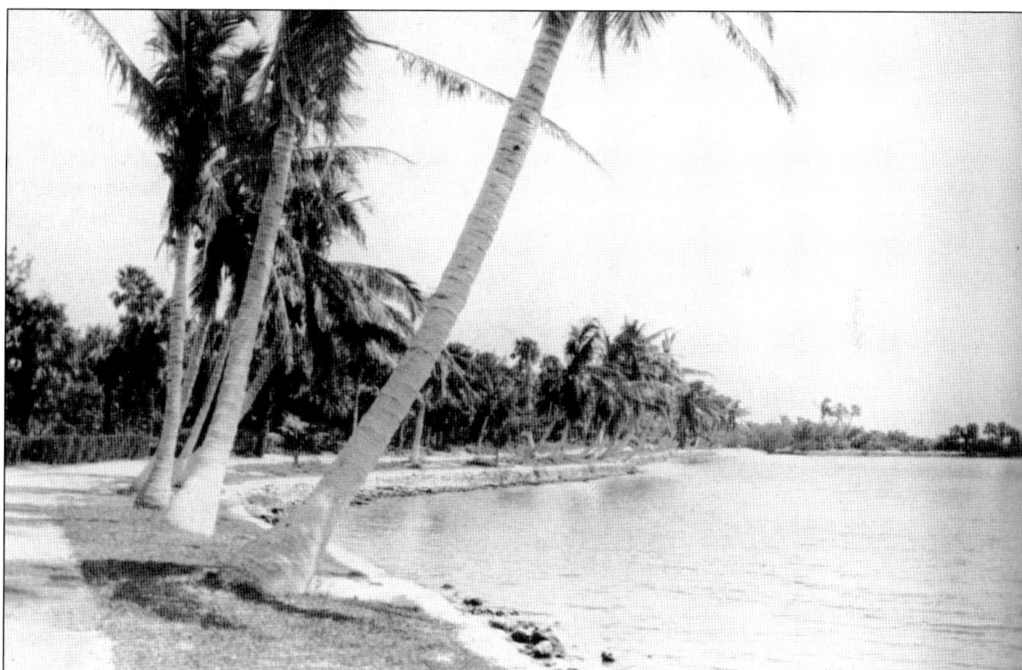

As early as 1918, realtors extolled Jupiter Island as an ideal winter resort. Seen here is a view from the inn found in the *Jupiter Island Book*, published as an advertising document in 1935 by the Hobe Sound Company. It was second only to Palm Beach in its appeal to the wealthier families. Today, this nine-mile barrier island remains a mecca for the rich and famous. Hidden behind tall hedges and at the end of long driveways live some of the nation's wealthiest families. Its seclusion is treasured by the old-money aristocracy, which has used the island as a retreat for generations. Some names are found on discreet markers outside of the gates. Those current and past residents come straight from the annals of American history and include Firestone, Roosevelt, Rockefeller, Weyerhaeuser, Mellon, Armour, Doubleday, Ford, Bush, DuPont, Whitney, Field, Woods, Dion, and Norman. (Courtesy of the Martin County Historical Society.)

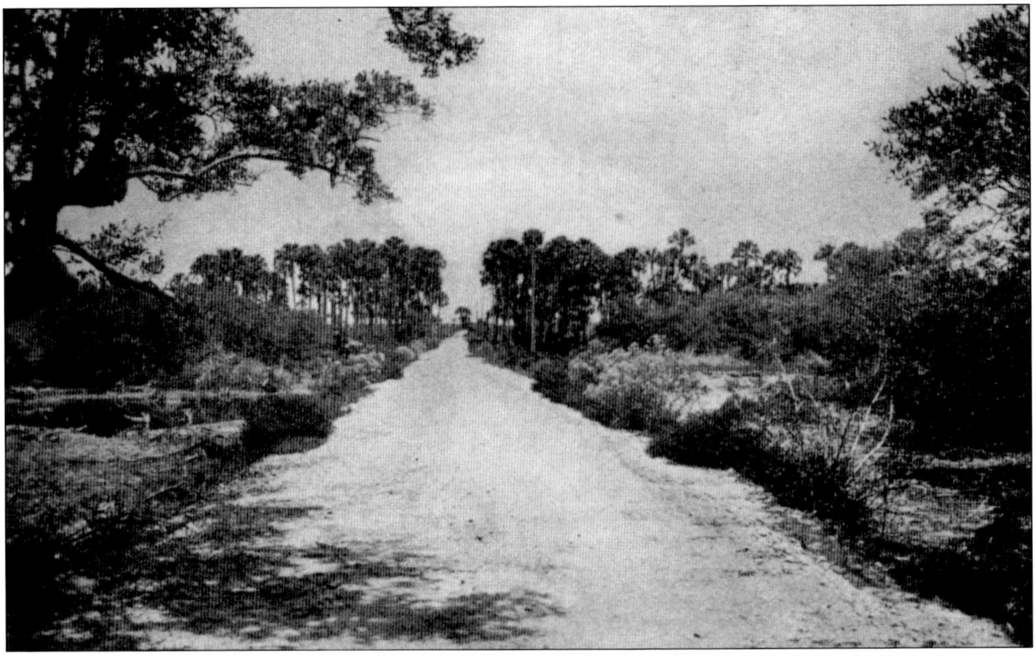

In these images, George Chapin captured the rugged beauty of Jupiter Island while it was in its infancy of development, in 1913. According to plans for the automobile road seen above, all garages had to be placed at the back of lots and the noise and dust kept away from residences and bungalows. Below is one of the earliest photographs of the rare "geyser" at Blowing Rocks Preserve. The wind and tide must align, which generally happens only after a strong nor'easter, to create a strong crashing of waves under the rocks. When this happens, the water can shoot 30–40 feet into the air. (Both, courtesy of the P.K. Yonge Library of Florida History, Special and Area Studies Collections, George A. Smathers Libraries, University of Florida.)

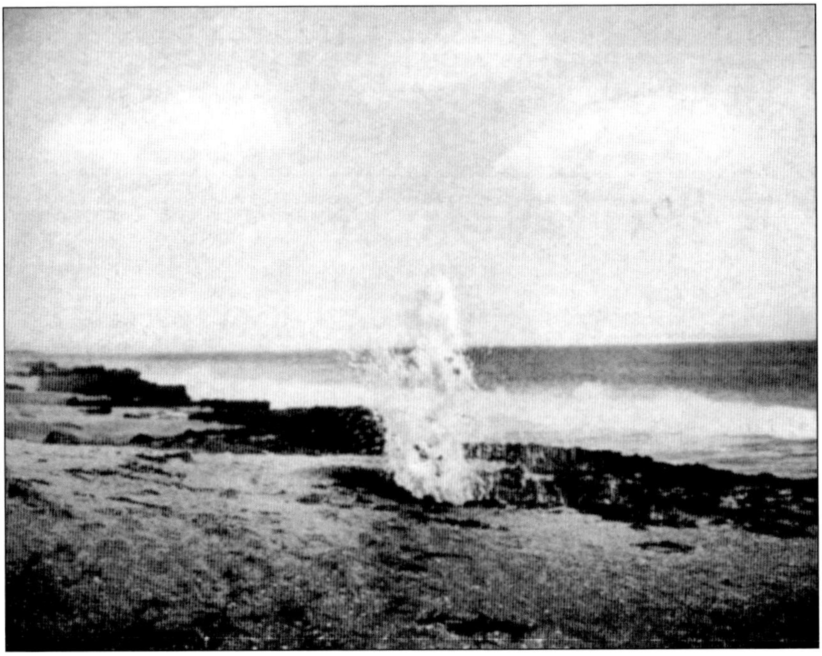

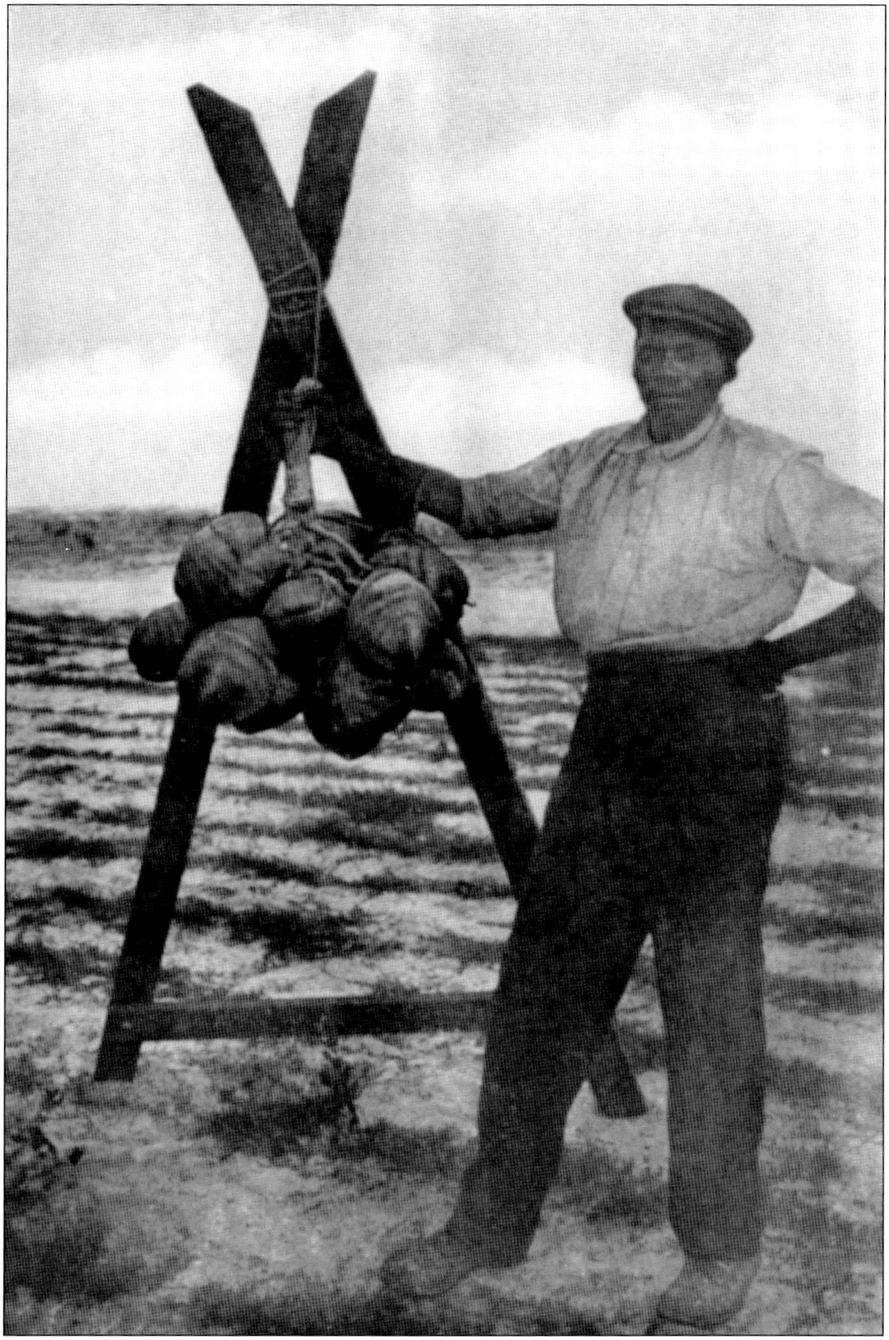

Coconuts are prevalent on Jupiter Island. Pictured is a man collecting coconuts in 1913. If harvesting the fruit for coconut water, it is ready six to seven months after emergence. The meat takes another five to six months. Along with timing, color is an indicator of ripeness. Green coconuts have the sweetest water, while brown ones have flesh that can be eaten. Coconuts were important to the early settlers as a means of food and water, with their shells being used for other purposes. (Courtesy of the P.K. Yonge Library of Florida History, Special and Area Studies Collections, George A. Smathers Libraries, University of Florida.)

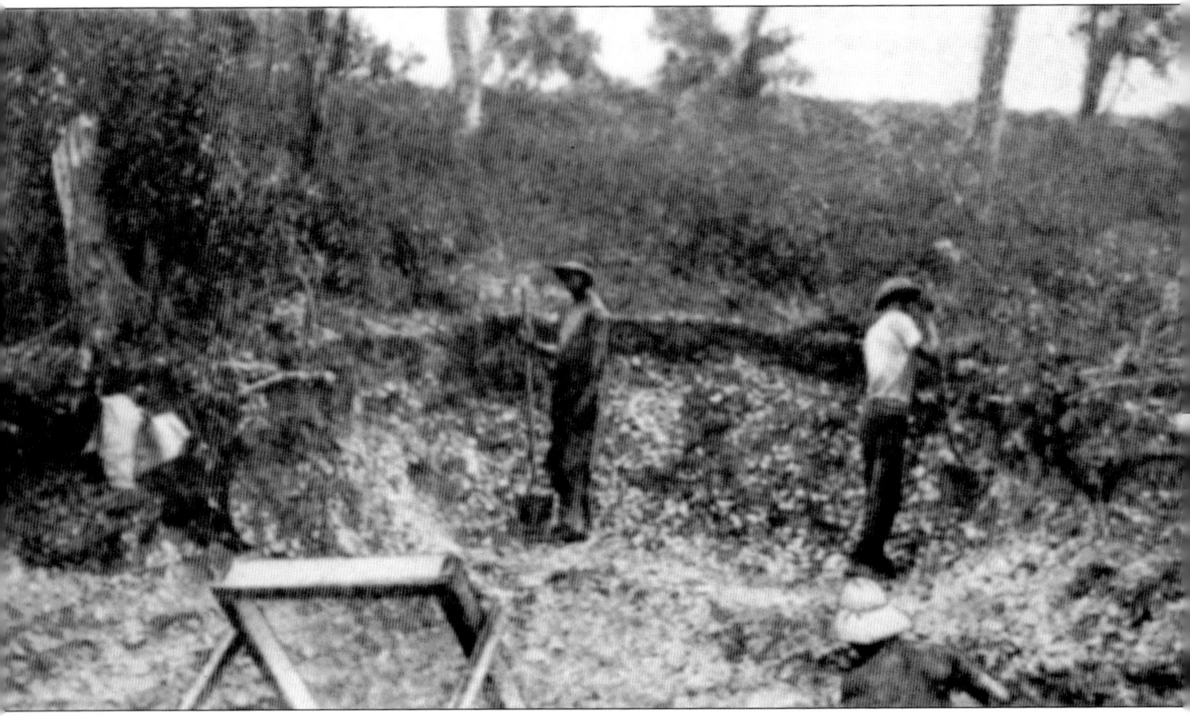

Coquina is a form of limestone composed of the shell fragments of ancient mollusks and other marine invertebrates, which over time are glued together by dissolved calcium carbonate in the shells. Coquina is also the name of a common tiny clam found everywhere on Florida beaches. As a building material, coquina is lightweight, easy to find (it is indigenous to the Florida coast), easy to use, and nearly indestructible. Here, coquina is being harvested for building on Jupiter Island in 1913. (Courtesy of the P.K. Yonge Library of Florida History, Special and Area Studies Collections, George A. Smathers Libraries, University of Florida.)

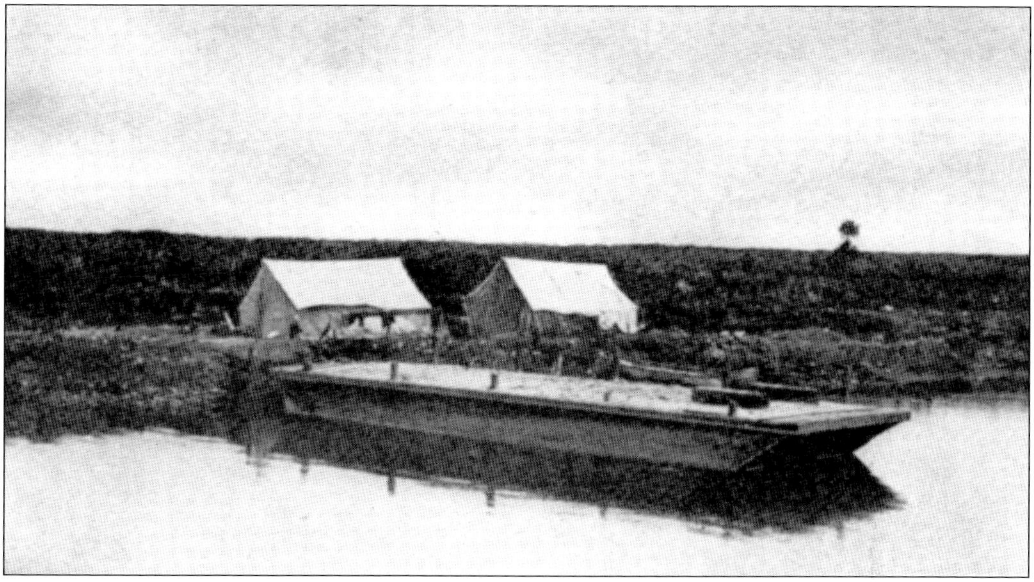

After 1900, the building of bungalows and residences picked up, and the necessity for building materials and roads provided the catalyst for a quarry on the island. Luckily, Mother Nature had provided an abundance of local materials. The Hobe Sound Stone Company operated a quarry from 1927 to 1930 on the island. This is a picture of the quarry on Jupiter Island. (Courtesy of the P.K. Yonge Library of Florida History, Special and Area Studies Collections, George A. Smathers Libraries, University of Florida.)

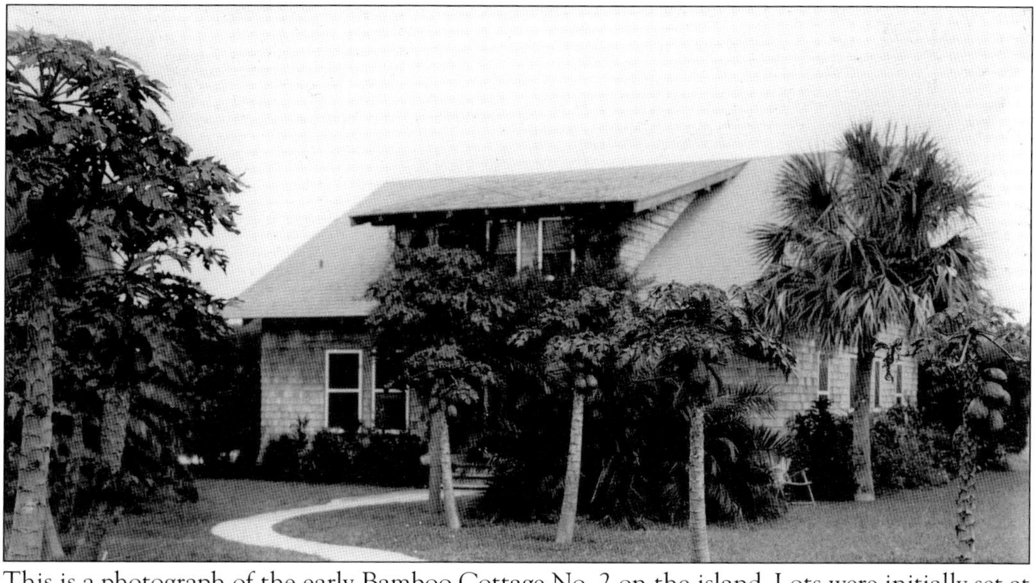

This is a photograph of the early Bamboo Cottage No. 2 on the island. Lots were initially set at one-third to one-fifth of an acre so as to minimize the necessity of a gardener during the summer months when no one was in residence. Setbacks were established at 10 feet from all sides, and fences could be no higher than 25 feet. (Author's collection.)

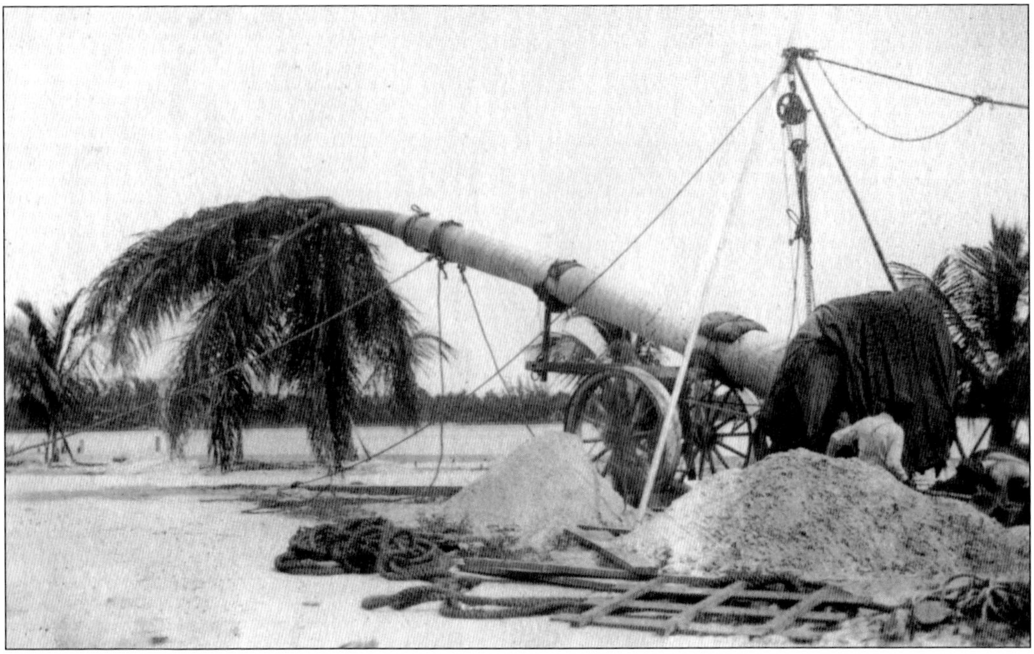

William Lyman Phillips (1885–1966) played a seminal role in the landscaping of Florida and in the history of landscape architecture, designing the world-famous Fairchild Tropical Garden in Miami (begun in 1938) as well as hundreds of other sites, four of them listed in the National Register. He studied under Frederick Law Olmsted at Harvard and then spent over 45 years pioneering the use of palms and other tropical plants, which had previously been largely ignored or treated with contempt by many. Above are palms being installed as part of the planned landscape on Jupiter Island around 1910. Below is a postcard showcasing the "Garden of the Gods" at Shuey's Inn on the Island. (Above, courtesy of the Martin County Historical Society; below, courtesy of Sandra Thurlow.)

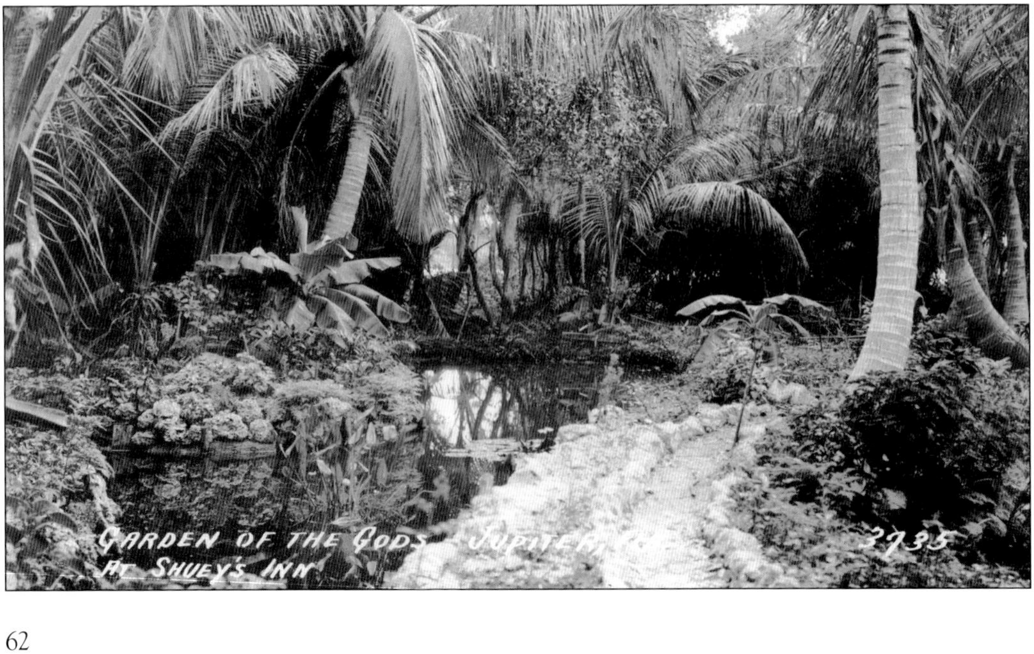

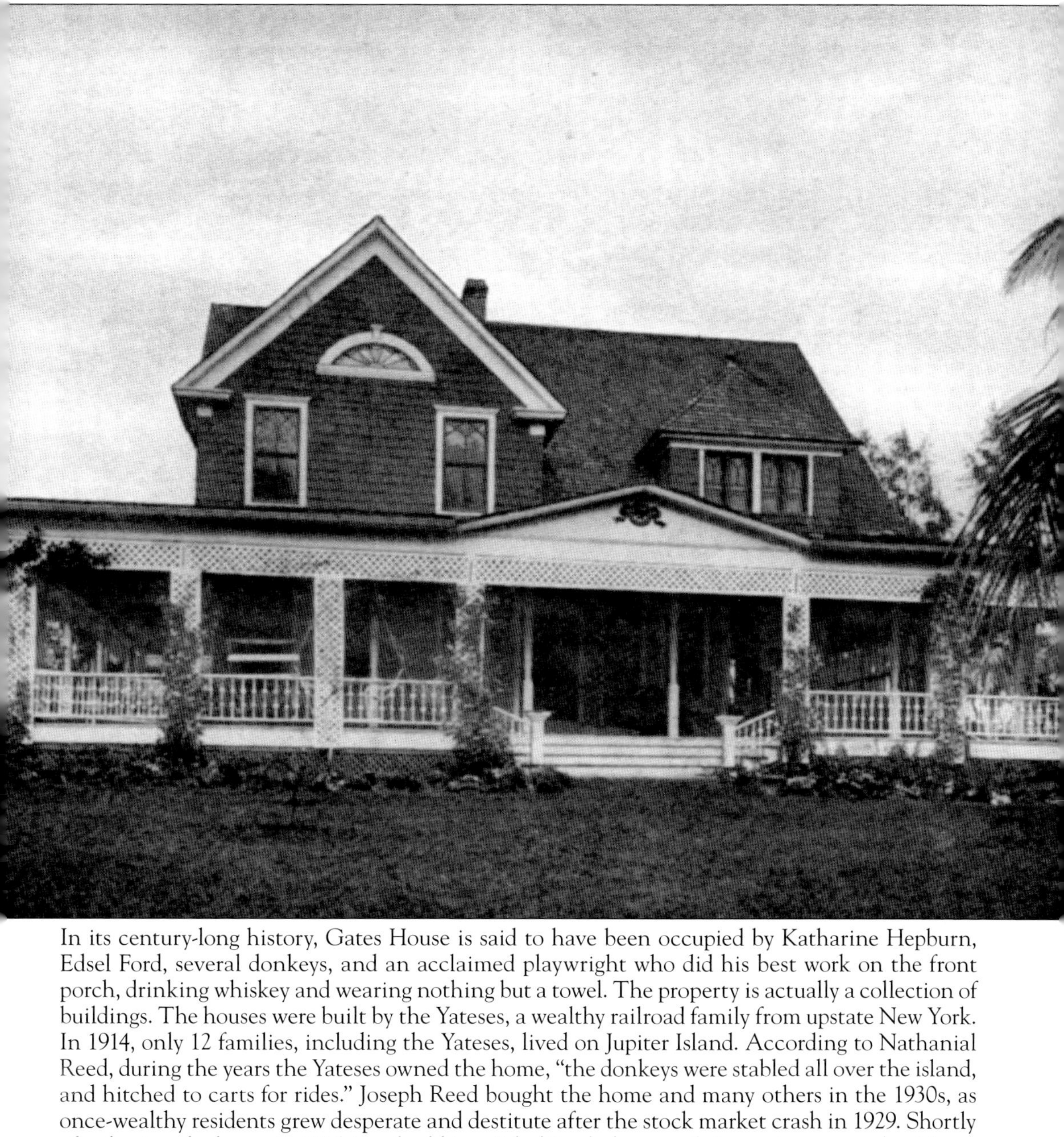

In its century-long history, Gates House is said to have been occupied by Katharine Hepburn, Edsel Ford, several donkeys, and an acclaimed playwright who did his best work on the front porch, drinking whiskey and wearing nothing but a towel. The property is actually a collection of buildings. The houses were built by the Yateses, a wealthy railroad family from upstate New York. In 1914, only 12 families, including the Yateses, lived on Jupiter Island. According to Nathanial Reed, during the years the Yateses owned the home, "the donkeys were stabled all over the island, and hitched to carts for rides." Joseph Reed bought the home and many others in the 1930s, as once-wealthy residents grew desperate and destitute after the stock market crash in 1929. Shortly after buying the home in 1935, Reed sold it to Edsel Ford, the son of pioneering automaker Henry Ford. A few years after he bought it, Ford sold Gates House to acclaimed playwright Philip Barry. A not-proven but often-talked-about rumor on the island is that Katherine Hepburn and Spencer Tracy rendezvoused at the home during their semi-secret 26-year love affair. (Courtesy of the P.K. Yonge Library of Florida History, Special and Area Studies Collections, George A. Smathers Libraries, University of Florida.)

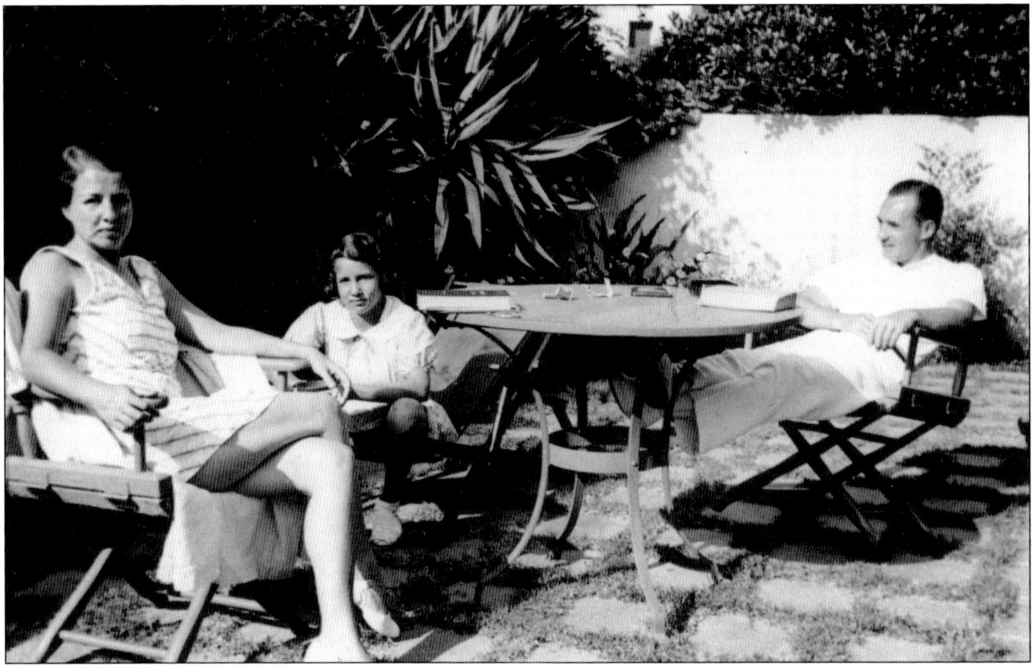

Edsel Ford was the president of Ford Motor Company from 1919 until his death in 1943. He is credited with the founding of the Model A in 1927 and the Mercury division, as well as the Lincoln-Zephyr and Lincoln Continental. In addition, he was behind the development of hydraulic brakes. He died of stomach cancer at the young age of 49 in 1943. Ford vacationed on Jupiter Island and purchased the Gates House in 1937. Above, he relaxes on the patio with his wife, Eleanor, and daughter Josephine. Below is Benson Ford, son of Edsel and grandson of Henry, in their driveway on Jupiter Island. (Both, courtesy of the collections of Ford House, 1986.2403 and 1986.4578.8.)

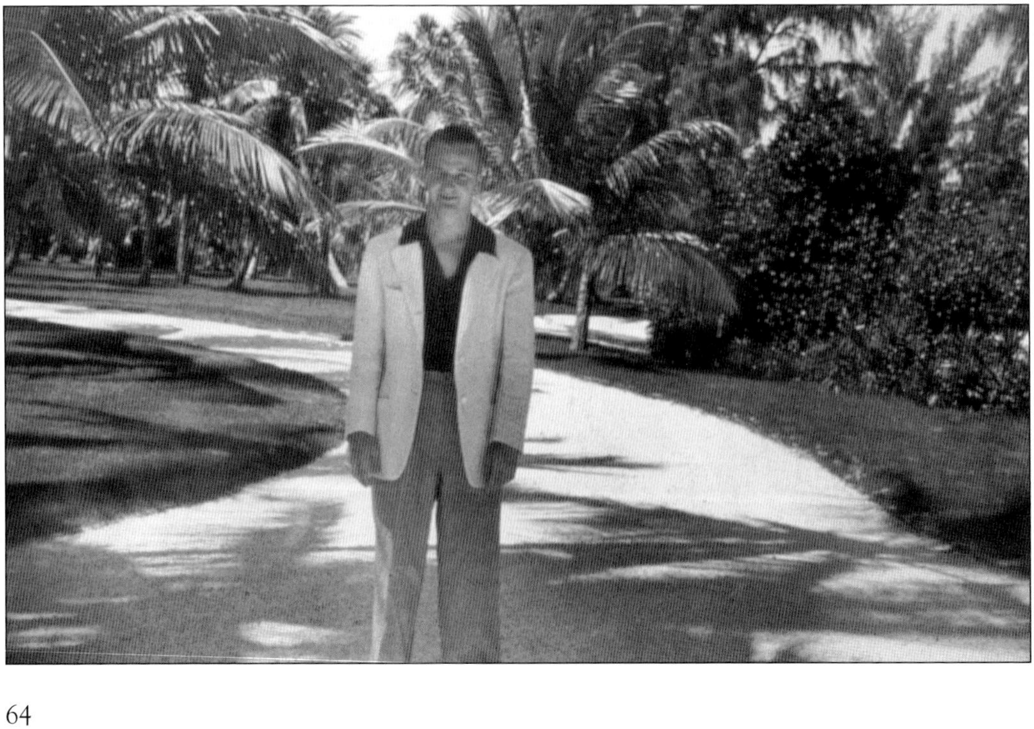

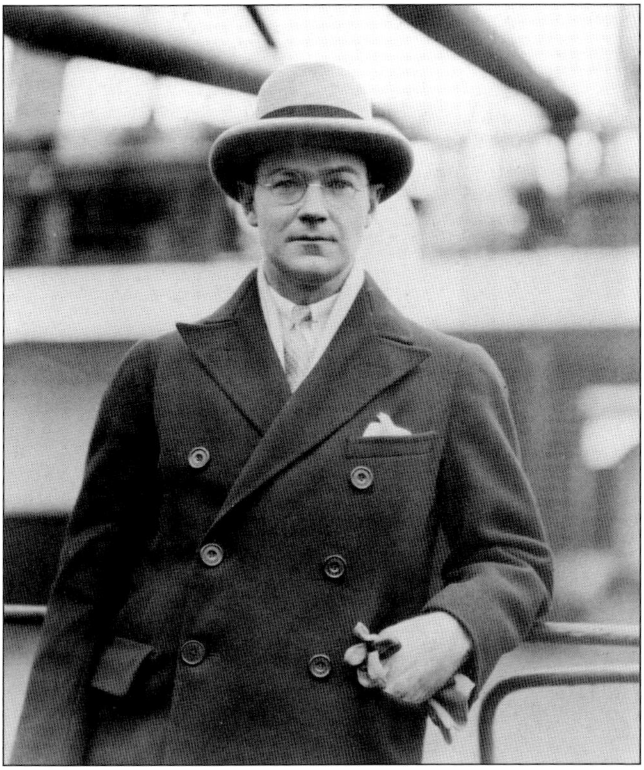

At right is Phillip Barry in 1928. Born in Rochester, New York, in 1896, Barry was a dramatist best known for his comedies of life and manners among the socially privileged. He bought the Gates House from Edsel Ford and used it as a writing retreat. It is said that he wrote *A Philadelphia Story* there. (Right, courtesy of George Grantham Bain Collection, Library of Congress; below, author's collection.)

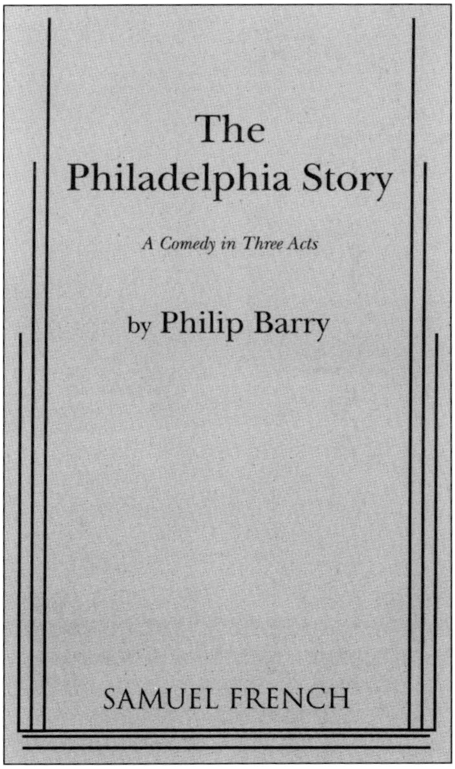

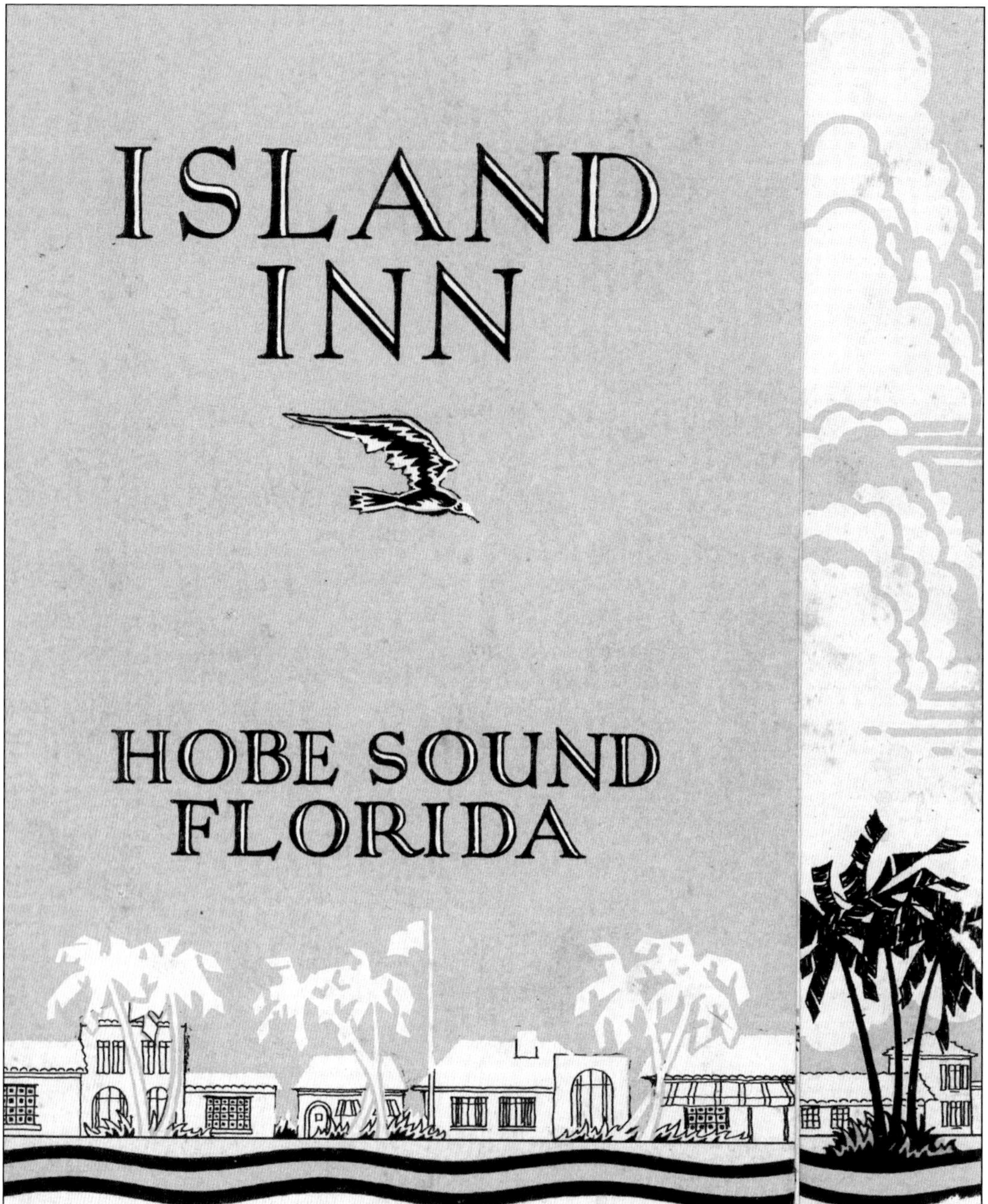

The Island Inn was constructed by William Angas in 1916 under the Indian River Association to host northerners during the winter season. It opened during the 1916–1917 winter season and hosted 150 guests in its first year. After several different owners and a period of disarray and neglect, it finally seemed to hit its stride by the late 1930s under the Hobe Sound Company. Seen here is a brochure from 1936 used to advertise the newly renovated resort. (Courtesy of the Martin County Historical Society.)

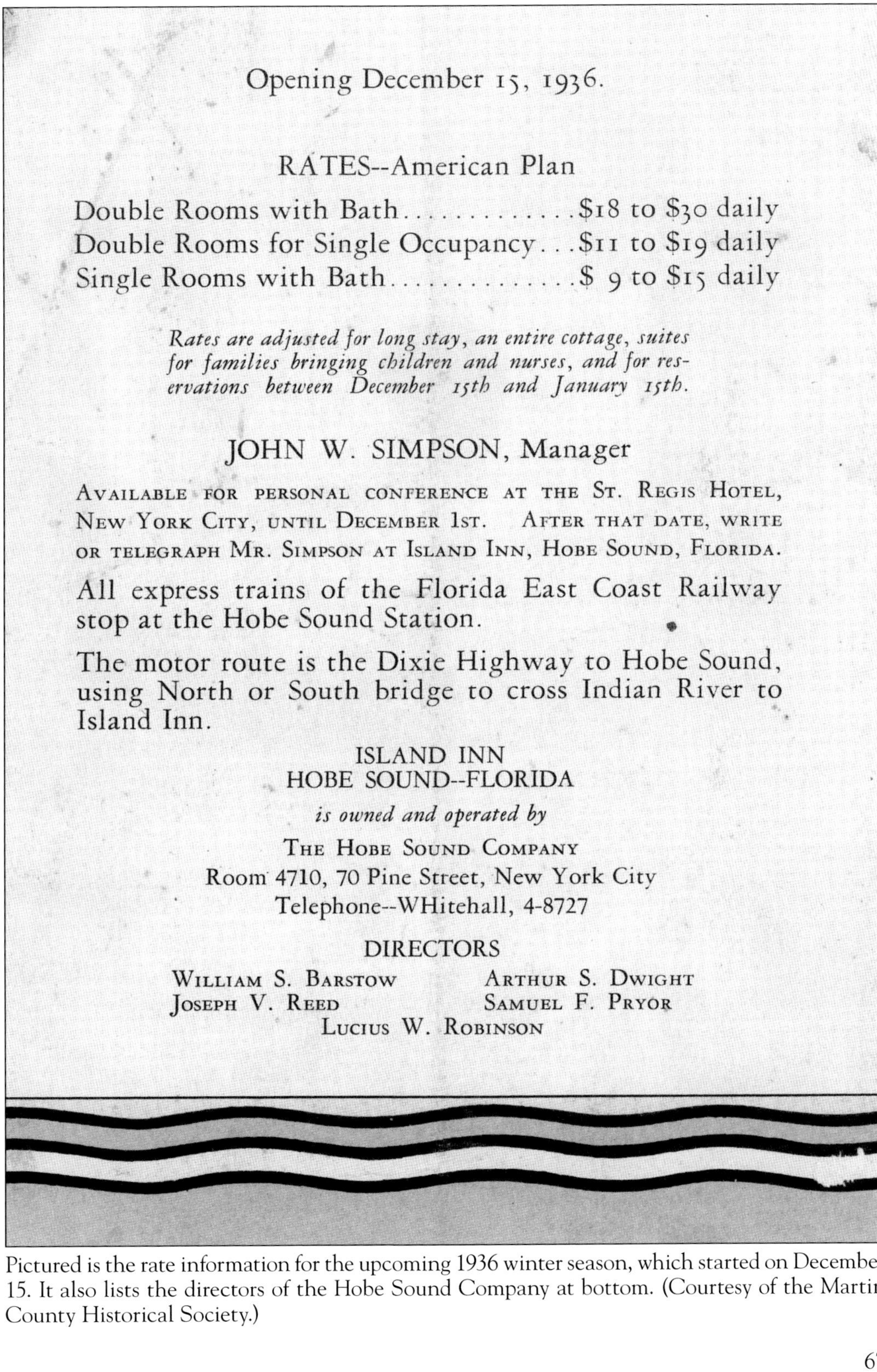

Opening December 15, 1936.

RATES--American Plan

Double Rooms with Bath............$18 to $30 daily
Double Rooms for Single Occupancy...$11 to $19 daily
Single Rooms with Bath.............$ 9 to $15 daily

Rates are adjusted for long stay, an entire cottage, suites for families bringing children and nurses, and for reservations between December 15th and January 15th.

JOHN W. SIMPSON, Manager

Available for personal conference at the St. Regis Hotel, New York City, until December 1st. After that date, write or telegraph Mr. Simpson at Island Inn, Hobe Sound, Florida.

All express trains of the Florida East Coast Railway stop at the Hobe Sound Station.

The motor route is the Dixie Highway to Hobe Sound, using North or South bridge to cross Indian River to Island Inn.

ISLAND INN
HOBE SOUND--FLORIDA
is owned and operated by
The Hobe Sound Company
Room 4710, 70 Pine Street, New York City
Telephone--WHitehall, 4-8727

DIRECTORS

William S. Barstow — Arthur S. Dwight
Joseph V. Reed — Samuel F. Pryor
Lucius W. Robinson

Pictured is the rate information for the upcoming 1936 winter season, which started on December 15. It also lists the directors of the Hobe Sound Company at bottom. (Courtesy of the Martin County Historical Society.)

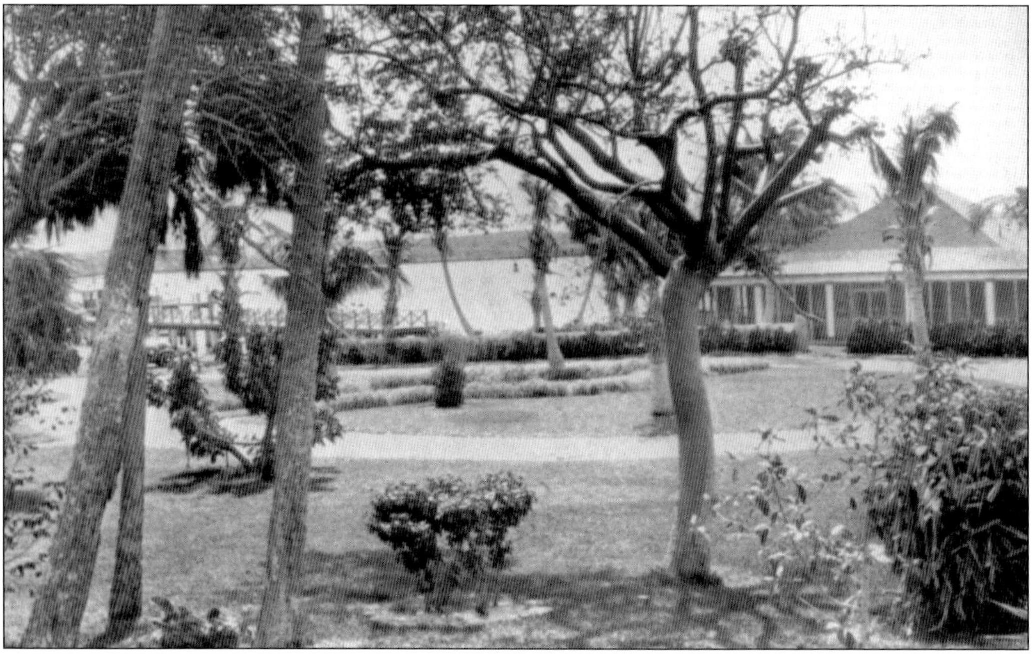

Above is the Jupiter Island Club recreation hall and boat dock in 1935. Below is a view of the inn from the lawn. (Both, courtesy of the Martin County Historical Society.)

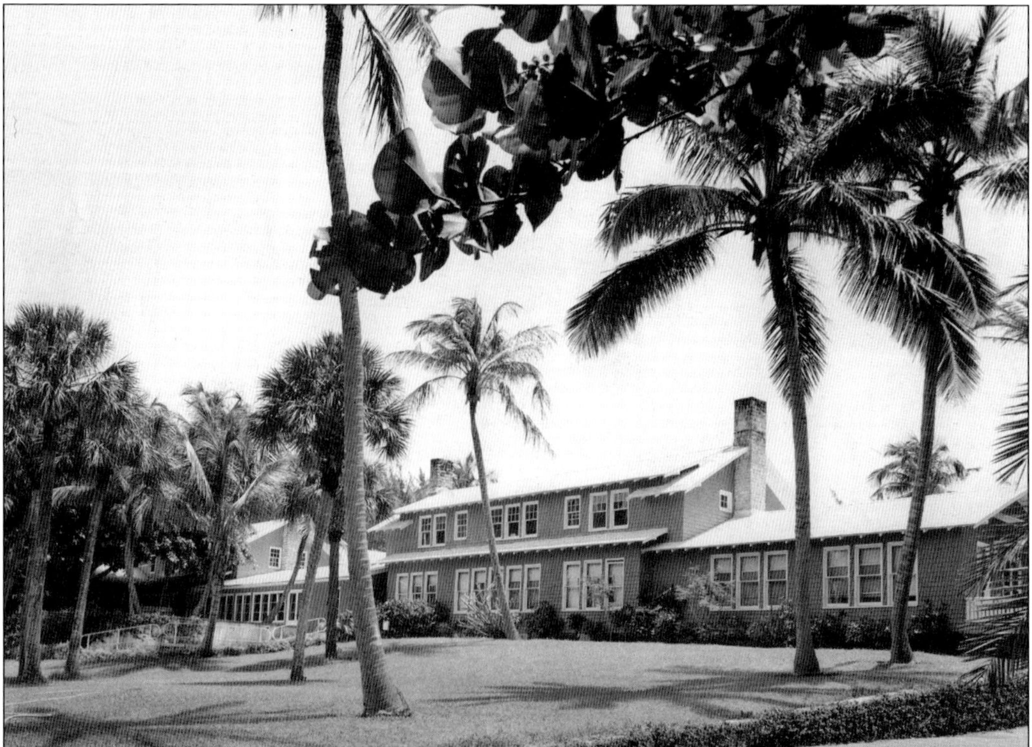

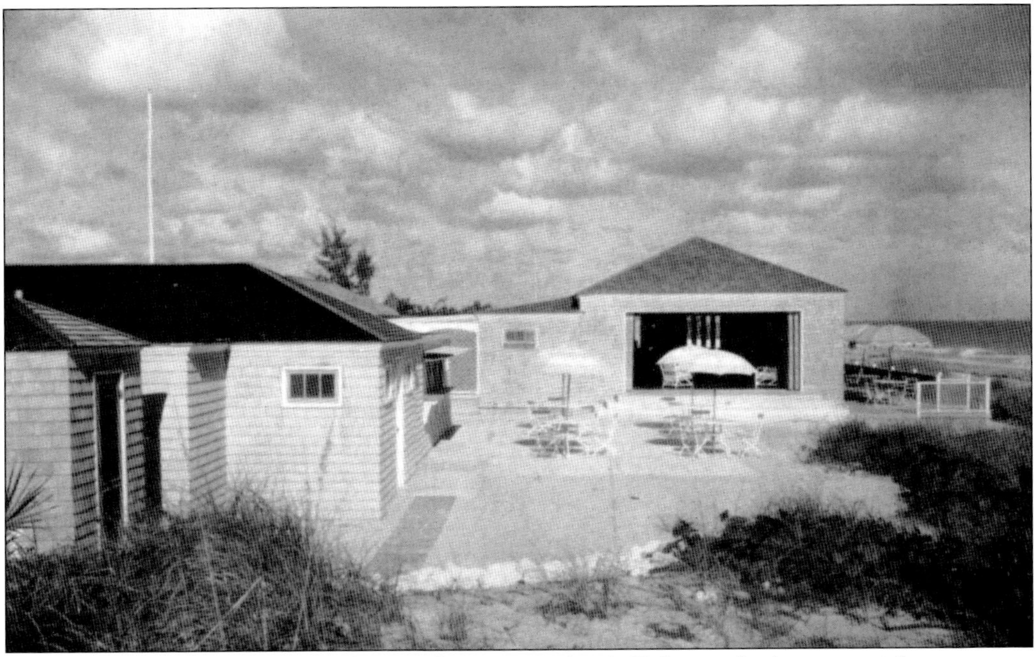

From the earliest days, membership in the Jupiter Island Club was the key to social acceptance here. Prospective members had to be sponsored by four current members. Original deeds on properties sold by the Hobe Sound Company, the company holding the land purchased by the Reeds in the 1930s, were sold subject to membership in the club. Today, anyone may buy a home on the island without seeking club membership, but it is still considered highly desirable. The Jupiter Island Beach Club, seen above in 1935 and below in 1954, is part of the Jupiter Island Club and provides a changing area as well as refreshment. (Above, courtesy of the Martin County Historical Society; below, courtesy of Library of Congress.)

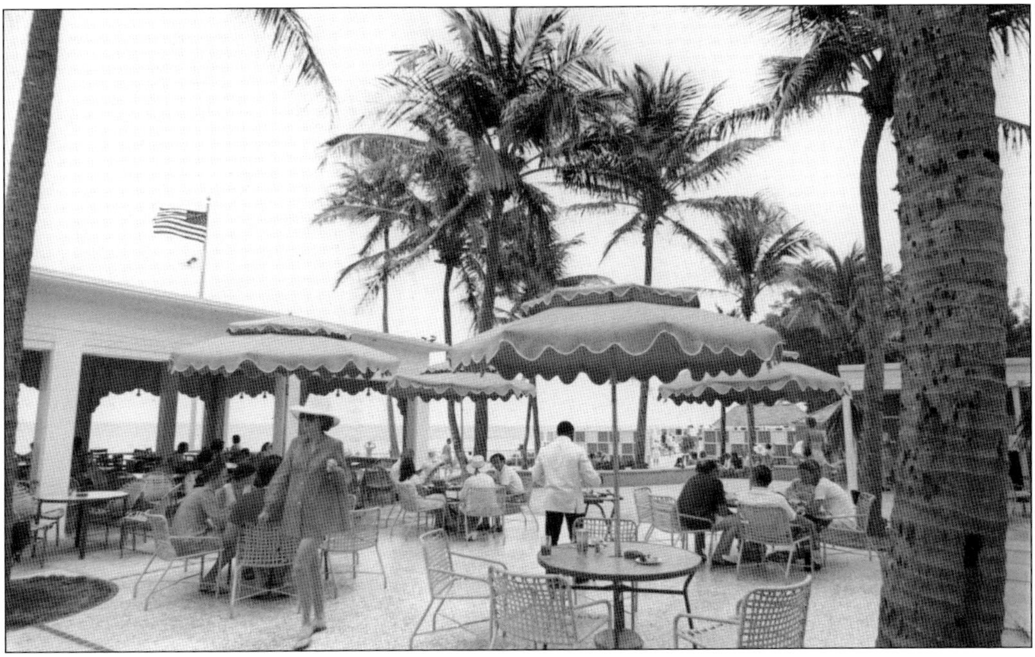

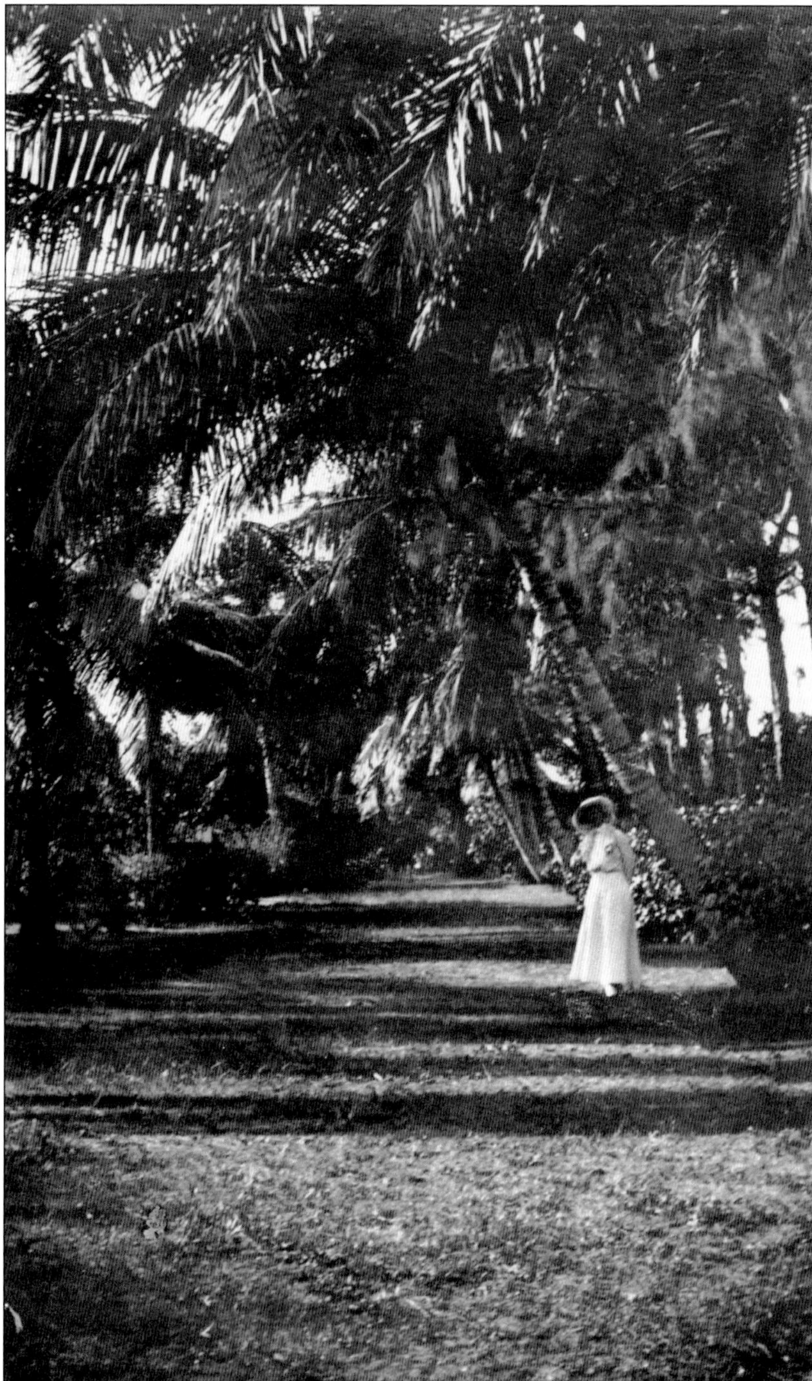

In the late 1800s and early 1900s, the "Sunshine State" was considered America's last frontier. Inns at the time were relatively small, modest, and had wood frames. Guests arrived by horse, boat, and later railroad. Visitors stayed for weeks or months. While the men fished, hunted, or played golf, the women took time to walk, visit with others, and read. Pictured is an elegant woman taking a stroll along an avenue of coconuts in 1913. (Courtesy of State Archives of Florida.)

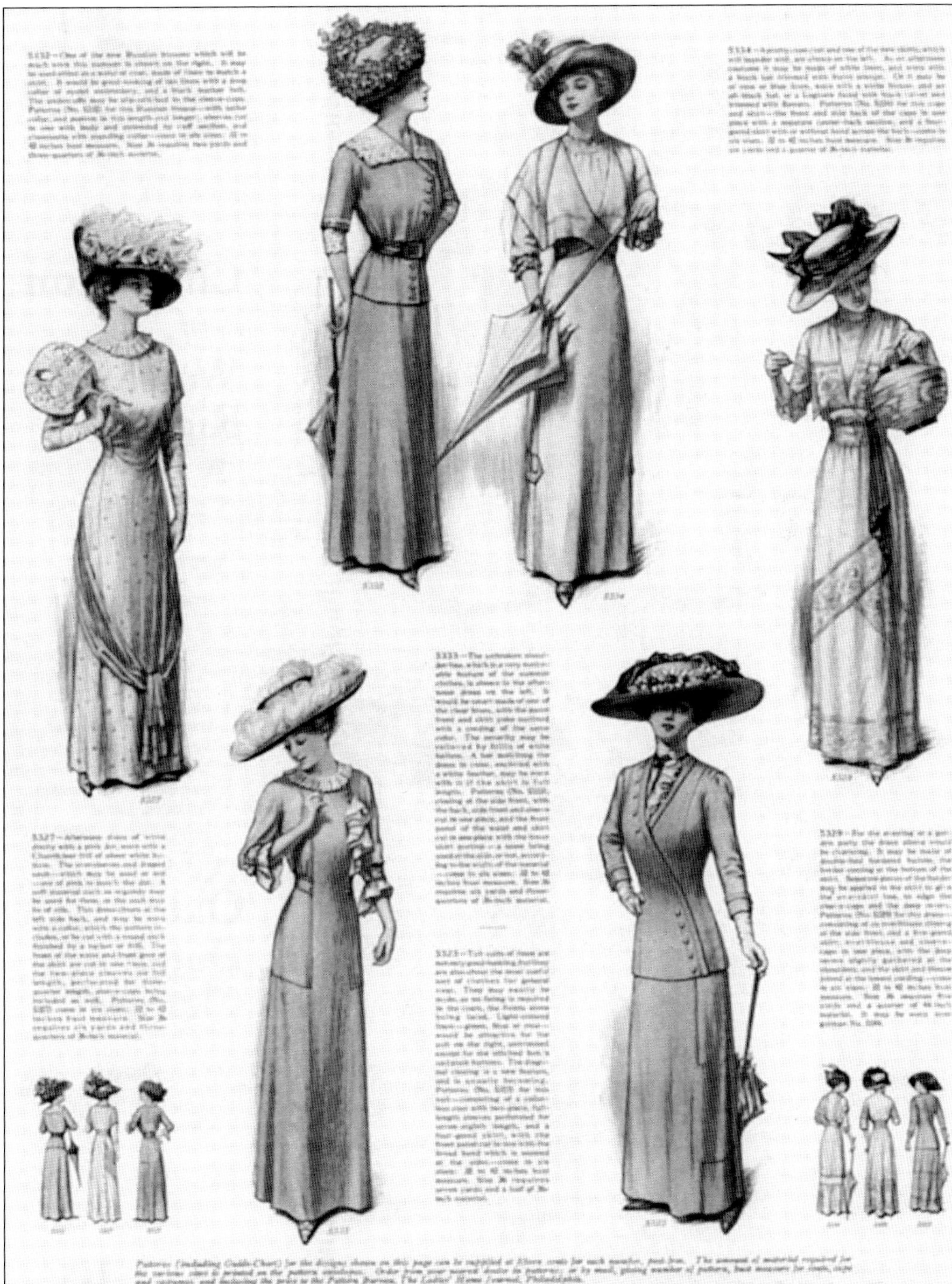

Fashions in the early 20th century used lighter materials for hot weather, but were still formal. As described in *Ladies Home Journal* in 1910, women's dress should be "Afternoon dress of white dimity with a pink dot, worn with a Chanticleer frill of sheer white batiste. For the evening or a garden party the dress above would be charming." (Courtesy of the Miriam and Ira D. Wallach Division of Art, Prints and Photographs, The New York Public Library.)

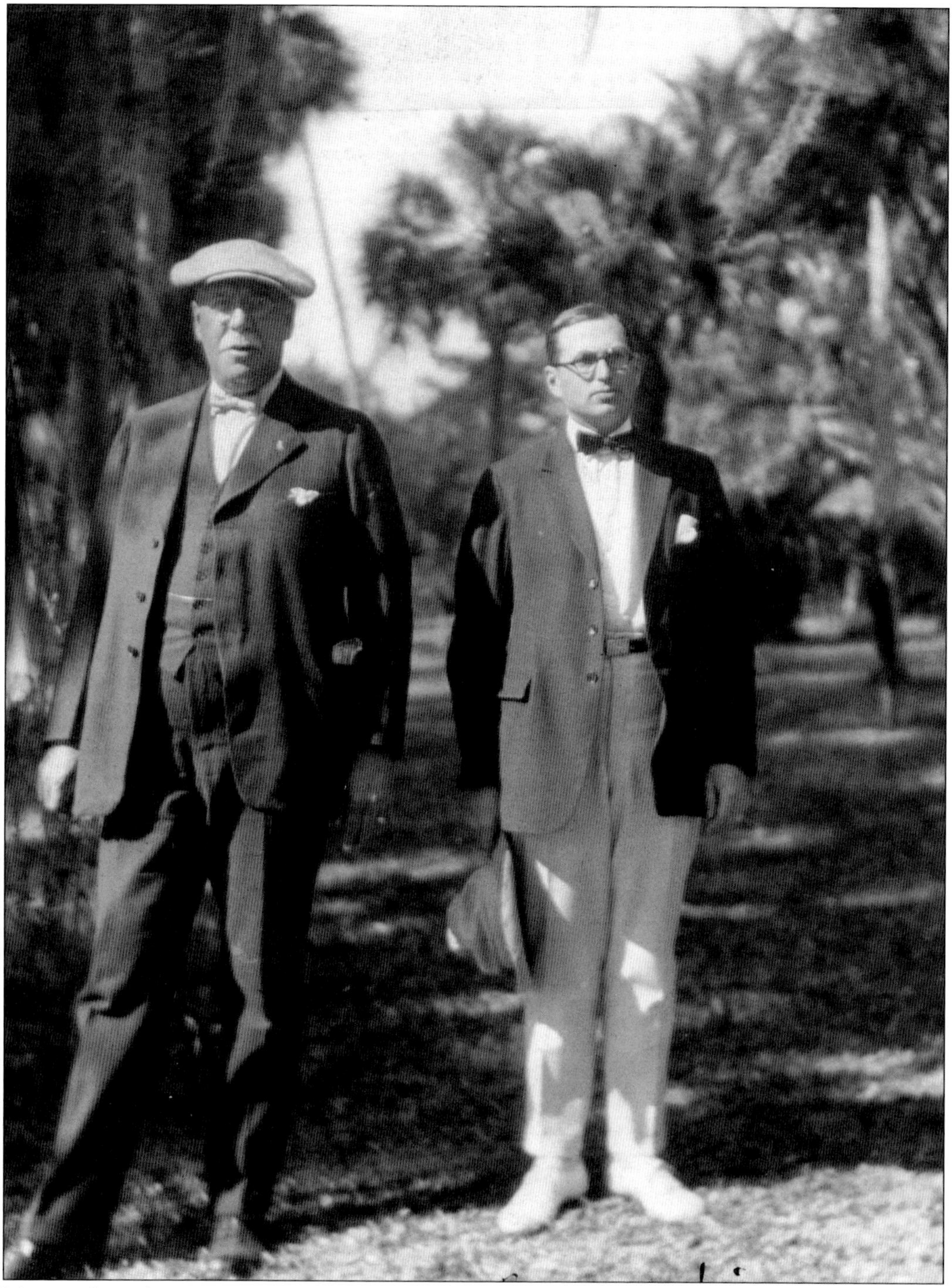

Men, such as these vacationing on Jupiter Island, would always have a hat and be in a suit. Not wearing a hat at that time would have been a significant fashion faux pas. The flat cap on the left was the most casual headwear of the era, worn on casual days or to sporting events by the middle and upper classes. Flat caps were also the choice of headwear for most working-class men. (Courtesy of the Martin County Historical Society.)

30 Gibbes St
Charleston, S.C. 29401
Jan. 4, 1969

Dear Vee,

Emma and I want you to know that we are sending you our love and best wishes on your birthday anniversary. We wish that we could in person join with family and friends on this festive occasion in being with you. We know that you are happy - having David home.

25 years ago at this time we were on Jupiter Island - our first experience there. You did so much to make that experience a happy one. Our best wishes to Ted, David and wife and, of course, you.

Robert E. Gribbin

This is a letter received by Lavenia "Vee" Chambers, a Hobe Sound resident, from a Jupiter Island resident thanking her for her hospitality over several decades. Vee and her family had moved to Hobe Sound in 1929. She and her husband, Ted, owned Chambers Electric, which is still in business today. She also had a property management company that catered to the residents of Jupiter Island. Vee is credited with helping bring the Indian River Community College to the area, and she was active in the PTA, on the school board, and in the historical society; she was considered a pillar of the Hobe Sound and Jupiter Island community. (Courtesy of Sandra Thurlow.)

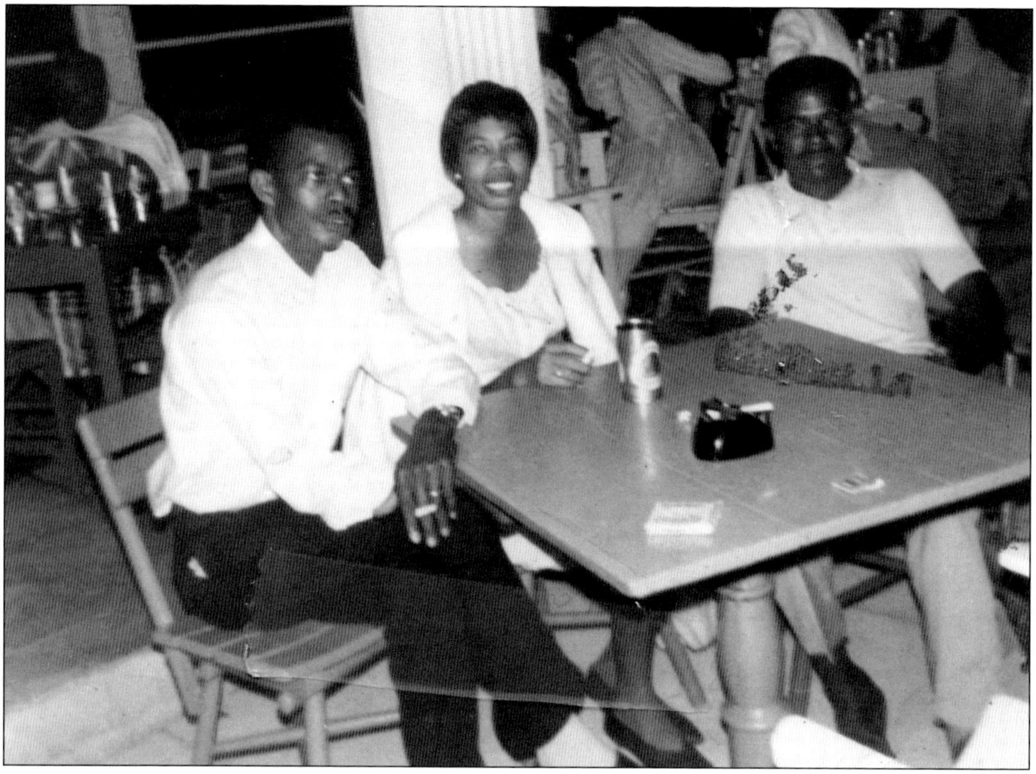

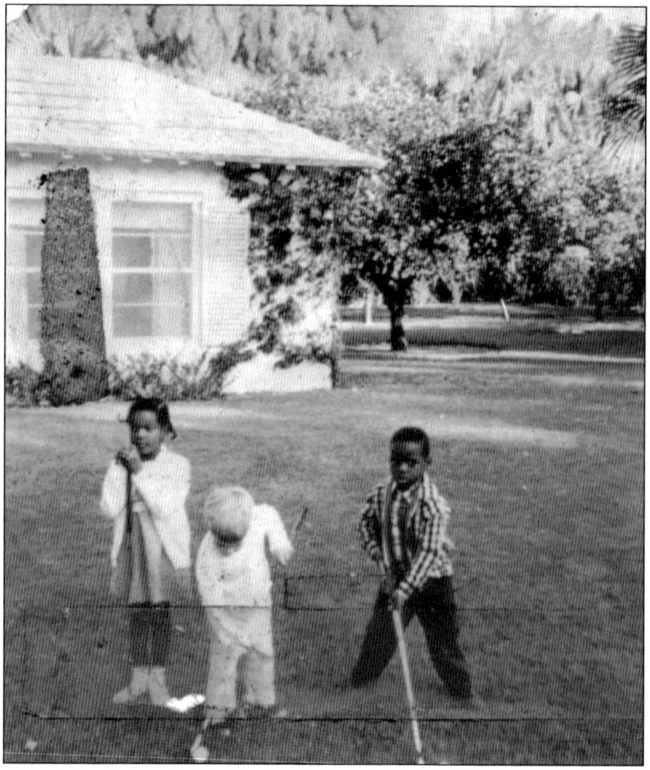

Seen above from left to right are Soney Pettway, Alice Ware, and Billy Harris in 1962 at an end of season party at the Jupiter Island Club. Many of the residents on the mainland were employed as staff in homes and at the Jupiter Island Club during the busy winter season. At left, from left to right are Sandra Pettway, a grandchild of Mr. and Mrs. Wells (Jupiter Island residents), and Kenneth Pettway playing with golf clubs on a Sunday afternoon in the late 1960s. (Both, courtesy of Annie Pettway.)

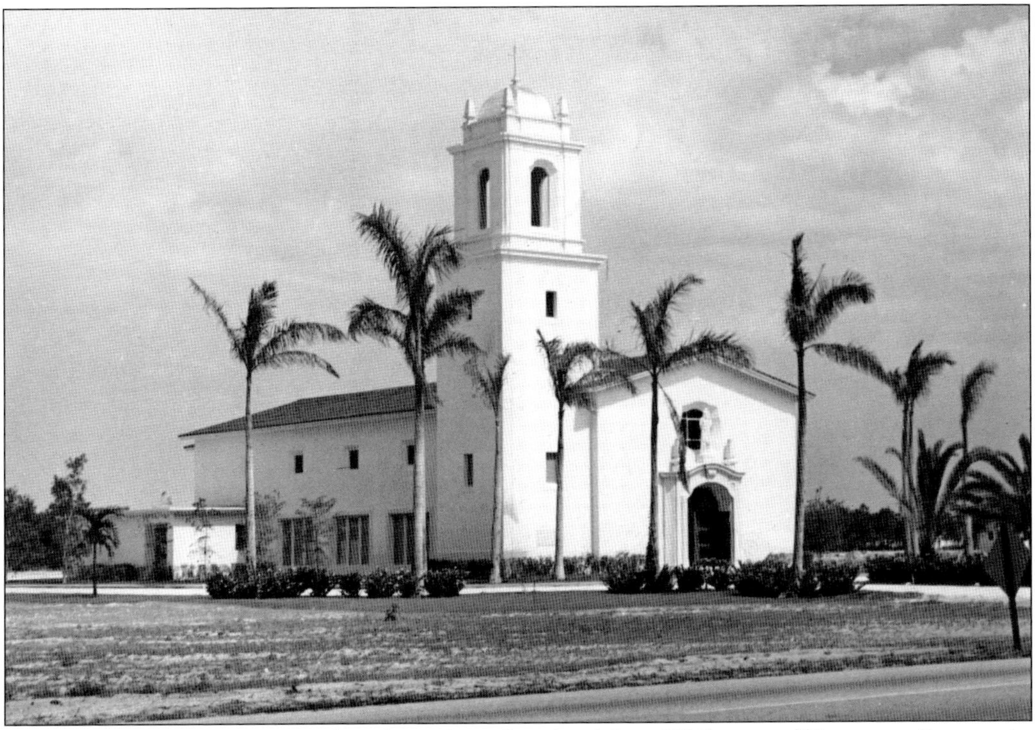

Pictured is Christ Memorial Chapel, a gift to the island from William and Francoise Barstow in memory of her sister Laura Fontenay Delespine Duclos. It was completed in 1939. Even though the church was consecrated by the Episcopal Church, Francoise Barstow hoped that it would always welcome members of every denomination, both residents and guests. (Courtesy of the Gottscho-Schleisner Collection, Prints & Photographs Division, Library of Congress.)

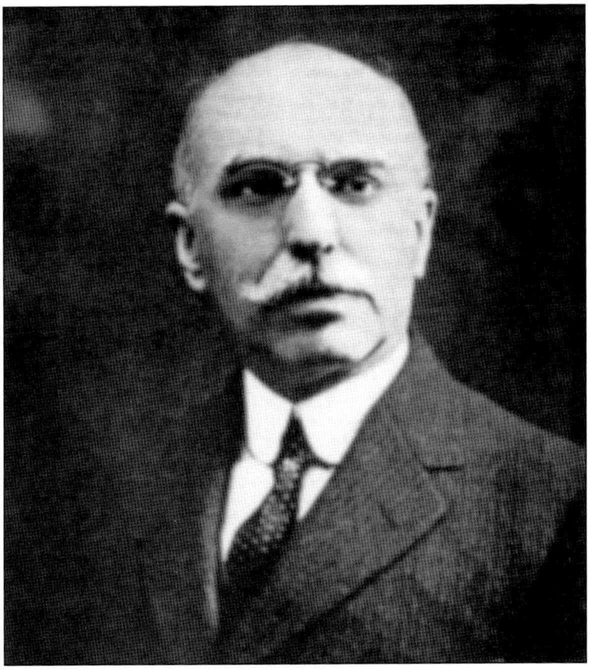

William Slocum Barstow was one of the nation's first electrical engineers. Against the advice of his professors who told him there was no future in electricity, he followed his hunch straight into an apprenticeship with Thomas Edison. By 1889, at age 23, Barstow found himself the electrical engineer of Edison Illuminating Company, then general superintendent, and eventually general manager. He went on to become the inventor of many products, including the first electric refrigerator, various electric railway systems, and a central street-lighting system. (Courtesy of the Great Neck Historical Society.)

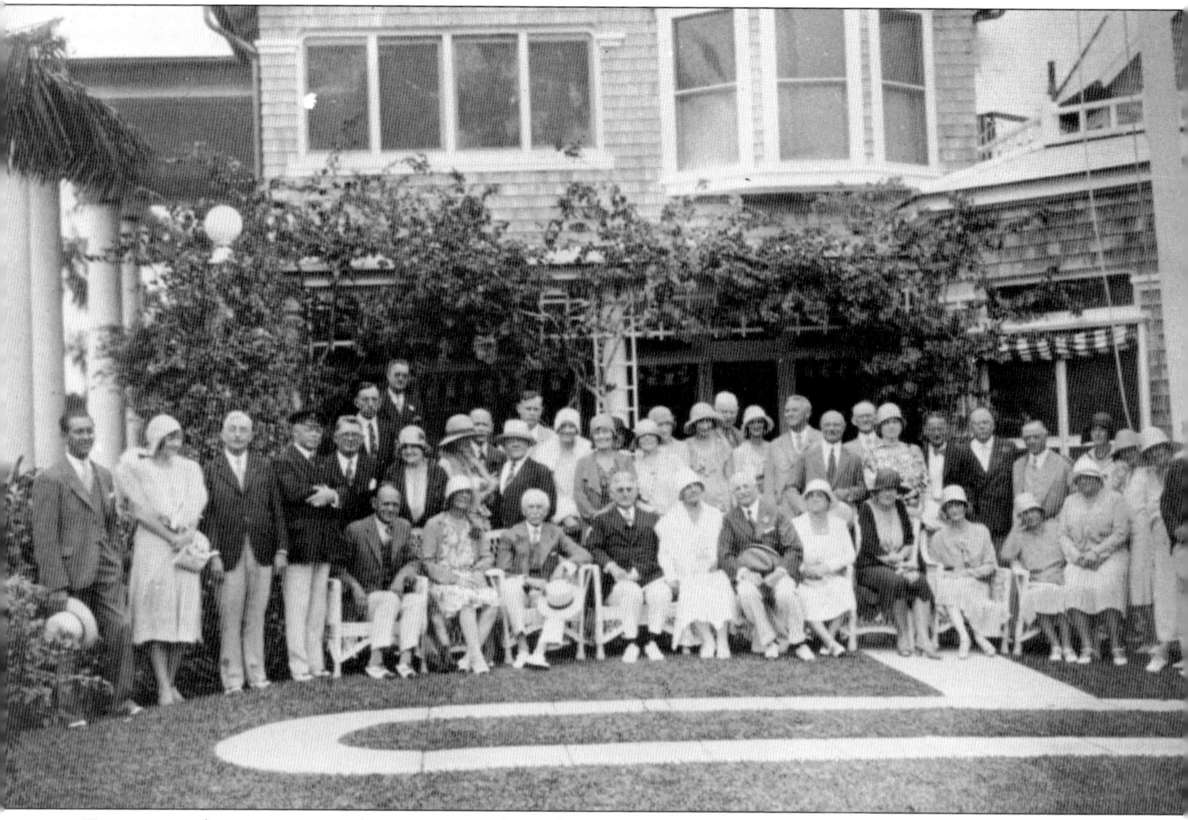

Every year beginning in the 1920s, Col. and Mrs. Thomas Edward Murphy held a party on St. Patrick's Day at their riverfront home on Jupiter Island. Seen here is the party in March 1928. Guests included Dr. and Mrs. John Newnham, Mr. and Mrs. Fred Hancock, Dr. and Mrs. Harry H. Hipson, and Mr. and Mrs. Stanley Kitching, all of Stuart. (Courtesy of the Martin County Historical Society.)

Four

Trade and Transportation

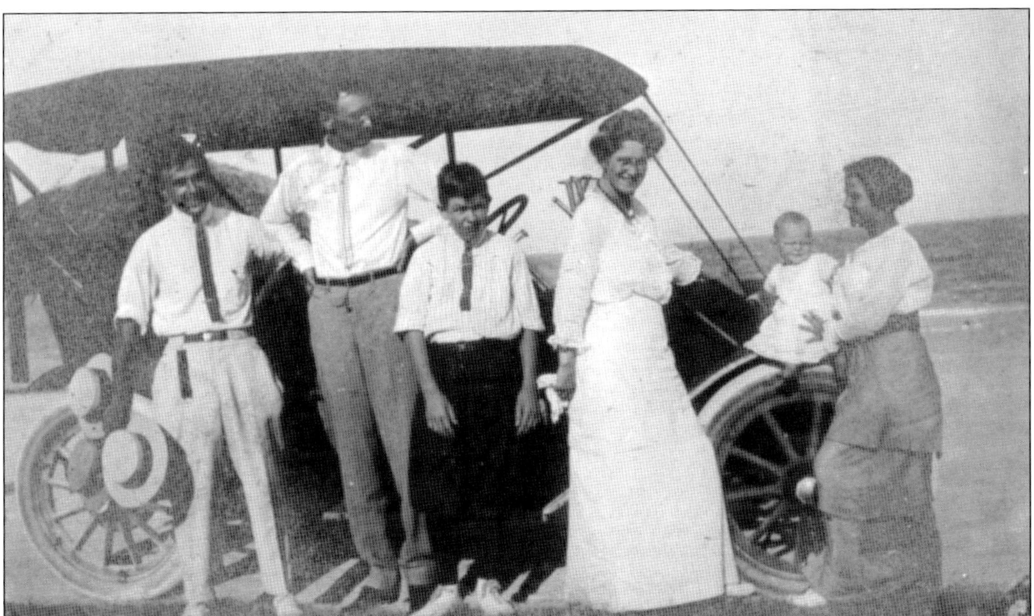

Martin County has been and remains decidedly agricultural in nature. There has been immense pressure to develop the area and Hobe Sound has been a focal point due to its close proximity to Jupiter. In times past, the innovation of steamships and railroads brought change to the area. In current days, it is the need for housing and the continued demand for restaurants and shops to service the thousands who come each winter. The images in this chapter represent transportation and trade within the community during the 19th and early 20th centuries. (Courtesy of the Martin County Historical Society.)

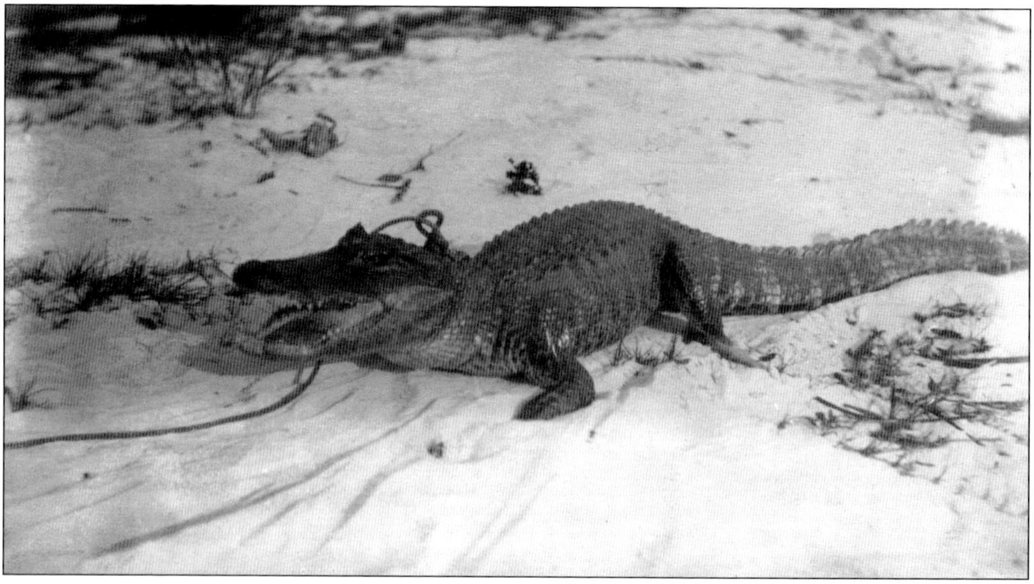

Alligators have been hunted throughout the 19th and 20th centuries for food, their skin, for sport, and out of fear. Hobe Sound and Martin County were no exception. In fact, in the early period of Florida statehood, trade in alligator leather was an important industry—exporting 280,000 skins annually, worth approximately $10 million today. Alligator meat and even eggs became a part of southeastern cuisine in the mid-1800s and continue to be offered today at many restaurants. Seen above is an alligator on the beach being caught, and below is a collection point for deceased alligators. (Both, courtesy of the Martin County Historical Society.)

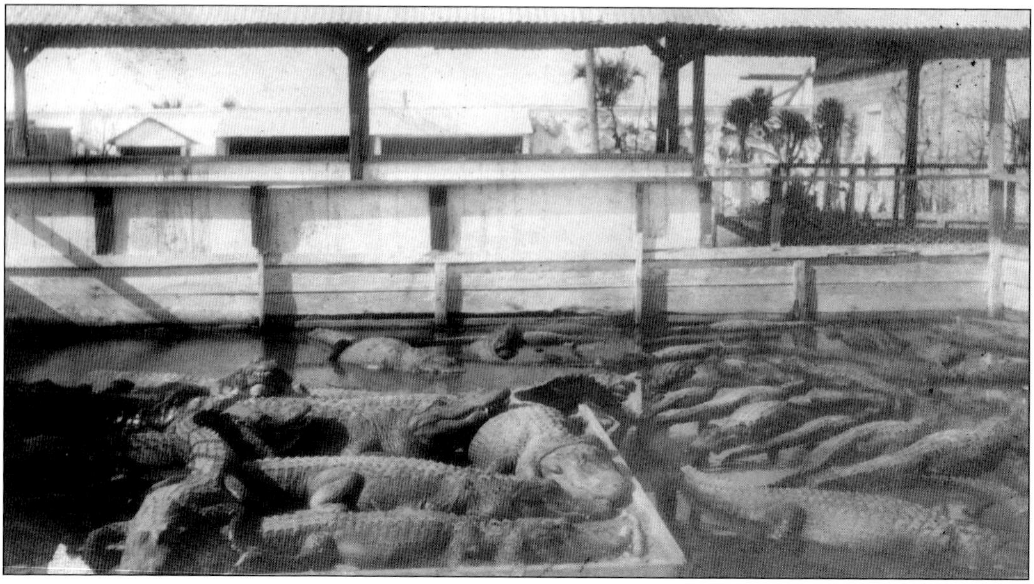

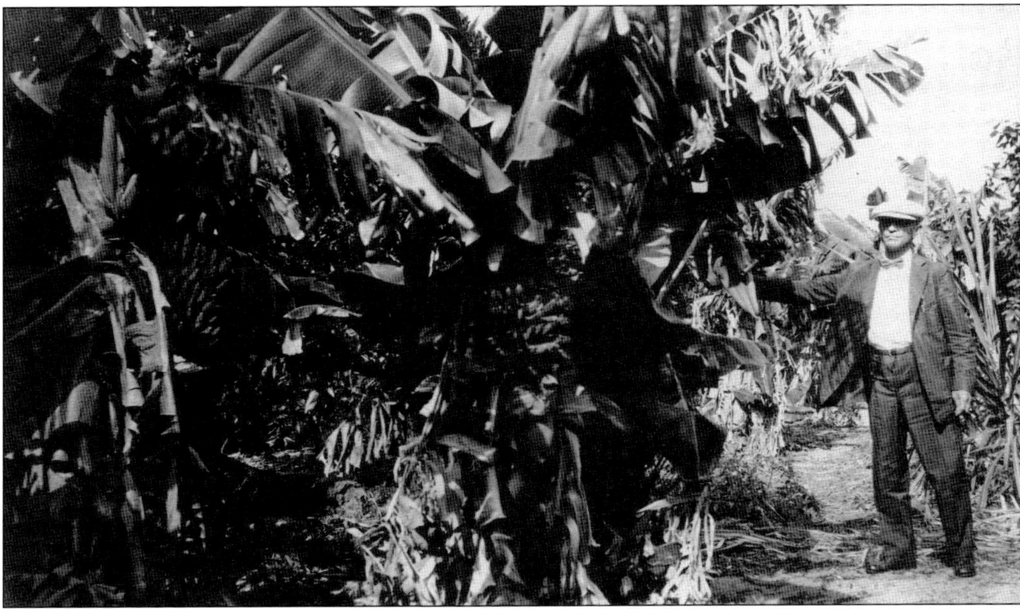

Bananas have been grown and scattered throughout Florida since their introduction during the 16th century by Spanish explorers. The first commercial banana farm in the United States was established in Florida near Silver Lake in 1876. Florida is second to Hawaii in banana production; however, Florida is the top exporter. Overall, current banana production in Florida is only about 500 acres. However, the banana remains an important affordable staple in the American diet, just as it did for the early settlers. Seen above is a small family-owned banana farm near Hobe Sound in 1925. Below is a family walking the land and inspecting the crop around the same time. (Both, courtesy of the Martin County Historical Society.)

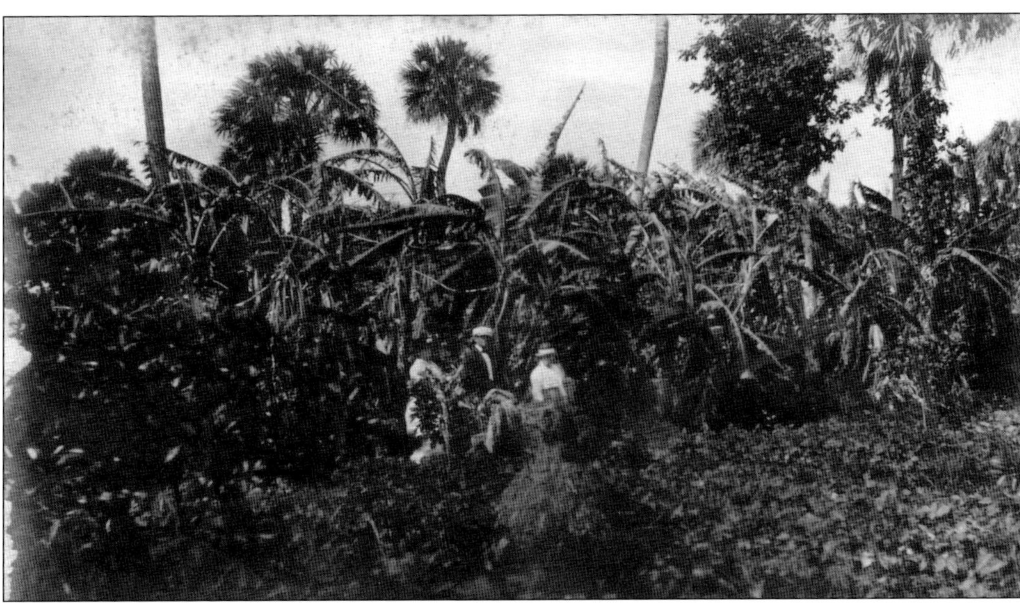

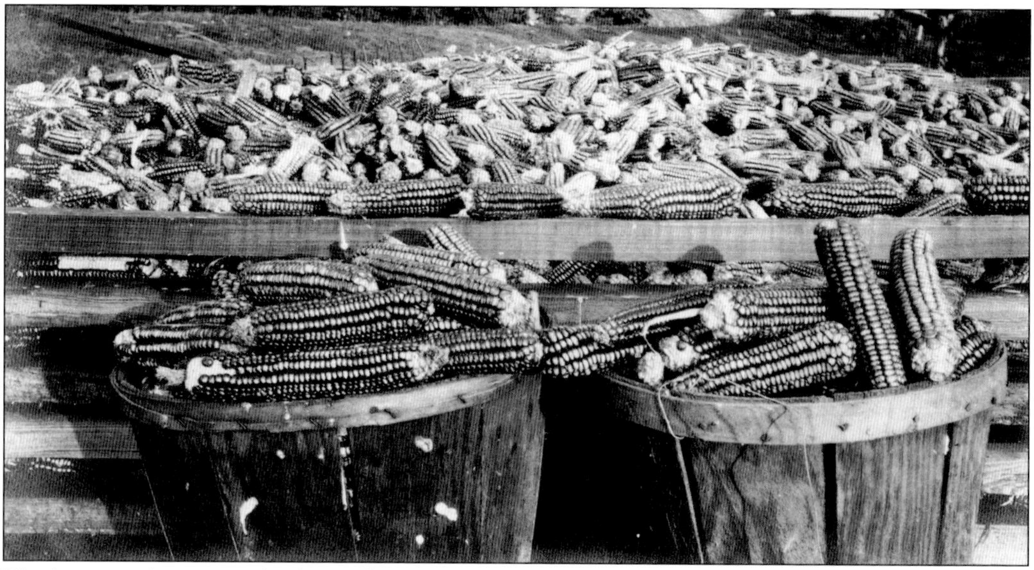

The history of corn goes back a millennium in Florida. It was a staple of the Native American diet and was adopted by Spanish explorers when they realized wheat would not grow here. Historically, the principal fresh sweet corn production region in Florida has been in the Everglades area, with over half of the state's production. Pictured is a corn harvest near Hobe Sound around 1924. (Courtesy of Martin County Historical Society.)

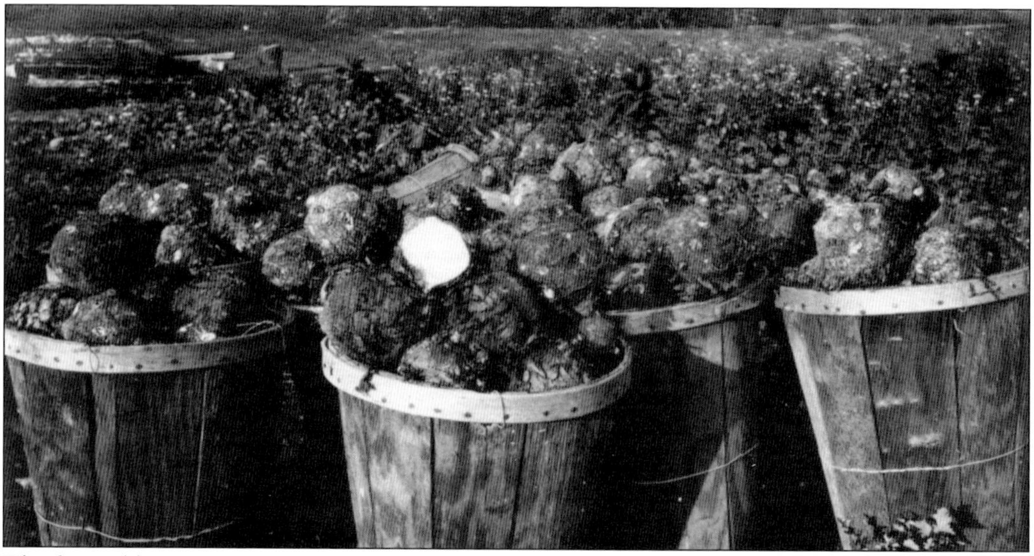

The first cabbage in America was brought by French explorer Jacques Cartier on his third voyage, 1541–1542. Due to Florida's warm climate, cabbage became a cash crop for early settlers. Florida remains a top producer of cabbage in the United States, bringing in an estimated $34 million a year. Seen here is a cabbage crop in Martin County in 1923. It is estimated that cabbage cost about 2¢ a pound in 1920. (Courtesy of the Martin County Historical Society.)

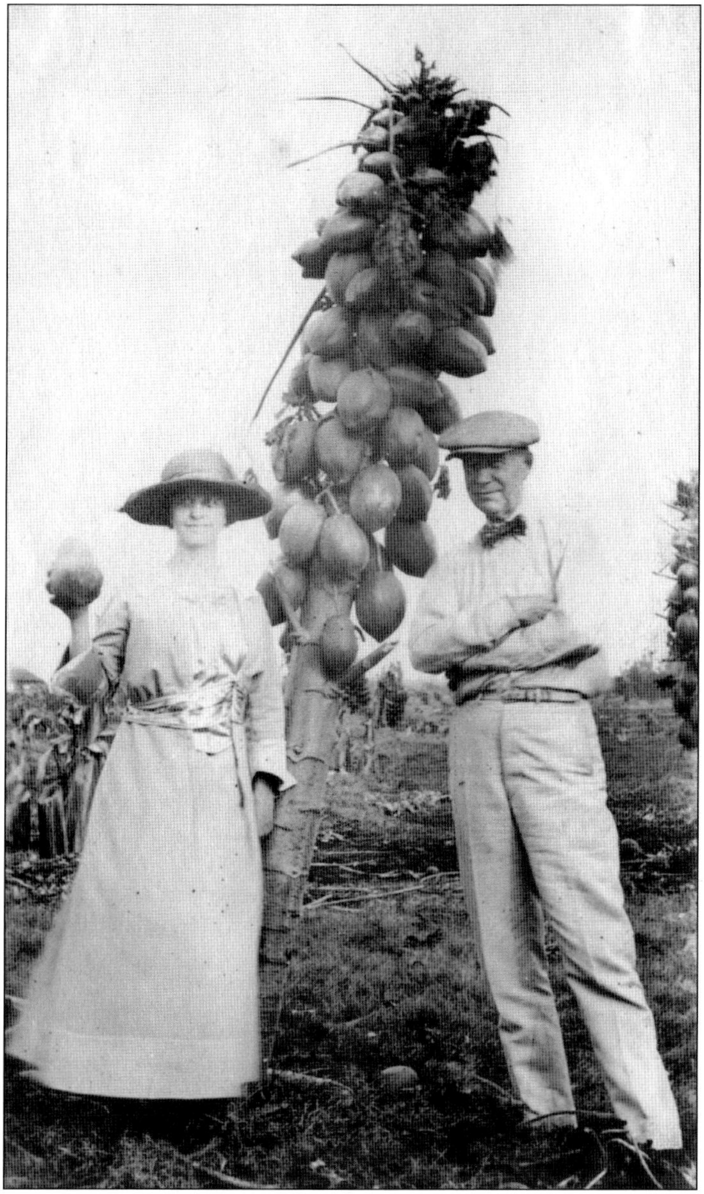

Not indigenous, but quite at home, coconuts were introduced to Florida by Spanish explorers in the 1500s. All coconuts can trace their history back to palms on the coasts of India or Southeast Asia. Humans have always been eager to bring coconuts along on their travels, and for good reasons. Coconuts are not only a source of both food and water; different parts of the coconut palm can also be used for other purposes. Alcohol and sugar can be extracted from its sap, and the nuts contain rich oil. Interestingly, by the early 1900s, coconut cream pie and coconut custard were all the rage in the United States. Coconut frosting topped all sorts of cakes, while grated coconut added its distinct aroma and flavor to cookies and confections. Coconuts, which originally were a survival food of early explorers and settlers, became a cash crop. In Florida, the coconut palm is successfully grown from Stuart on the east coast and Punta Gorda on the west coast, south to Key West. Seen here is an unidentified couple harvesting coconuts around 1926 in Martin County. (Courtesy of Martin County Historical Society.)

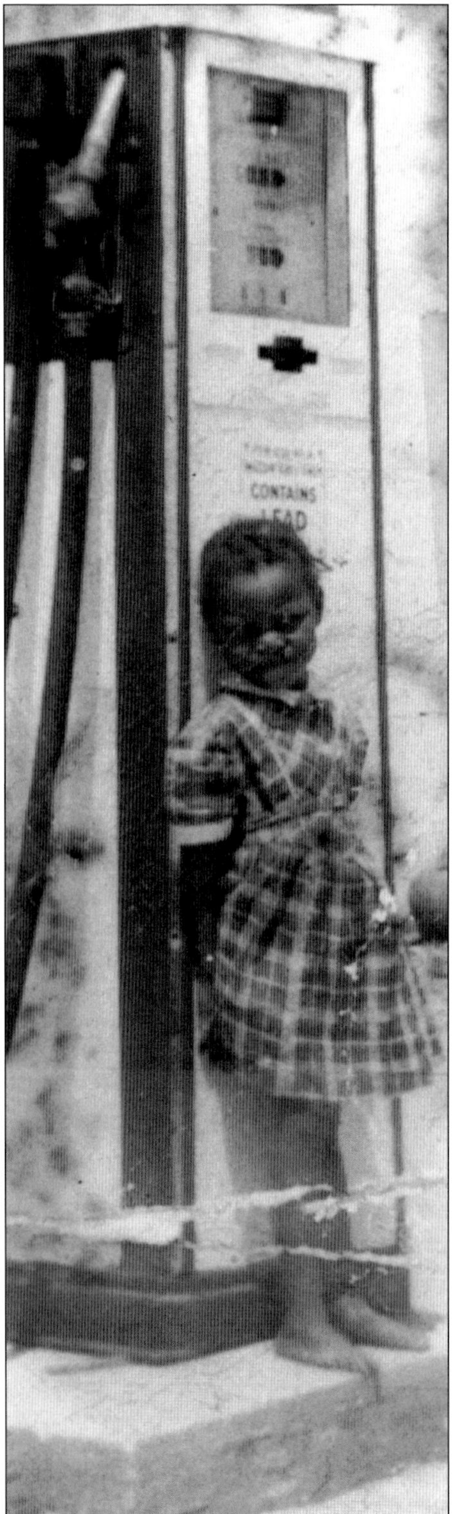

Pictured is Annie Pettway in 1946 standing in front of a gas pump in front of the Pettway grocery store. A gallon of gas cost 21¢. Annie can be found each day at the store on the corner of Pettway Street and Dixie Highway (A1A.) (Courtesy of Annie Pettway.)

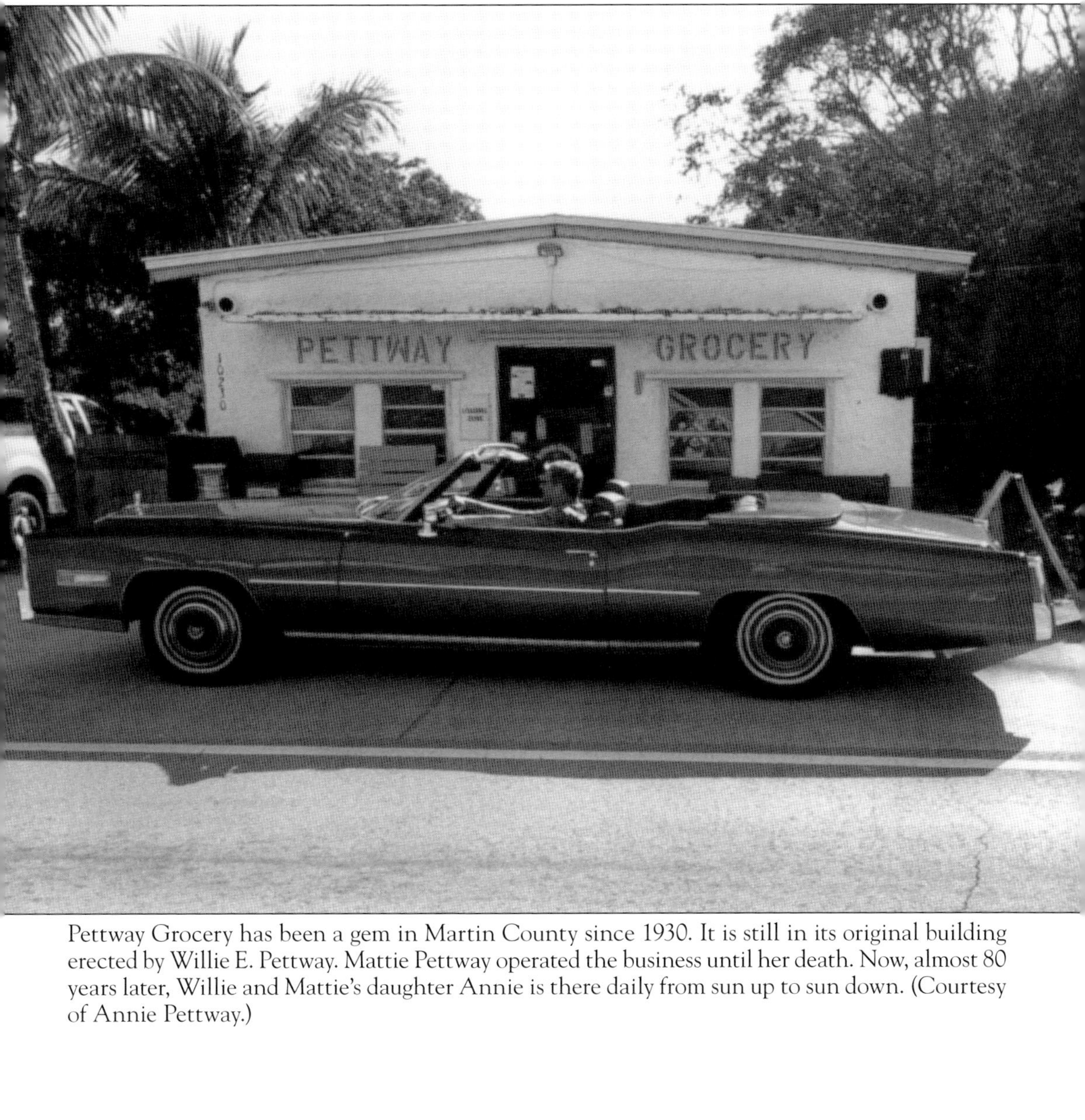

Pettway Grocery has been a gem in Martin County since 1930. It is still in its original building erected by Willie E. Pettway. Mattie Pettway operated the business until her death. Now, almost 80 years later, Willie and Mattie's daughter Annie is there daily from sun up to sun down. (Courtesy of Annie Pettway.)

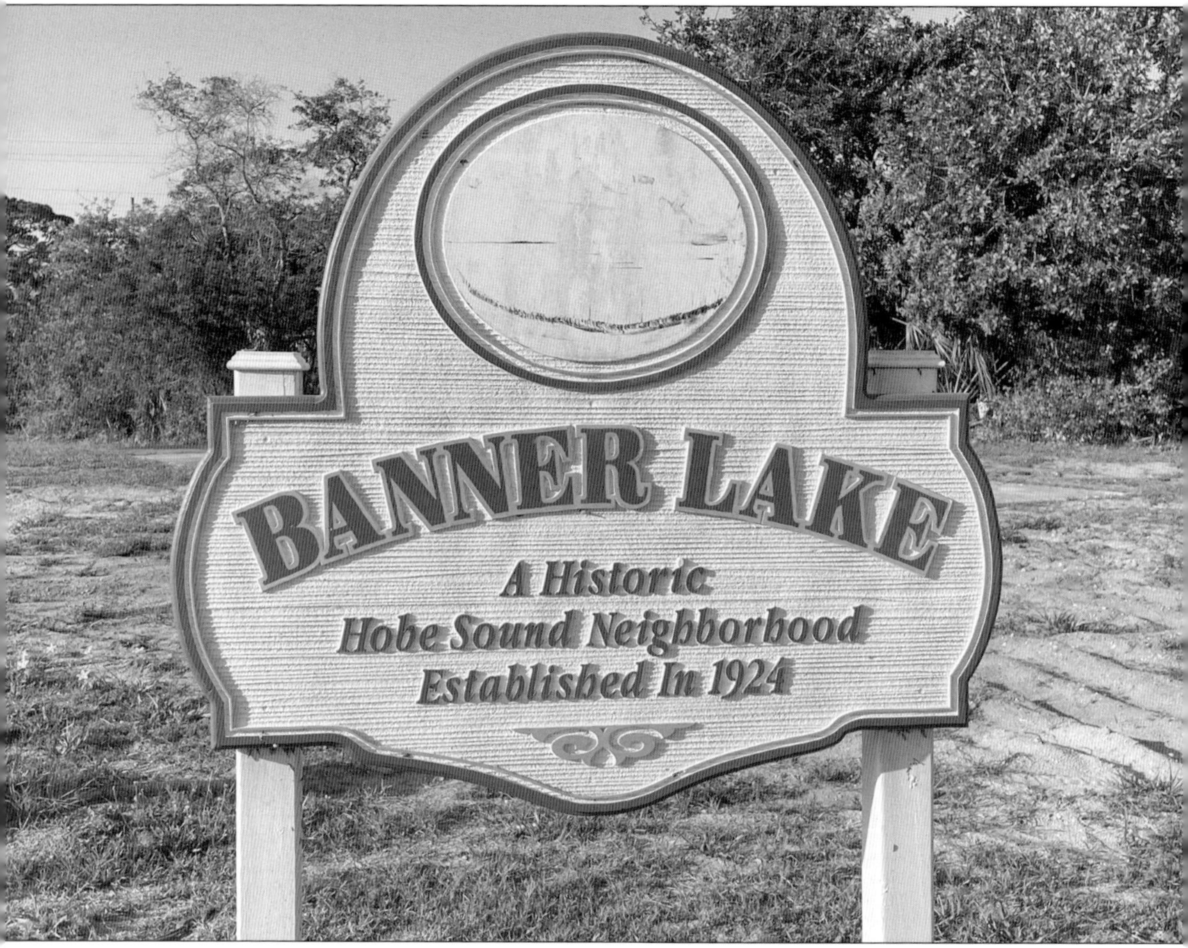

Those of African American and Caribbean descent in Hobe Sound originally settled near the Intracoastal Waterway in the Gomez Avenue area and eked out a living on small farms. Many worked on the pineapple and coconut plantations on Jupiter Island, while others worked on the flower farms along the Gomez corridor. As Jupiter Island developed in the early 1920s, the African American residents were employed as housekeepers, nannies, gardeners, and cooks. By the early 1930s, the wealthy Jupiter Island families, including William S. Barstow and Norman Banner, realized that those workers needed homes and a community to live in. They helped to establish the first homes on Florida Avenue in what was then called Banner Lake Village Inc. Over time, the community became self-sufficient, with its own cafes, grocers, restaurants, dry cleaners, contractors, tree service, a gas station, barber and beauty shops, teen clubs, and juke joints, along with its own elementary school due to segregation. The community still exists today. (Author's collection.)

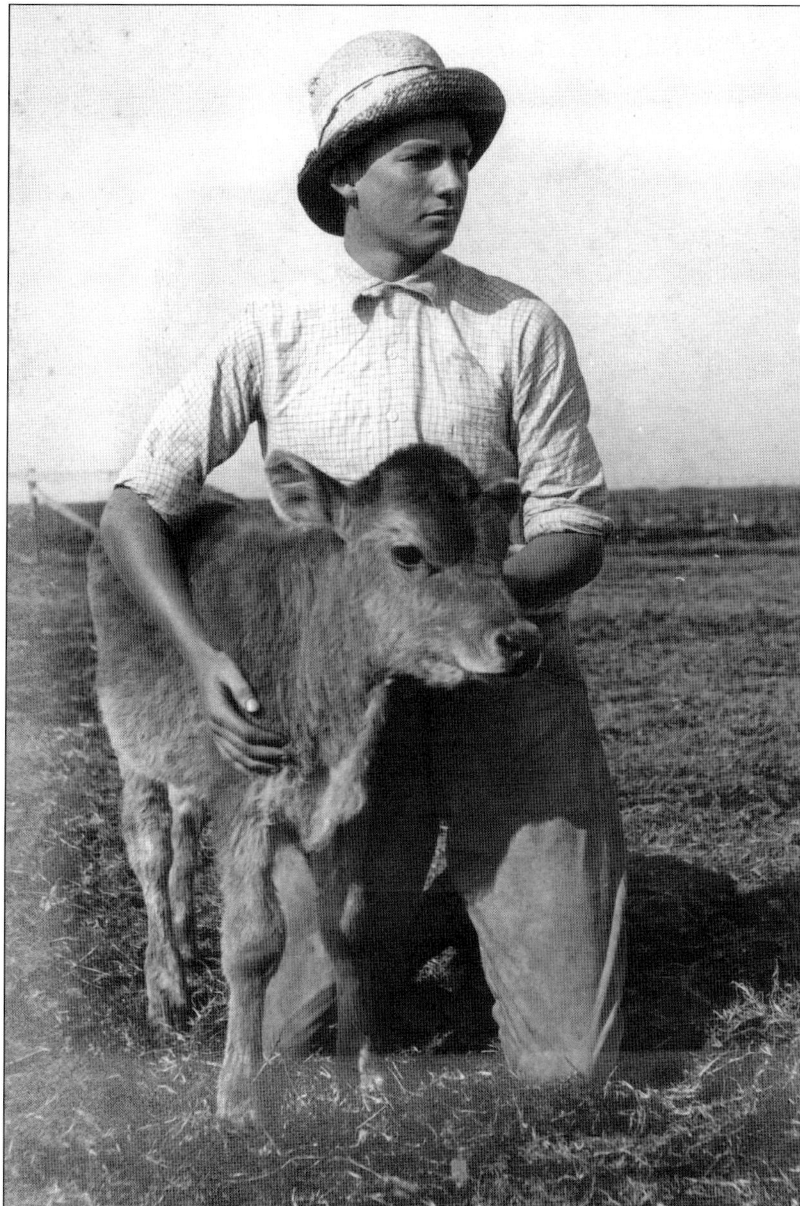

Florida's Andalusian/Caribbean cattle were the first in the United States. Some scholars believe that cattle were brought by the expeditions of Ponce de Leon in 1521 and Don Diego de Maldonado in 1540 that escaped and survived in the wild and formed the original herds. Organized ranching began with the founding of St. Augustine in 1565, when cattle from Spain and Cuba formed the basis of herds that fed the garrison and surrounding communities. In addition to herds owned by the Spanish and Indians, wild cattle flourished in the rangelands and prairies. Since the late 1920s and early 1930s, cattle have been an important economic driver in Florida including Martin County and the town of Hobe Sound. This is still true and seen today while traveling west on Bridge Road. Almost 50 percent of the county's land remains in agricultural production, with cattle ranches comprising the largest percentage. Seen here is a young Martin County boy in 1925. (Courtesy of Martin County Historical Society.)

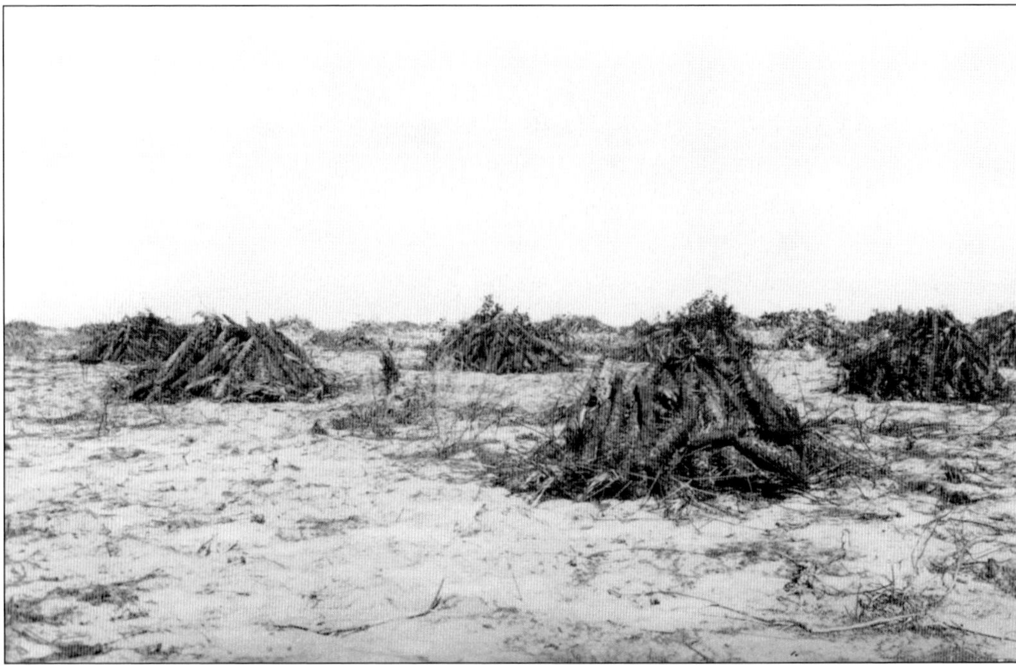

Saw palmetto berries were used by Native Americans for their healing properties, and the plant plays an important part in the Florida ecosystem. Once early settlers realized that pineapples flourished in the sandy soil along the Indian River and Jupiter Island, palmettos were cleared as fast as possible to begin planting pineapples. In this photograph is a heavily wooded saw palmetto patch on Jupiter Island being cleared around 1905. (Courtesy of State Archives of Florida.)

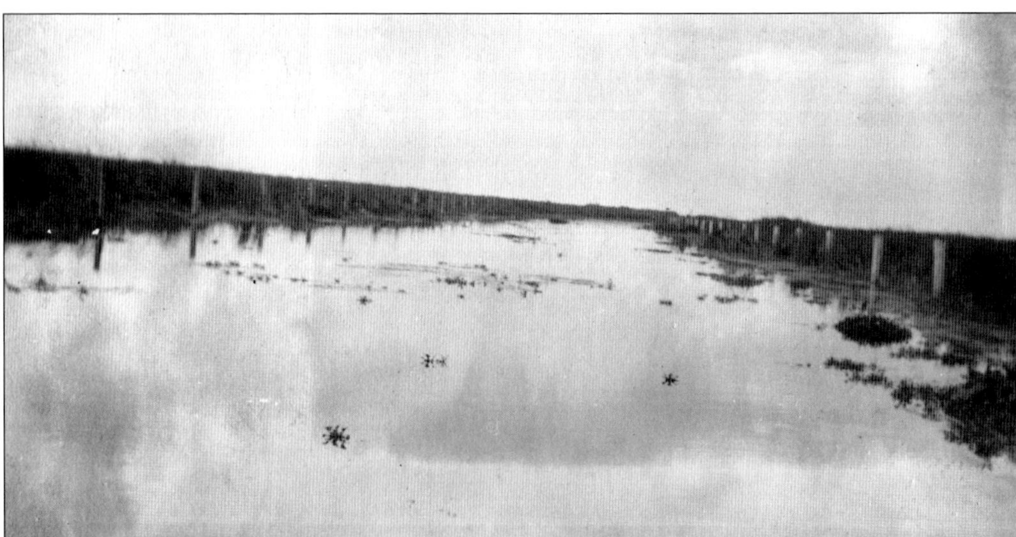

Seen here are the western lands of Hobe Sound in what is now the Okeechobee Watershed District post–Okeechobee hurricane of 1928. Agriculture was affected significantly, with the storm destroying what may have been the largest citrus crop in the history of the industry. Approximately 6 percent of oranges and 18 percent of grapefruit were ruined, and 278 livestock and 47,389 poultry were killed, respectively. (Courtesy of the Martin County Historical Society.)

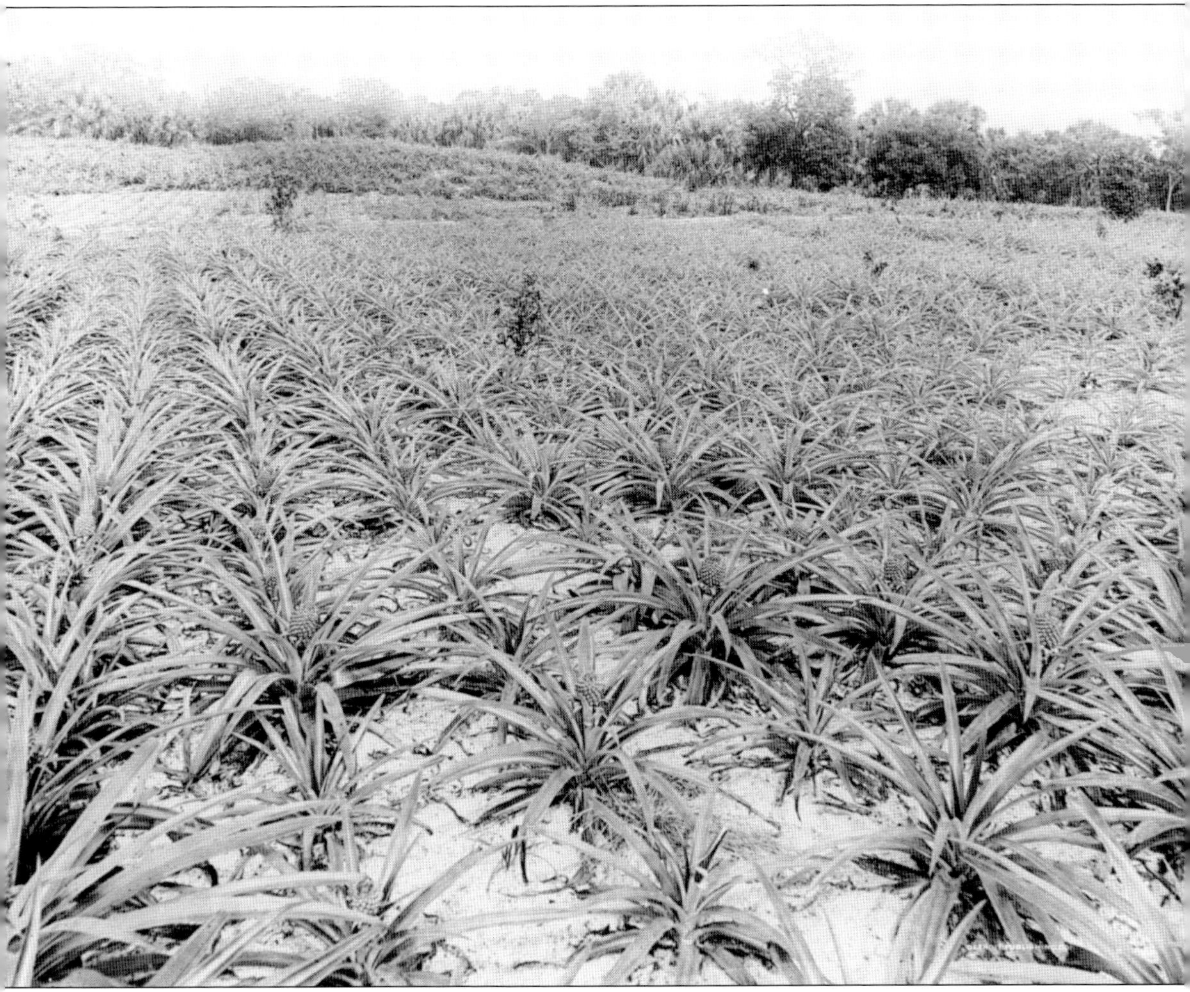

The earliest pineapple cultivation in Florida started in Key West in the 1860s. Around the same time, a Mr. Brantley was producing pineapples on Merritt Island, and close by, John Laurence Jensen set up his pineapple plantation that became the town of Jensen Beach. By 1895, Jensen was called the "Pineapple Capital of the World," shipping over one million boxes of pineapples each year. This is a photograph of a local pineapple plantation. (Courtesy of the William Henry Jackson Collection, Library of Congress.)

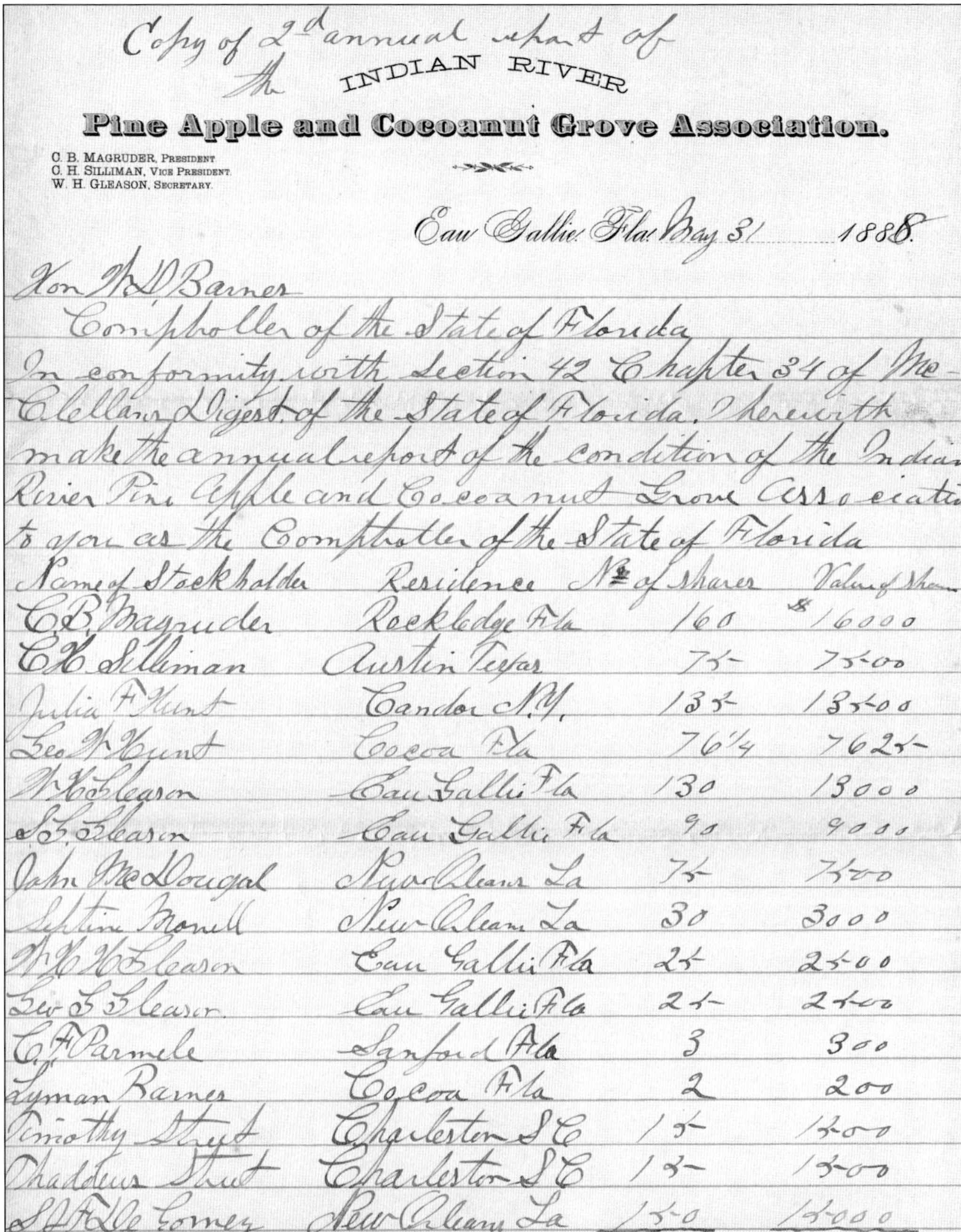

Copy of 2d annual report of the

INDIAN RIVER

Pine Apple and Cocoanut Grove Association.

C. B. MAGRUDER, PRESIDENT
C. H. SILLIMAN, VICE PRESIDENT.
W. H. GLEASON, SECRETARY.

Eau Gallie Fla May 31 1888

Hon W D Barnes
Comptroller of the State of Florida
In conformity with Section 42 Chapter 34 of McClellans Digest of the State of Florida I herewith make the annual report of the condition of the Indian River Pine Apple and Cocoanut Grove Association to you as the Comptroller of the State of Florida

Name of Stockholder	Residence	No of shares	Value of Shares
C B Magruder	Rockledge Fla	160	$16000
C H Silliman	Austin Texas	75	7500
Julia F Hunt	Candor N.Y.	135	13500
Geo W Hunt	Cocoa Fla	76 1/4	7625
W H Gleason	Eau Gallie Fla	130	13000
S G Gleason	Eau Gallie Fla	90	9000
John McDougal	New Orleans La	75	7500
Septime Morell	New Orleans La	30	3000
W H H Gleason	Eau Gallie Fla	25	2500
Geo G Gleason	Eau Gallie Fla	25	2500
C F Parmele	Sanford Fla	3	300
Lyman Barnes	Cocoa Fla	2	200
Timothy Street	Charleston S C	15	1500
Thaddeus Street	Charleston S C	15	1500
S J H De Gomez	New Orleans La	150	15000

In the 1880s, the Indian River Association acquired the Gomez grant and a subsidiary of the company, the Pineapple and Cocoanut Grove Association. It allocated a series of lots west of the Indian River and on Jupiter Island for pineapple production. Seen here is the original document of incorporation and the initial shareholders. (Courtesy of the P.K. Yonge Library of Florida History, Special and Area Studies Collections, George A. Smathers Libraries, University of Florida.)

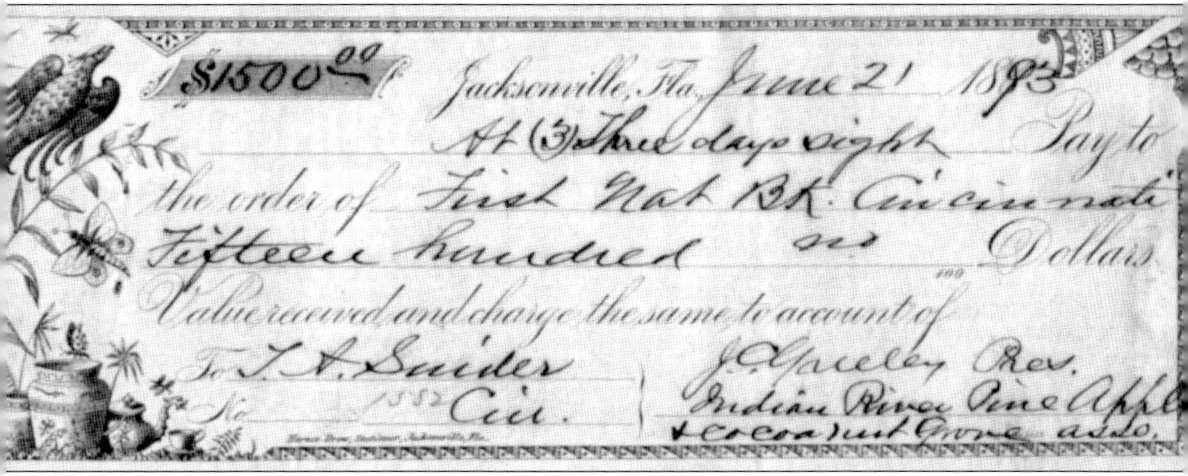

On May 31, 1886, the Indian River Pine Apple and Cocoanut Grove Association was formed with $125,000 in capital. The land purchased ran from the mouth of the St. Lucie River down to Jupiter Inlet and included Jupiter Island and 10,000 acres of the former Gomez Grant, including present-day Hobe Sound. The corporation expressed that its purpose was "the cultivation of pine apples, cocoanuts, oranges, lemons, limos, citrons, bananas, plantains, and other tropical fruits, gardening, horticulture, stock raising and general agriculture," along with "The purchasing of real estate, selling, leasing and improving the same." (Courtesy of the P.K. Yonge Library of Florida History, Special and Area Studies Collections, George A. Smathers Libraries, University of Florida.)

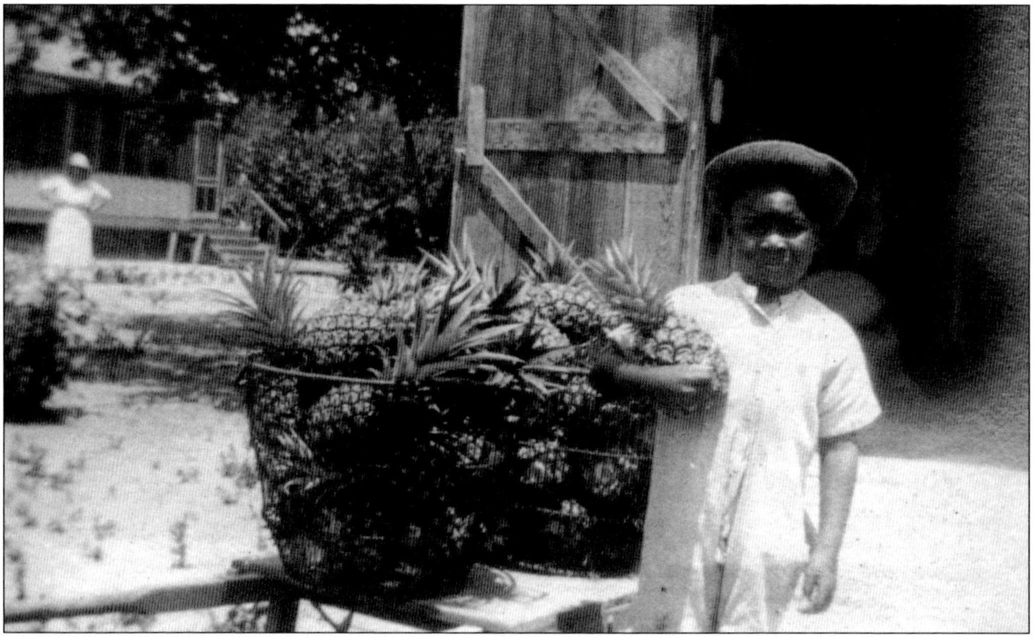

By 1876, there was "hardly a settler from New Smyrna Beach to Jupiter that did not have his pineapple patch," wrote H.R. Saunder, an early shipper of the sweet fruit. Pineapple plants were easy to grow and needed minimal care. Besides offering a healthy food option for a minimal cost to many early families, many early settlers were hoping to make money off "pine crops." The average cost of a pineapple in 1924 was 40¢. Pictured is a young boy with a basket of pineapples. (Courtesy of Martin County Historical Society.)

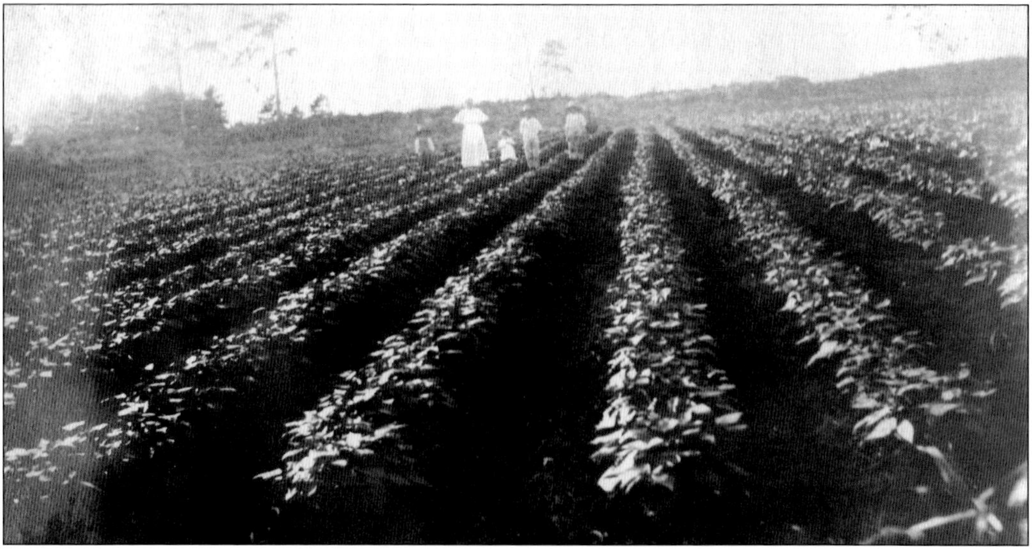

In 1920, Florida grew and shipped one-fifth of the lettuce grown in the United States. Practically all of it was the Big Boston, or butter-head, type. With the introduction of the crisp head iceberg type, perfected in California's Imperial Valley, which won immediate popularity, demand for the local product dropped from more than 3,000 carloads annually to less than 300. In 1920, three heads of lettuce cost 25¢. Pictured is a local lettuce field. (Courtesy of the Martin County Historical Society.)

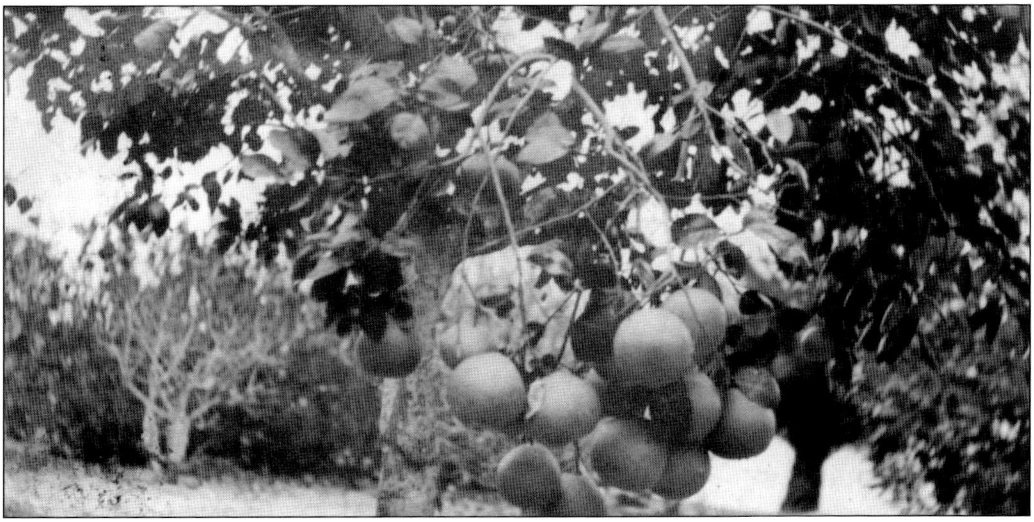

Early Spanish explorers (most likely Ponce de Leon) planted the first orange trees near St. Augustine in the 1500s. Commercial production began nearly 300 years later—after the Civil War—when the development of the railroad allowed citrus growers to ship their products across the country. In 1894 and 1895, freezes destroyed much of Florida's citrus crops. Not to be defeated, many citrus growers moved south and began growing again. Seen here is a personal orange grove in Hobe Sound around 1908. (Courtesy of Martin County Historical Society.)

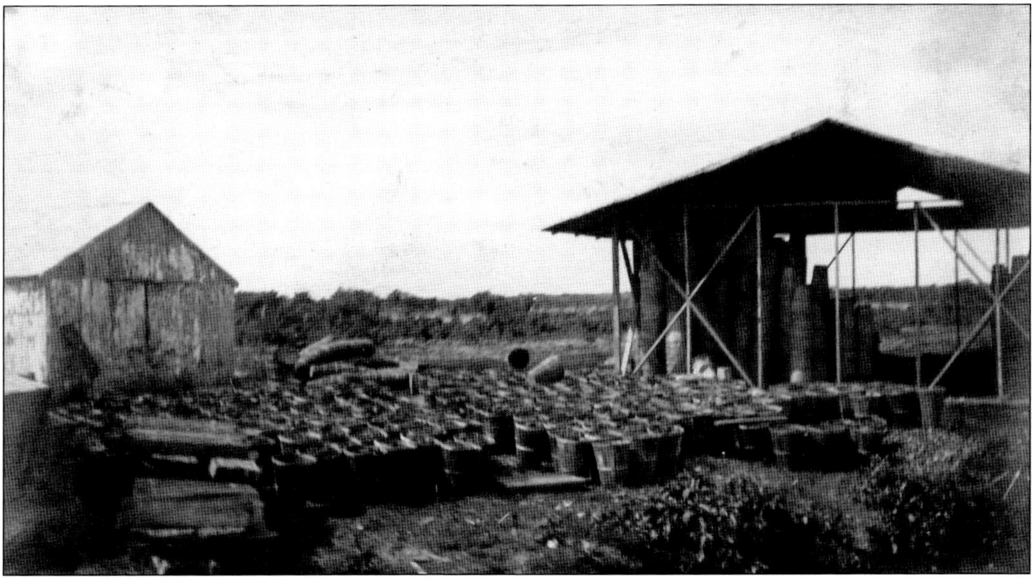

The expansion of railroads into southern Florida contributed to the growth of the citrus and agricultural industry in the late 19th century and early 20th centuries. With the railroads came an increase in population and in acreage devoted to citrus and crop cultivation. Packing sheds were constructed in central locations to store, process, grade, sort, and pack agricultural products for sale. Seen here is a packing shed near Hobe Sound in the early 1900s. (Courtesy of Martin County Historical Society.)

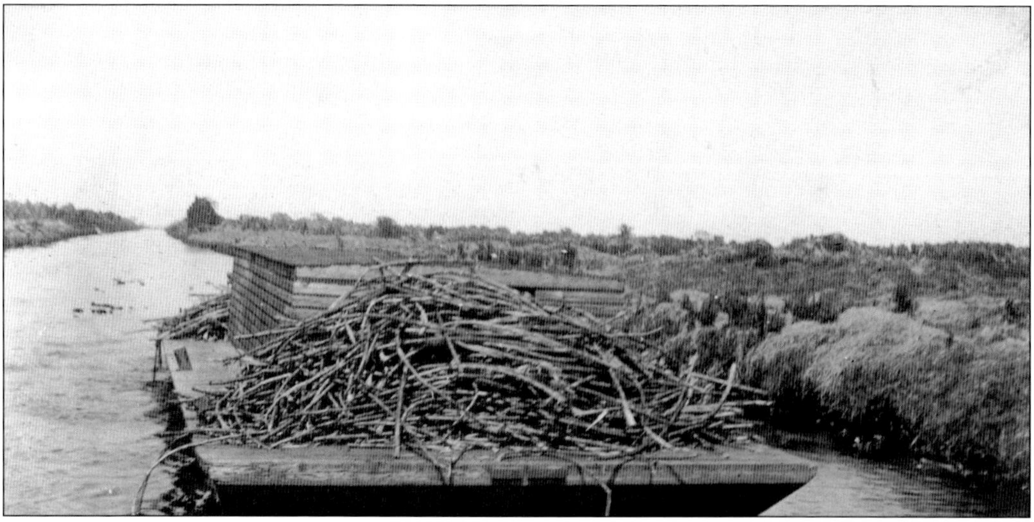

The Indian River Lagoon was originally known on early Spanish maps as the "Rio de Ais," after the Ais Indian tribe, who lived along the east coast of Florida. The full length of the Indian River Lagoon is 156 miles extending from Ponce de Leon Inlet in Volusia County to Jupiter Inlet in Palm Beach County. Prior to the arrival of the railroad, the Indian River Lagoon and Loxahatchee River were essential transportation links. Seen here is a load of sugarcane being transported north around 1924. (Courtesy of the Martin County Historical Society.)

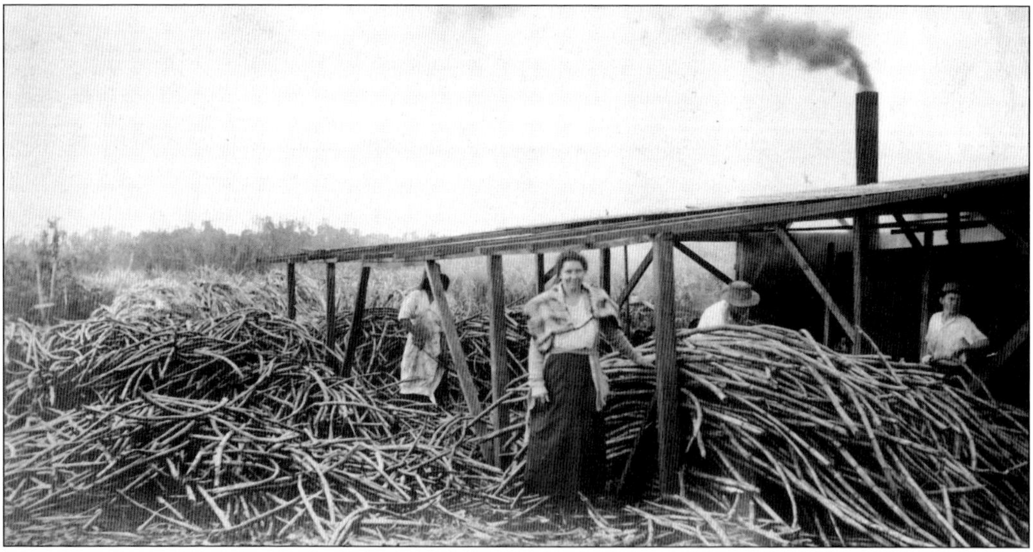

Sugarcane was brought to St. Augustine by Spanish colonial governor Menendez in 1565. However, production of sugarcane did not begin until 1767 in Florida near New Smyrna Beach. Early pioneers tried to scale up what was initially small operations of only a few acres, with the cane grown and cut by hand. Unpredictable weather and bad soil forced production south to the Lake Okeechobee area, including Martin County east toward Hobe Sound around the 1860s. In the 1920s, the US government began building and dredging canals and draining Everglades land south of the lake for agriculture, and paying subsidies to sugar growers. Even with government help, the sugar industry stayed small until 1959 and the Cuban revolution. It was then, with an embargo on sugar, that local production soared. Pictured is a processing mill in Martin County around 1908. (Courtesy of Martin County Historical Society.)

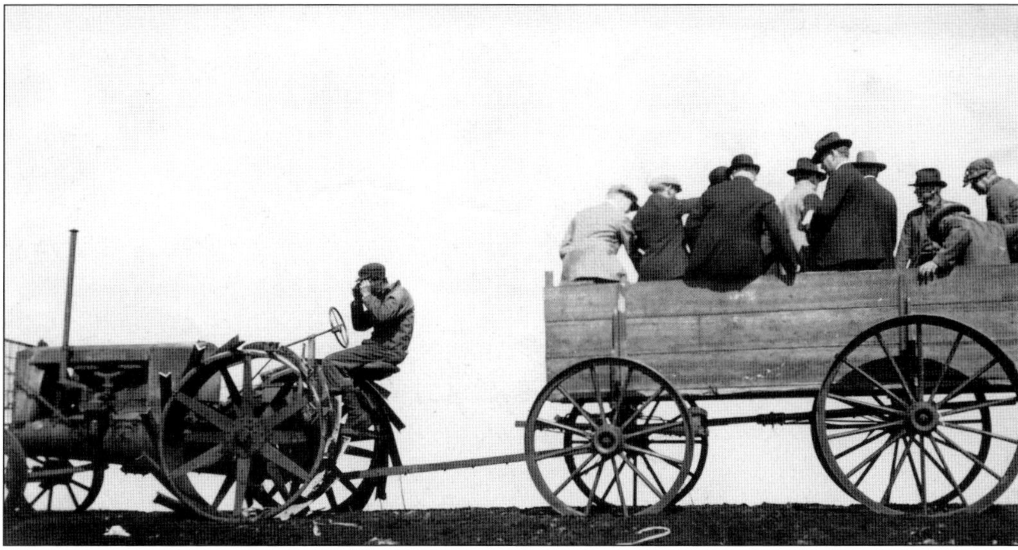

By the late 1800s, innovators had begun experimenting with internal combustion engines that ran on petroleum-based fuels, as coal- or wood-fueled traction engines proved difficult to maintain and operate. In 1910, the Gas Traction Company launched one of the earliest successful tractor brands, the Big 4. The tractor, with 96-inch diameter rear wheels, ran on gas or kerosene and earned its name from the four-cylinder engine that powered it. Farm tractors became one of the most important and easily recognizable technological components of modern agriculture in the United States. Their development in the first half of the 20th century fundamentally changed the nature of farm work, significantly altered the structure of rural America, and freed millions of workers to be absorbed into the rapidly growing manufacturing and service sectors of the country. Seen above and below are two images taken in the fields in south Martin County around 1910. (Both, courtesy of Martin County Historical Society.)

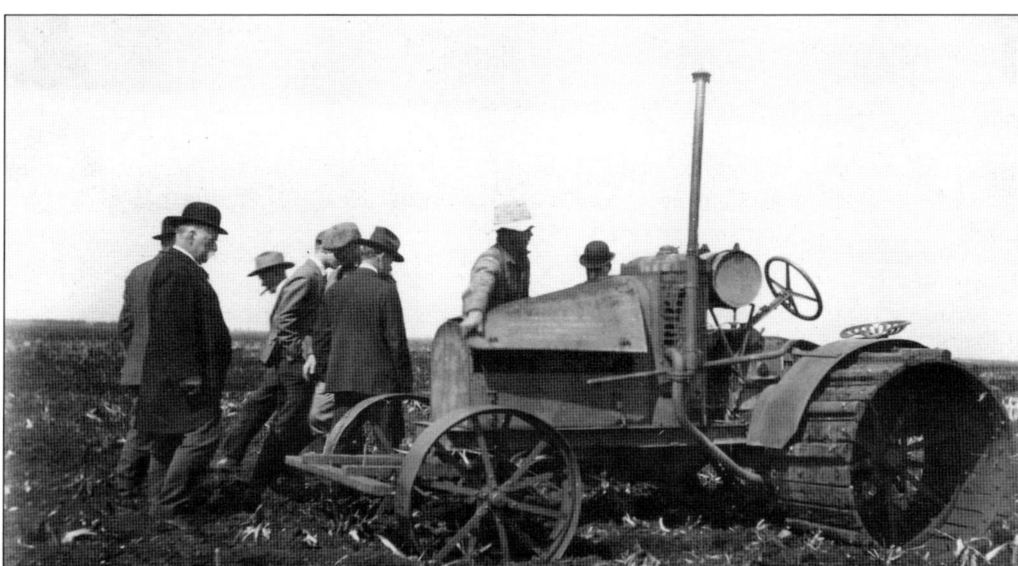

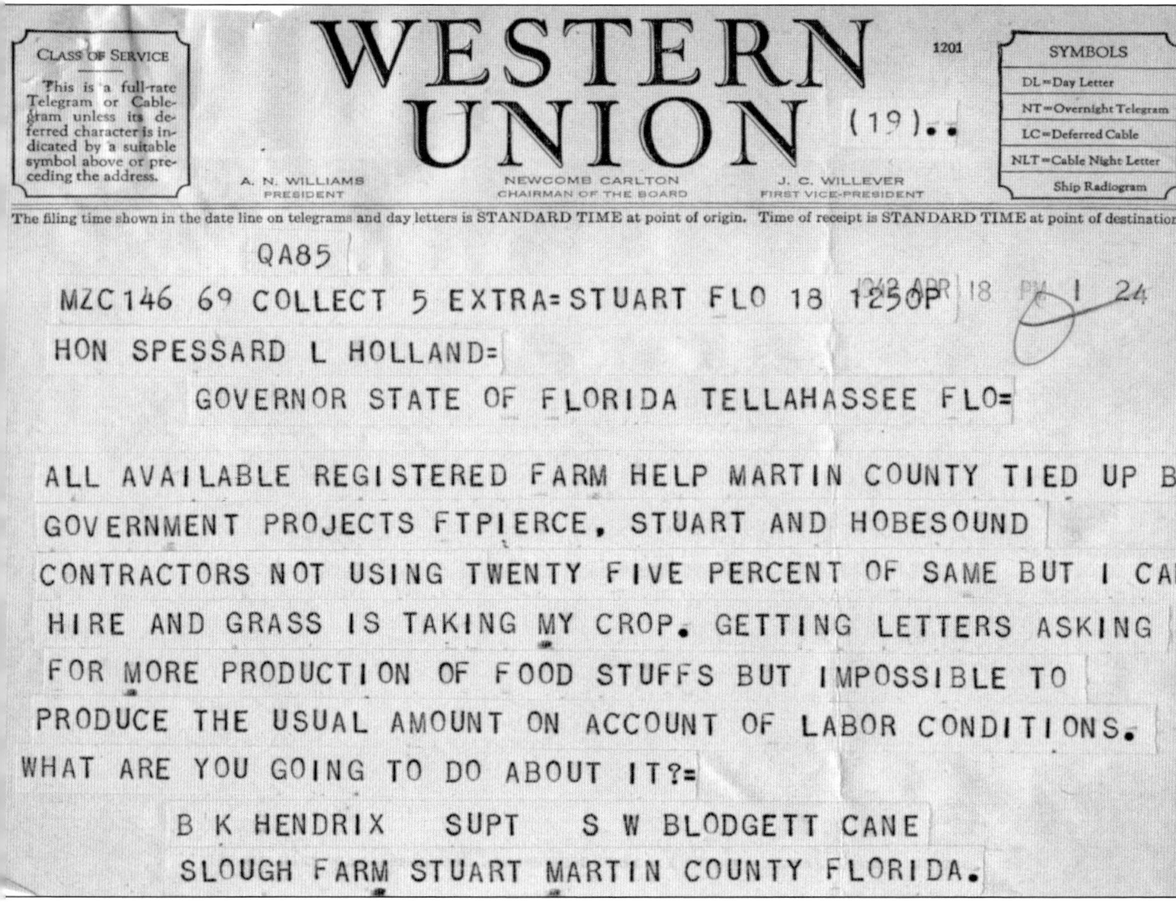
CLASS OF SERVICE
This is a full-rate Telegram or Cablegram unless its deferred character is indicated by a suitable symbol above or preceding the address.

WESTERN UNION

1201

(19)..

SYMBOLS
DL=Day Letter
NT=Overnight Telegram
LC=Deferred Cable
NLT=Cable Night Letter
Ship Radiogram

A. N. WILLIAMS PRESIDENT — NEWCOMB CARLTON CHAIRMAN OF THE BOARD — J. C. WILLEVER FIRST VICE-PRESIDENT

The filing time shown in the date line on telegrams and day letters is STANDARD TIME at point of origin. Time of receipt is STANDARD TIME at point of destination

QA85

MZC146 69 COLLECT 5 EXTRA=STUART FLO 18 1250P 1942 APR 18 PM 1 24

HON SPESSARD L HOLLAND=

GOVERNOR STATE OF FLORIDA TELLAHASSEE FLO=

ALL AVAILABLE REGISTERED FARM HELP MARTIN COUNTY TIED UP BY GOVERNMENT PROJECTS FTPIERCE, STUART AND HOBESOUND CONTRACTORS NOT USING TWENTY FIVE PERCENT OF SAME BUT I CAN HIRE AND GRASS IS TAKING MY CROP. GETTING LETTERS ASKING FOR MORE PRODUCTION OF FOOD STUFFS BUT IMPOSSIBLE TO PRODUCE THE USUAL AMOUNT ON ACCOUNT OF LABOR CONDITIONS. WHAT ARE YOU GOING TO DO ABOUT IT?=

B K HENDRIX SUPT S W BLODGETT CANE SLOUGH FARM STUART MARTIN COUNTY FLORIDA.

On Farm Mobilization Day, January 12, 1943, Pres. Franklin D. Roosevelt delivered a nationwide address in which he underscored the important role to be played by American agriculture in winning the war. Throughout the wartime years, the need for workers in agriculture, as well as in manufacturing and the military, was unprecedented. The Bureau of Agricultural Economics reported that between April 1940 and July 1942, more than two million men left agricultural jobs. One of the least known aspects of World War II in the United States is the crucial role played by the many women who plowed the ground, planted the seeds, cultivated the plants, and harvested much of the nation's crops from 1942 through 1945. Without their contributions, food would have been even scarcer, both at home and on the fighting fronts. Seen here is a 1942 telegram from local farmer B.K. Hendrix to the governor of Florida, Spessard Holland, begging for help in 1942. (Courtesy of State Archives of Florida.)

Winter Vegetables a Gold Mine

We quote below a tabulated list showing conservative and average returns and yield of various kinds of truck, all of which is invariably sold f. o. b. loading station:

Celery	800	crates per acre, at	$1.25	$1,000.00
Eggplant	700	crates per acre, at	1.00	700.00
Lettuce	500	baskets per acre, at	1.25	625.00
Peppers	600	crates per acre, at	1.00	600.00
Cucumbers	200	crates per acre, at	1.50	300.00
Squash	500	crates per acre, at	.60	300.00
Onions	300	bushels per crate, at	1.00	300.00
Cauliflower	200	crates per acre, at	1.50	300.00
Tomatoes	200	crates per acre, at	1.50	300.00
Beans	200	crates per acre, at	1.50	300.00
Irish Potatoes	50	barrels per acre, at	3.00	150.00
Sweet Potatoes	200	bushels per acre, at	.50	100.00

and many others; in fact, you can successfully grow practically everything raised in the north, besides many varieties of tropical fruits —all at an immense profit.

Bear in mind that these figures represent the returns from but one crop, and that two, three and sometimes four crops can be raised on the land during the year.

Some Florida Fruits

Strawberries	4,000 quarts	$ .20	$ 800.00	per acre
Bananas	600 bunches	.20	150.00	per acre
Pineapples		250.00	500.00	per acre
Watermelons		75.00	100.00	per acre
Cantaloupes		125.00	200.00	per acre
Oranges		6 year trees	420.00	per acre
Oranges		10 year trees	1,400.00	per acre

Boosters promoted Florida as a paradise on earth: the climate cured all aliments and the soil produced wealth with little effort. Pictured is an advertisement for Hobe Sound around 1952. Florida's economy, which had been largely agricultural in nature, became more diverse after World War II with growth in tourism and other industries. Farming in the 1950s and 1960s had serious challenges as millions of farmers left for jobs in towns and cities. (Courtesy of Martin County Historical Society.)

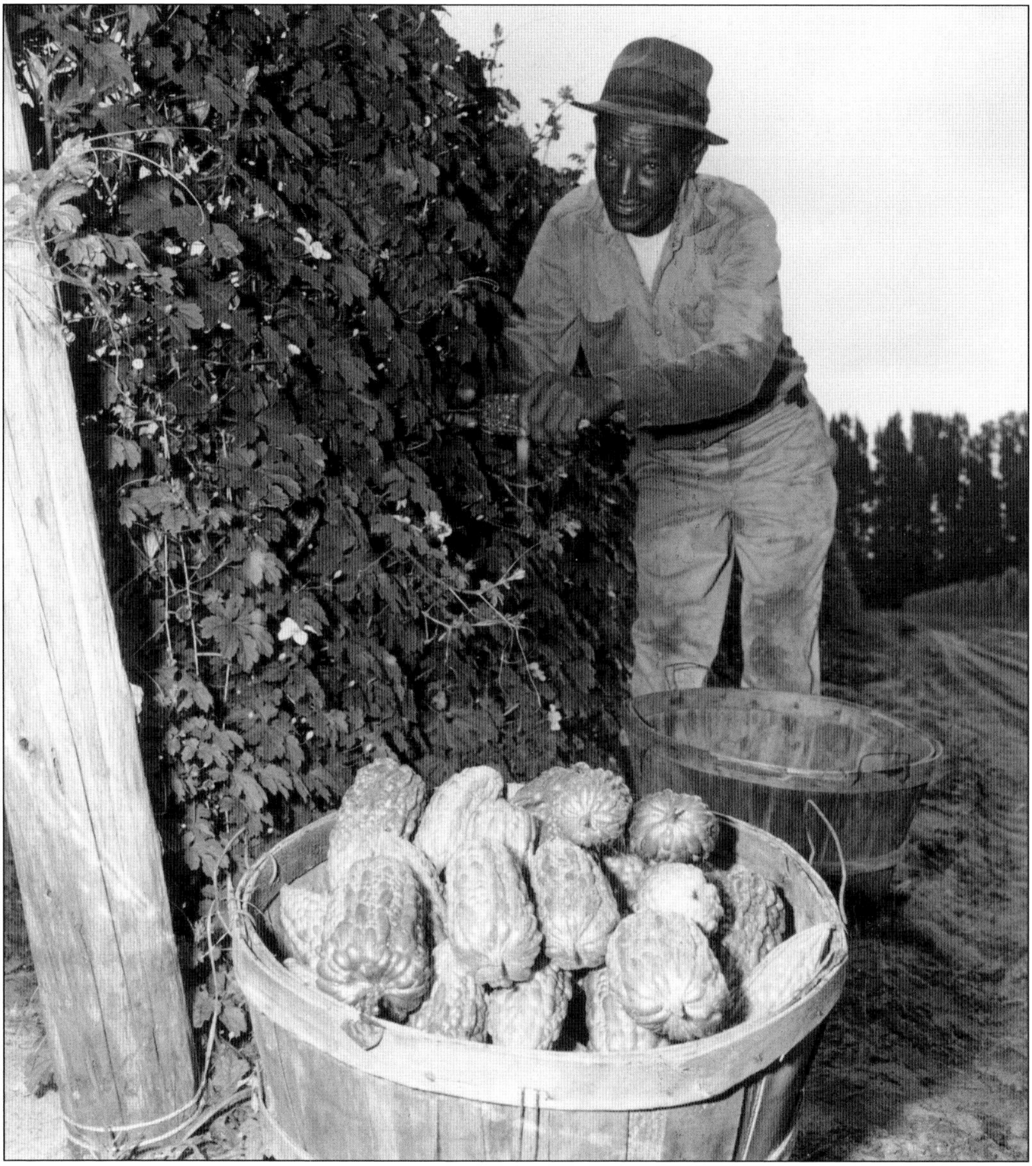

A worker gathers produce in the fields. Established in the 1950s the Sang Lee farm was famous for foot-long okra, 28-to-32-inch pole beans, extra-long taro, soup melons, Chinese cabbage, squash, bok choy, Napa, and kohlrabi. Produce was shipped daily to Chinatown in New York City, Chicago, and other cities. The farm was very successful during the 1960s, 1970s, and into the early 1980s, increasing to 500 acres. Unfortunately, a severe freeze in 1982 ruined 50 percent of the Sang Lee farm's crops. The family never recovered financially, and the farm closed on May 9, 1990. (Courtesy of the State Archives of Florida.)

Martin County is also known as the "Chrysanthemum Capital of the World." Miniature mums were developed here. Palm City had the world's largest lily-growing operation, and Hobe Sound had Peter Nissen's Sunshine State Carnation farm off Gomez Avenue since 1962. The flower industry took off in the 1950s and was very profitable well into the 1960s due to the creation of artificial lighting. (Courtesy of the Martin County Historical Society.)

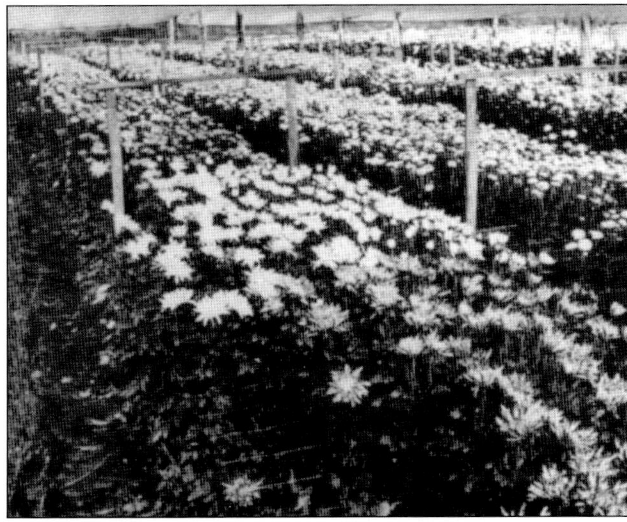

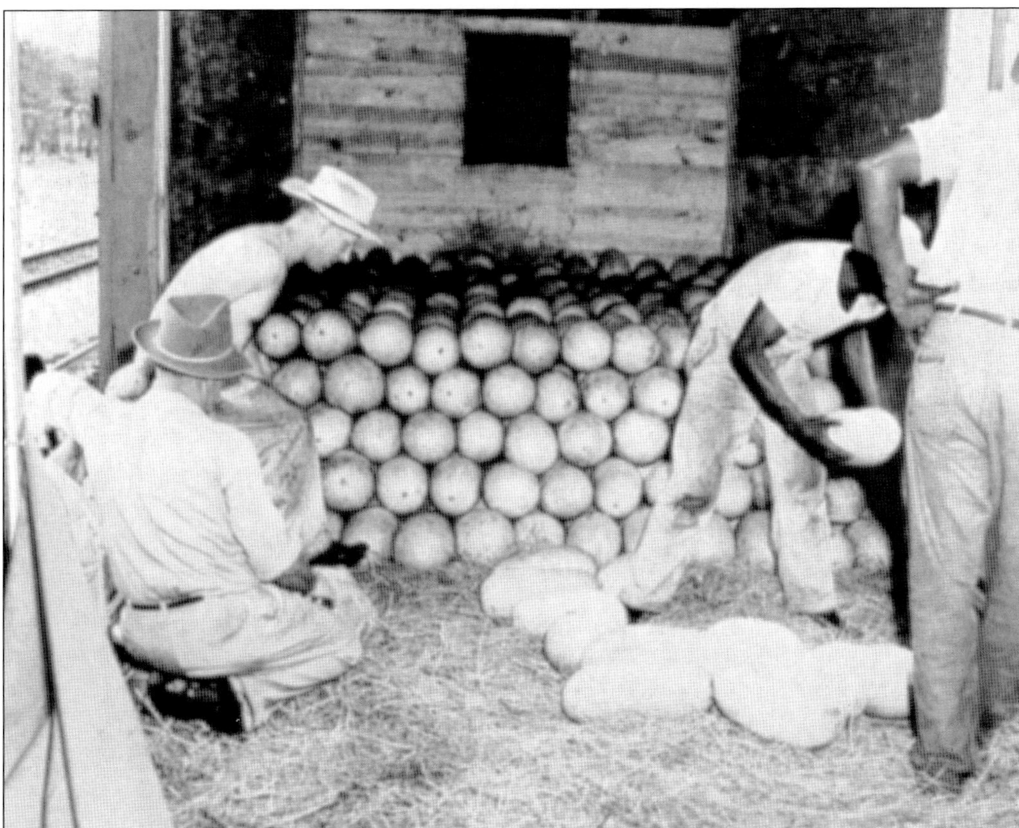

The watermelon's history dates back 5,000 years to South Africa, where the tough, drought-tolerant ancestor of the fruit thrived. Watermelons were brought to America by European colonists. The first ones were grown in Florida in the 16th century. While it is generally considered a summer fruit, Florida is the only state in the country that produces watermelon from December to April. Pictured is a watermelon packing shed in Hobe Sound around 1945. (Courtesy of Martin County Historical Society.)

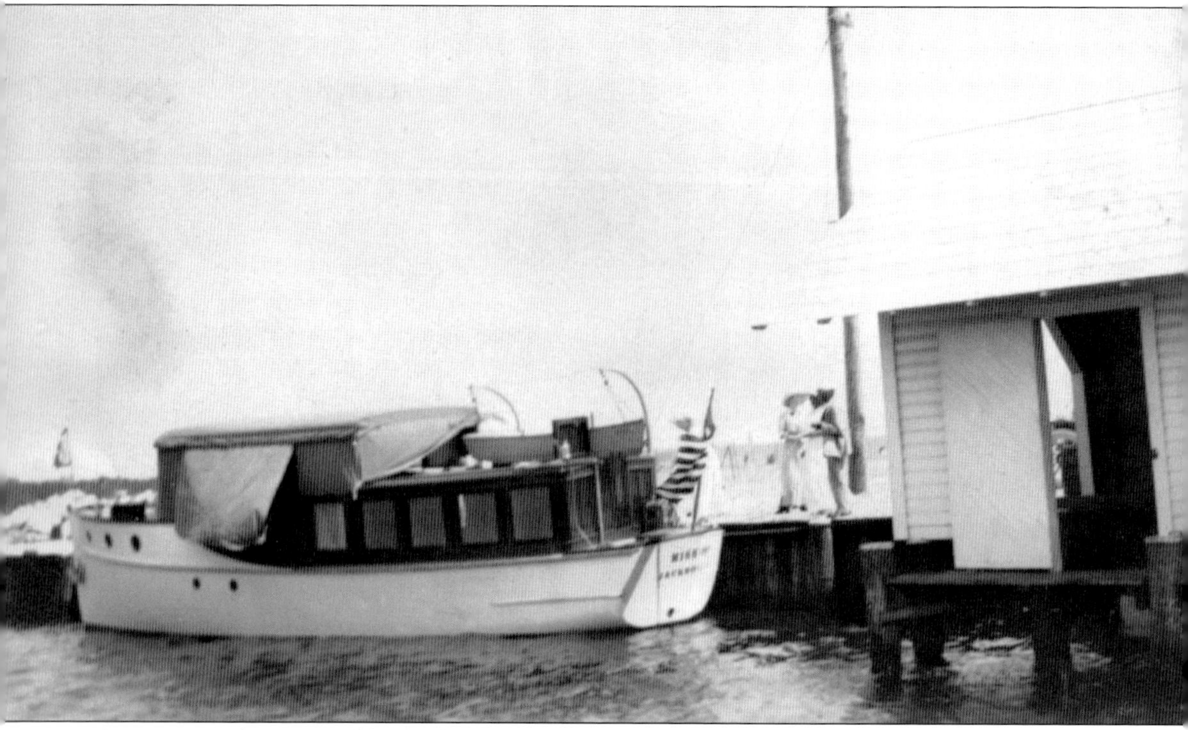

Annie Peacock Corse and her husband, Montgomery Corse, were prominent citizens of Jacksonville. Montgomery ran a shingle mill turning out cedar shakes after having trouble with the family's orange grove on the St. Johns River due to freezing temperatures. The family spent time traveling throughout the state. Annie was an accomplished musician, artist, and photographer, and her collection of photographs documented their travels. Here, the *Miss Anne* is docked in Hobe Sound Harbor. (Courtesy of State Archives of Florida.)

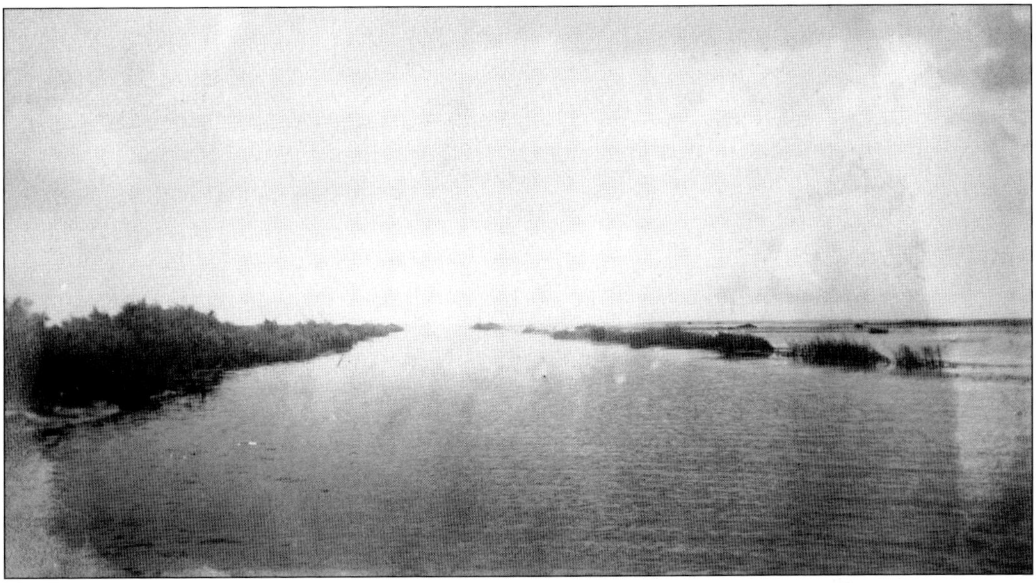

From at least 6,000 years ago, the native people of Florida traveled the waterways and coasts by canoe, facilitating communication and trade among the tribes. Following statehood in 1845, Florida's economy became stronger, and the principal ports shipped vast quantities of citrus, cotton, lumber, and other products to the Atlantic states, the Caribbean, and Europe. Waterways and a growing network of railroads linked the frontier with the eastern cities. Produce moved on small boats along canals and rivers from the farms to the ports. Seen above is the Indian River Lagoon in the Jupiter Narrows area in 1890 unblemished and undeveloped. Below are early settlers transporting goods up the Loxahatchee River around 1924. (Above, courtesy of the William Henry Jackson Photo Collection, Detroit Publishing Company, Library of Congress; below, courtesy of Martin County Historical Society.)

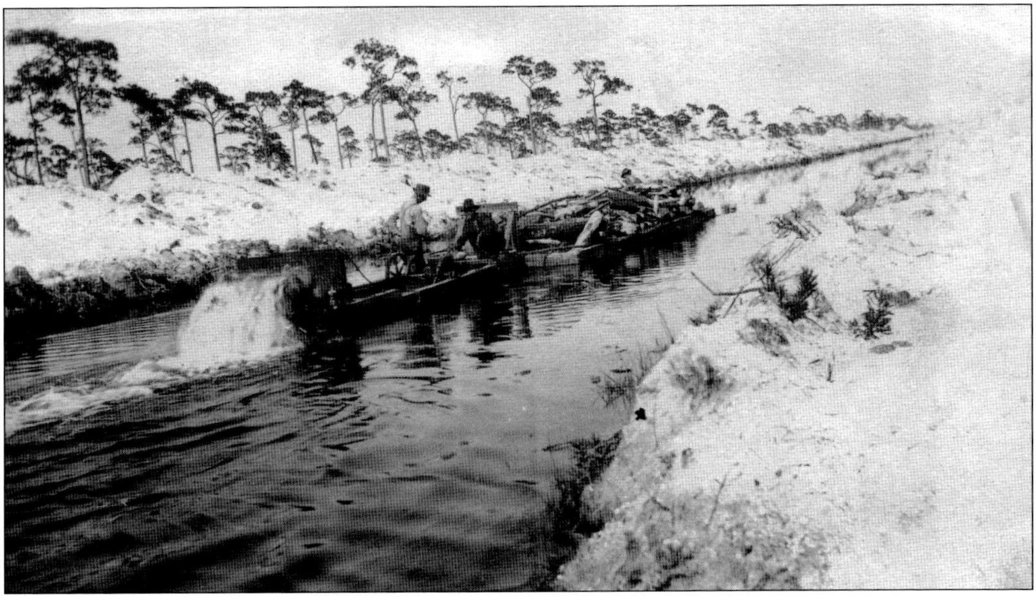

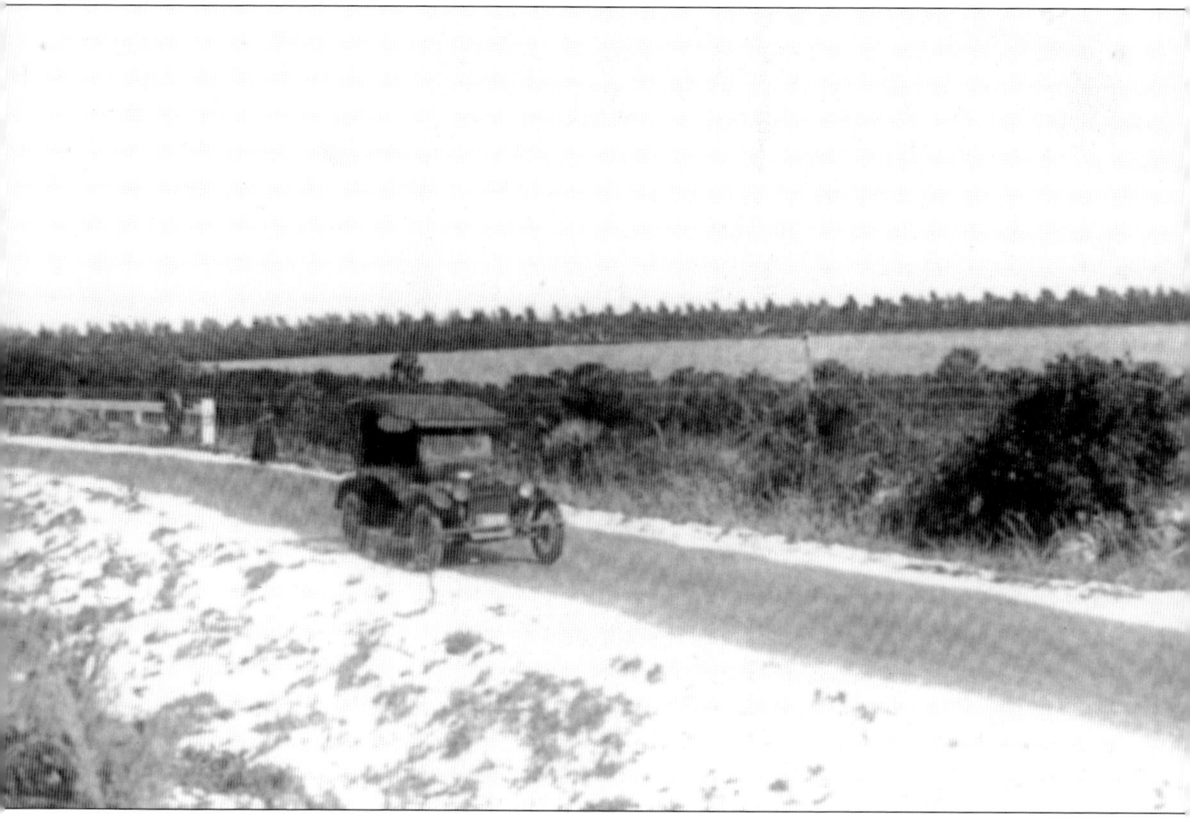

An automobile drives along the Indian River Lagoon on what is now Dixie Highway in the early 1900s. This was the main thoroughfare through Hobe Sound before the construction of US Route 1. (Courtesy of the Martin County Historical Society.)

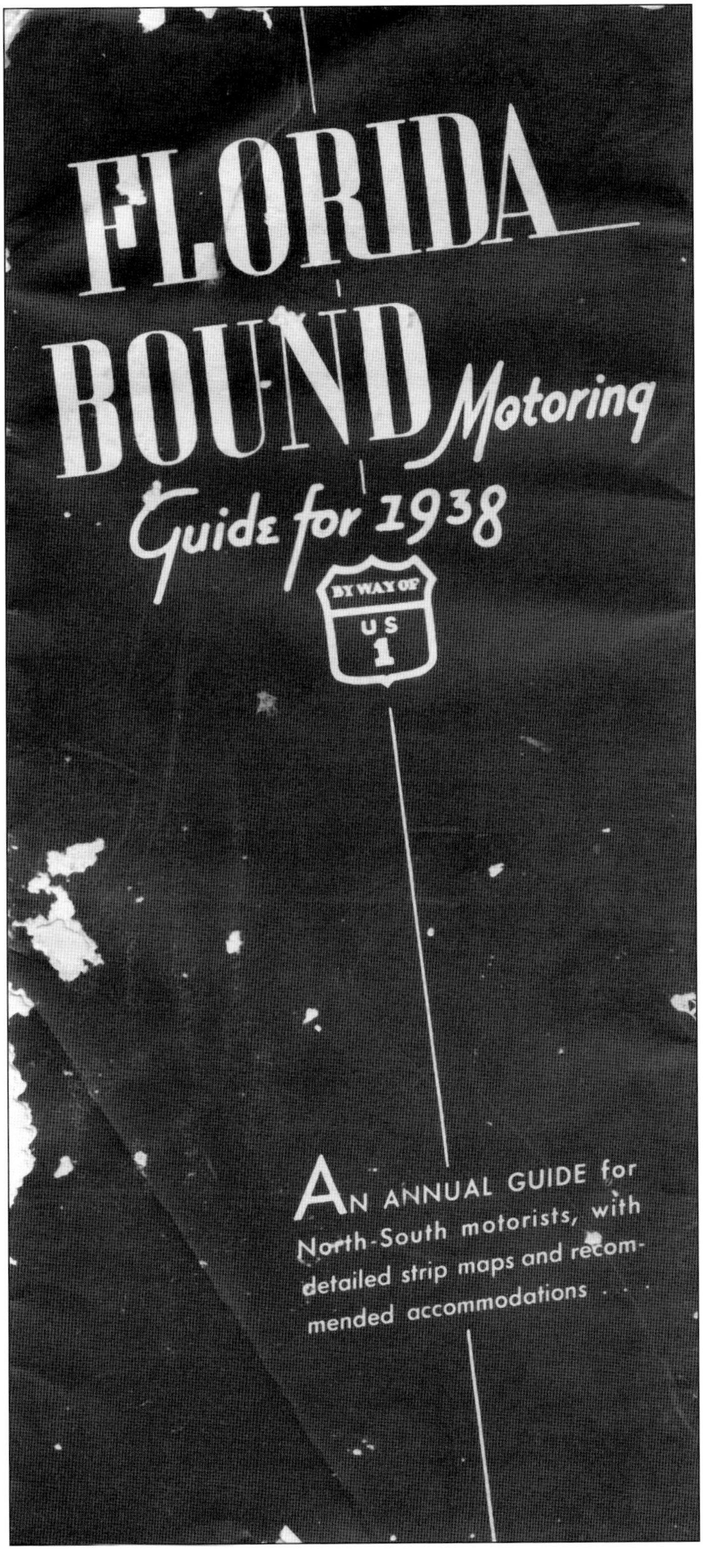

Despite exponential growth in car sales in the 1910s, and the annual publication of a route guide called *The Official Automobile Blue Book*, trips still proceeded from point to point on local, often unpaved and unidentified roads. Rain and mud limited travel, and snow precluded it. In the 1920s, the government sought to improve long-distance auto travel with the introduction of the US Highway System by 1926. In the 1920s and 1930s, the amenities offered by modern highways were few and far between. There were limited places to stop and eat, and travelers had to plan carefully for gas. Starting in the 1930s, booklets like this one were published each year to help motorists. (Both, courtesy of the Martin County Historical Society.)

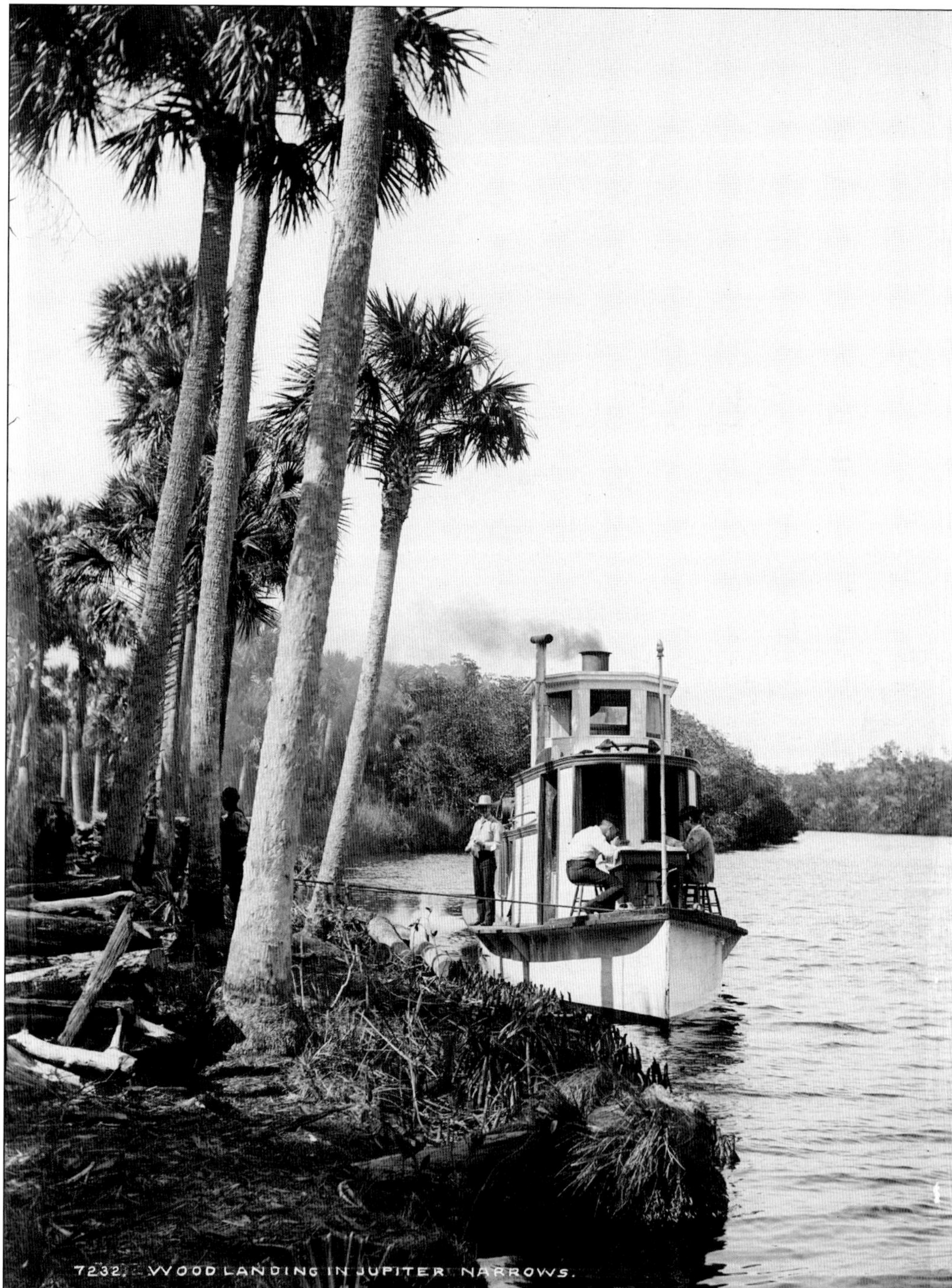

"Queens of the River" was the phrase a newspaper reporter used to describe the first steamboats that plied the Indian River Lagoon in the late 1870s. Between 1877 and 1905, more than 200 steamboats chugged up and down the lagoon carrying cargo and people. Here, on the Indian River Lagoon at Jupiter Narrows, a steamship is tied up in the late 1800s. (Courtesy of the William Henry Jackson Photo Collection, Detroit Publishing Company, Library of Congress.)

Five

Recreation and Leisure

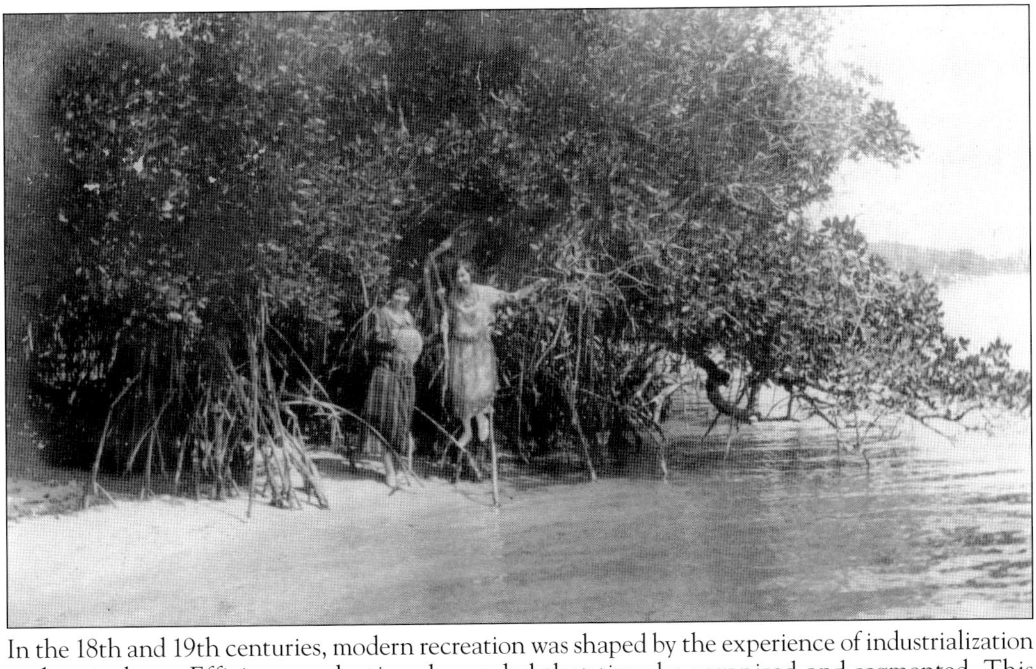

In the 18th and 19th centuries, modern recreation was shaped by the experience of industrialization and agriculture. Efficient production demanded that time be organized and segmented. This meant that recreation too became regimented and bound by time, both hindering and enabling play. The typical workday was 11 hours long, and by 1894, the half-day Saturday that was paid became commonplace. The idea of vacation also appeared, though it was unpaid. Hobe Sound offered many forms of recreation and leisure both on land and in the water. Seen here are friends posing for the camera while playing in the mangroves along the Indian River Lagoon. (Courtesy of the Martin County Historical Society.)

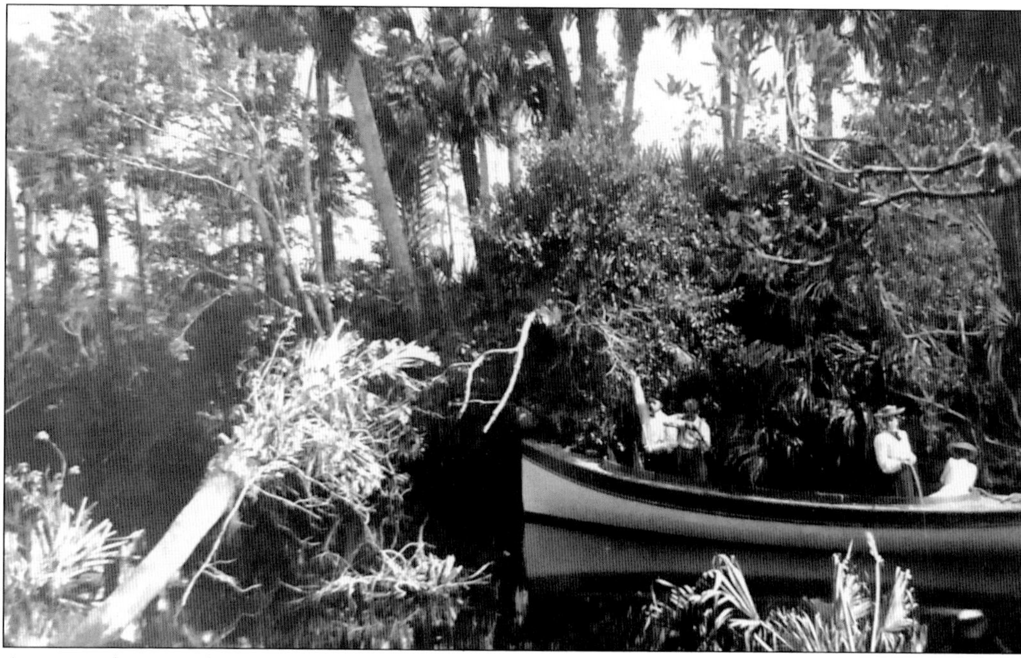

A group of men and women are pictured on the Loxahatchee River near Hobe Sound in the early 1900s. The Loxahatchee was a federally designated wild and scenic river in 1985, one of only two in Florida. Today in Jonathan Dickinson State Park, people continue to enjoy the river on boats, kayaks, and paddleboards. (Courtesy of the Martin County Historical Society.)

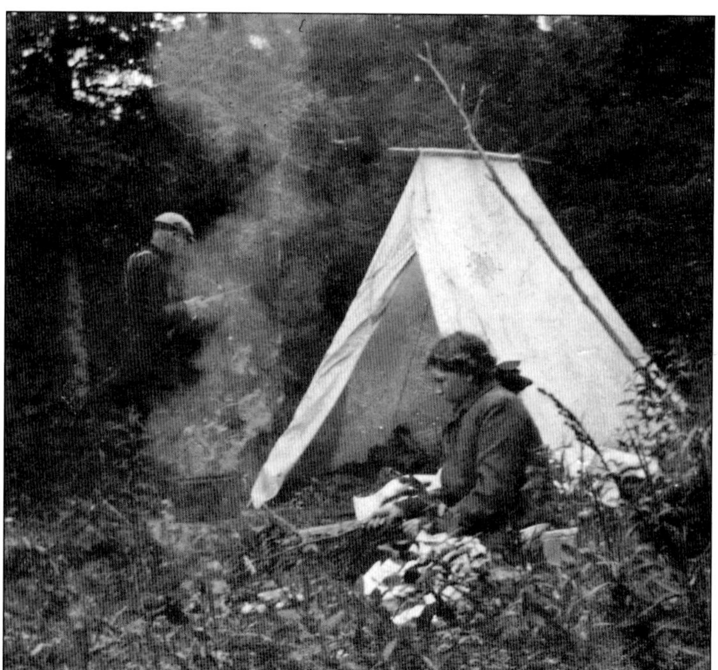

As American cities grew at the beginning of the 20th century, consuming more and more land with concrete and construction, experiencing nature became a journey. Camping was increasingly popular, and new cars helped facilitate weekend excursions, even doubling as mobile accommodations. Pictured is a family camping in Martin County around 1908. (Courtesy of the Martin County Historical Society.)

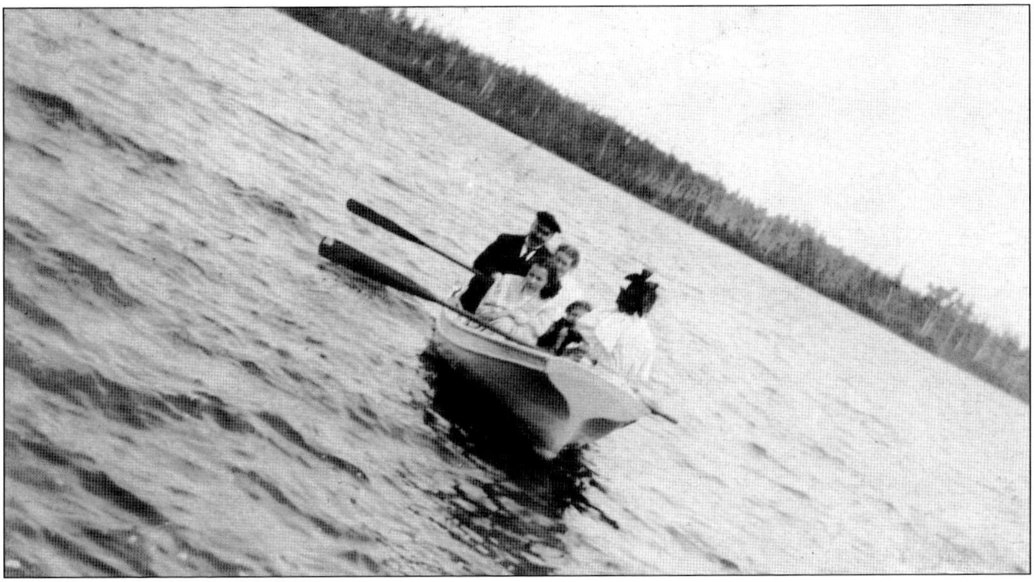

Prior to the early 1900s, boats were made of natural materials, mostly wood, and oars or sails were used for power. Soon after the invention of the Evinrude outboard motor in 1909, new boat designs and materials were developed. By the 1920s, there were the original runabouts. They were still made of wood, with mahogany hulls and planking and oak framing, but the design had changed significantly. Above is a group of women being rowed on the Indian River in Hobe Sound. Below are people diving off their wooden boat around 1908. (Both, courtesy of the Martin County Historical Society.)

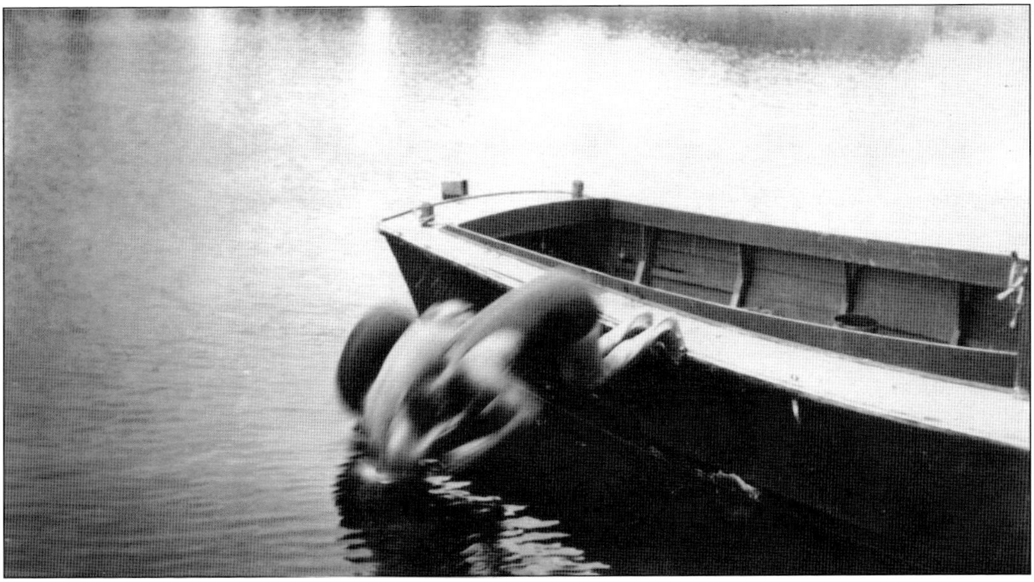

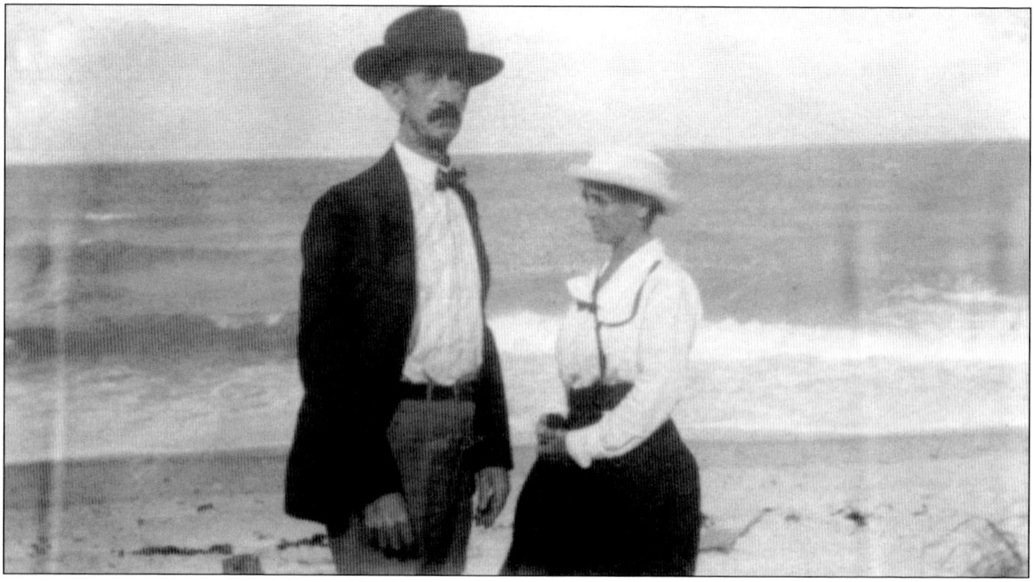

The seashore used to be a scary place, then it became a place of respite and vacation. Around the mid-19th century, European elites began touting the curative qualities of fresh air, exercise, and sea bathing, and by the late 19th century, it was gaining popularity in America. The coastal landscape, once dangerous and deadly, became a site of transformative experience, where individuals could enjoy and embrace nature. Above is a couple walking along the beach on Jupiter Island. Below is a c. 1908 photograph taken on the local beach with many residents enjoying the sun and sand. (Both, courtesy of Martin County Historical Society.)

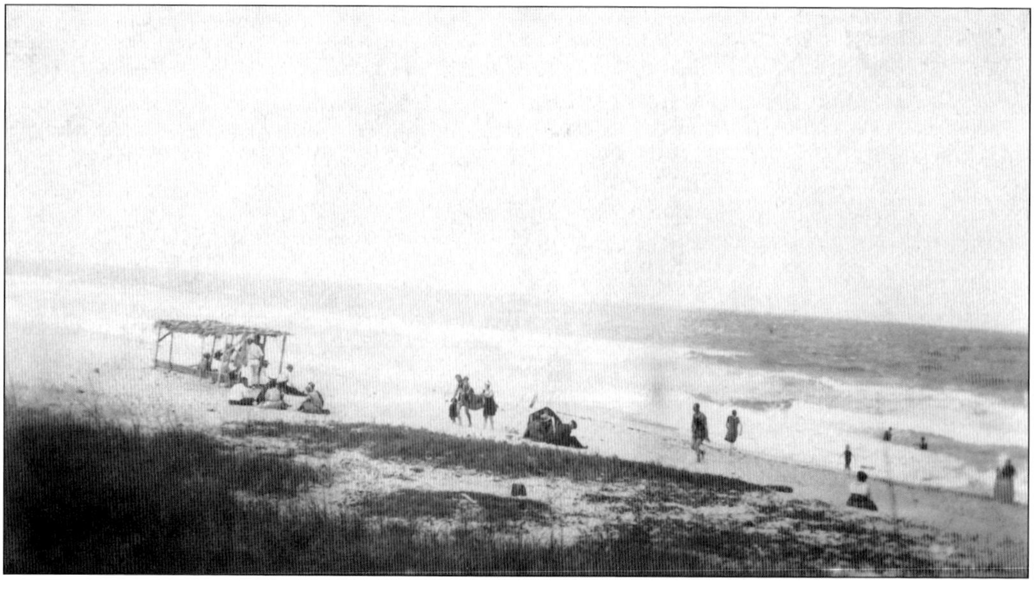

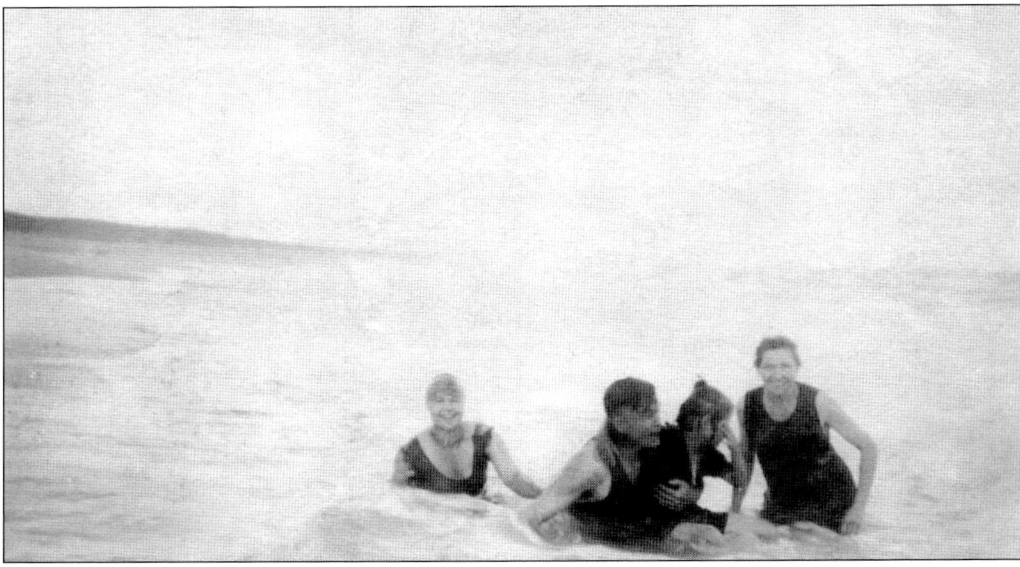

Living near the sea, summer means going to the beach and having a swim or getting a tan. This seems so natural for many during warm summer days. However, the beach was not always seen as a destination to relax. The things people do at the beach today would be seen as immodest and offensive not long ago. It was not until the 1840s that Europeans began to escape the industrial cities and go to the seaside for vacations. This trend spread to America in the late 19th century. Above is a family in the early 1900s enjoying Hobe Sound Beach. Below is a swimmer. (Both, courtesy of the Martin County Historical Society.)

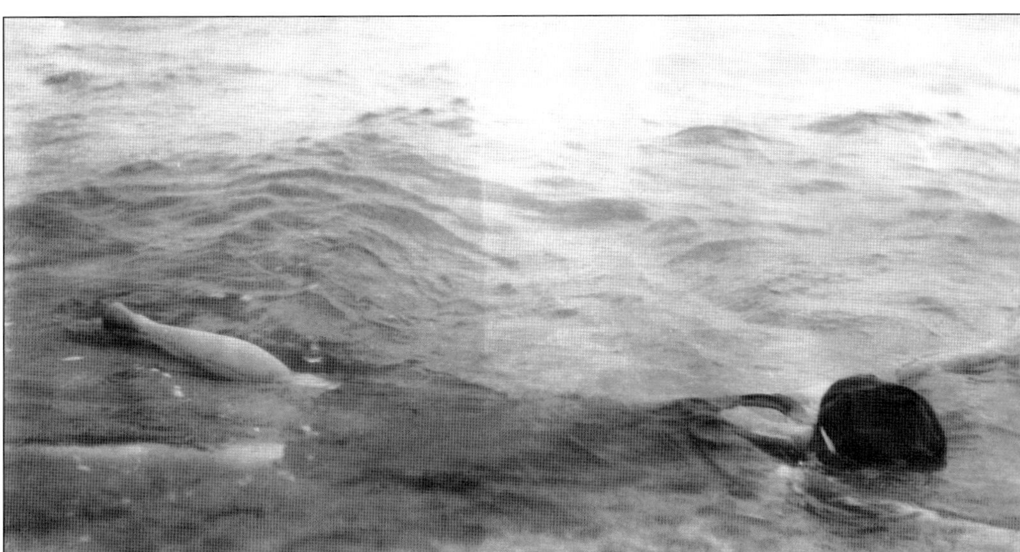

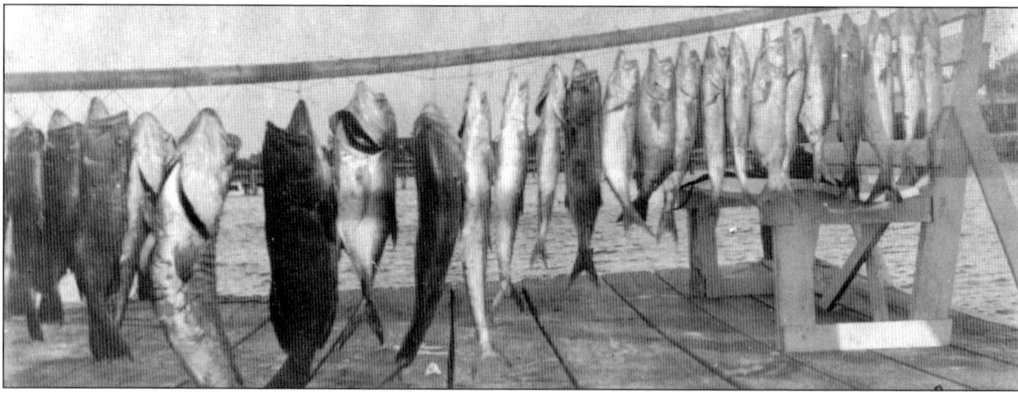

The Gulf Stream is a 20-to-60-mile-wide current that brings warm water from the Gulf of Mexico to the Atlantic Ocean. It extends all the way up the eastern coast of the United States and Canada then makes its way towards northwestern Europe. It has an average speed of about four miles per hour off the coast of Florida but slows to about one mile per hour as it widens in the north. First discovered in 1513 by Juan Ponce De Leon, it was extensively used by Spanish ships as they traveled from the Caribbean to Spain. Benjamin Franklin later mapped the current. The Gulf Stream runs closer to Jupiter Island than anywhere else in the United States. This brings many benefits and makes for a sportfishing paradise, whether by boat or on shore. Above is a prize catch after a day of fishing in 1908. The c. 1940s image below highlights the famous Hobe Sound Beach shore fishing. (Both, courtesy of the Martin County Historical Society.)

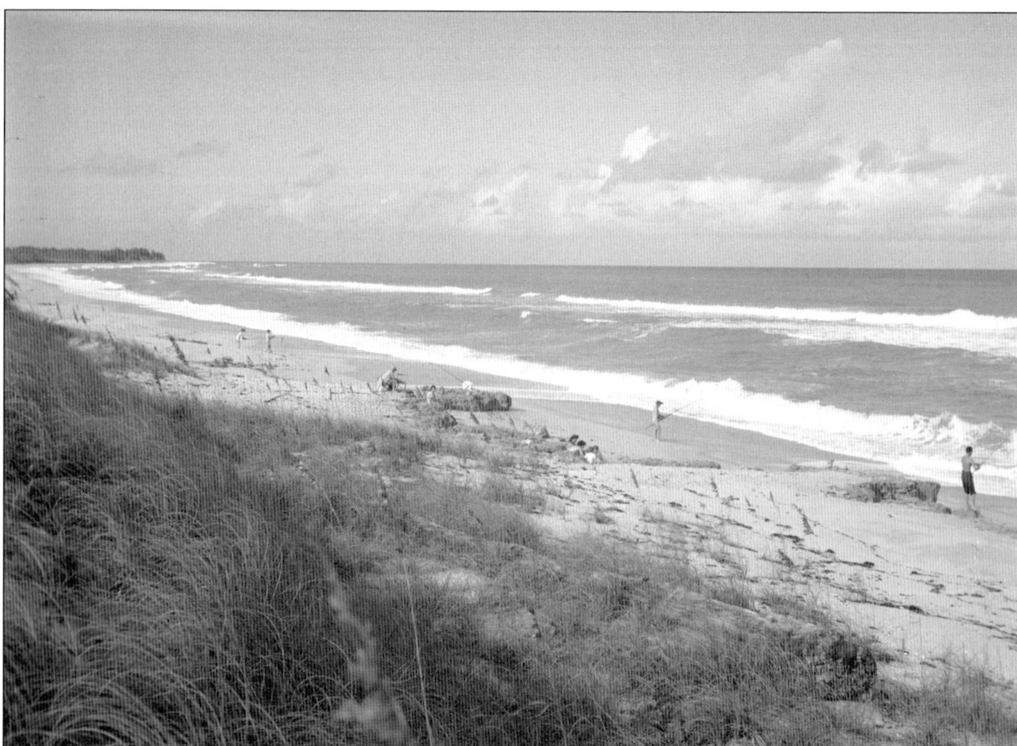

In the 19th century, women wore long bathing gowns with matching drawers. The number-one priority for women who took part in water-based activities was to maintain their modesty. Bathing outfits would consist of a bathing dress, drawers, and stockings, often made of wool or cotton. Speedo, the Australian clothing company, started to experiment with swimwear in 1914. For both sexes, the all-in-one garments tended to have short-sleeve or vest-style tops with long legs. Tanned skin was not a concern and was seen as a characteristic of the working class up until World War II. Pictured here are Hobe Sound residents enjoying the beach. (Both, courtesy of the Martin County Historical Society.)

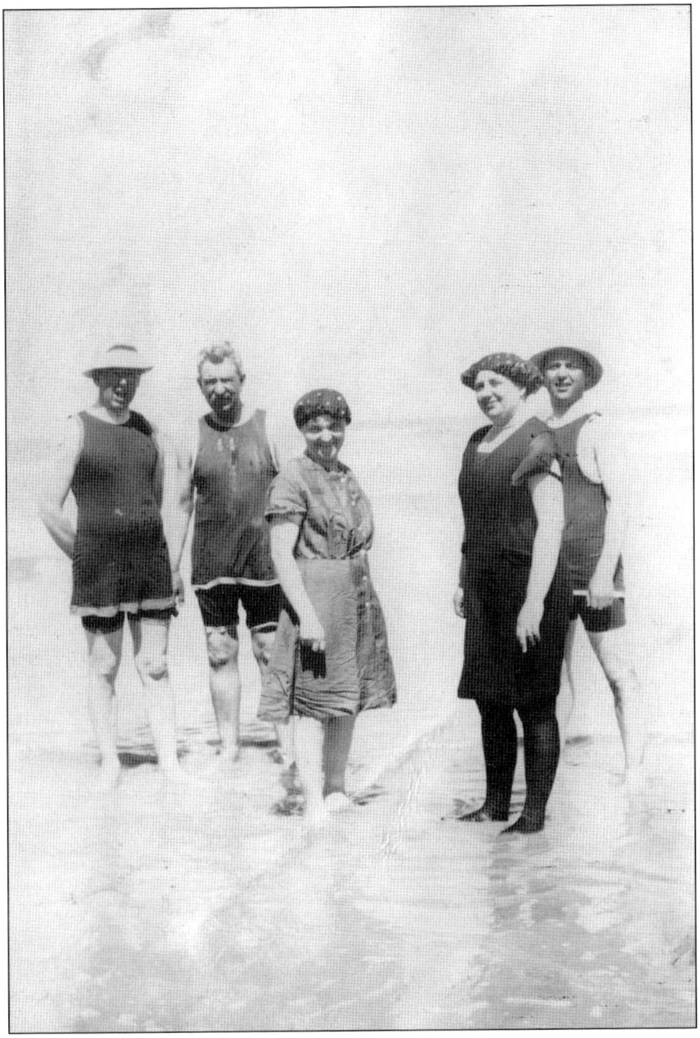

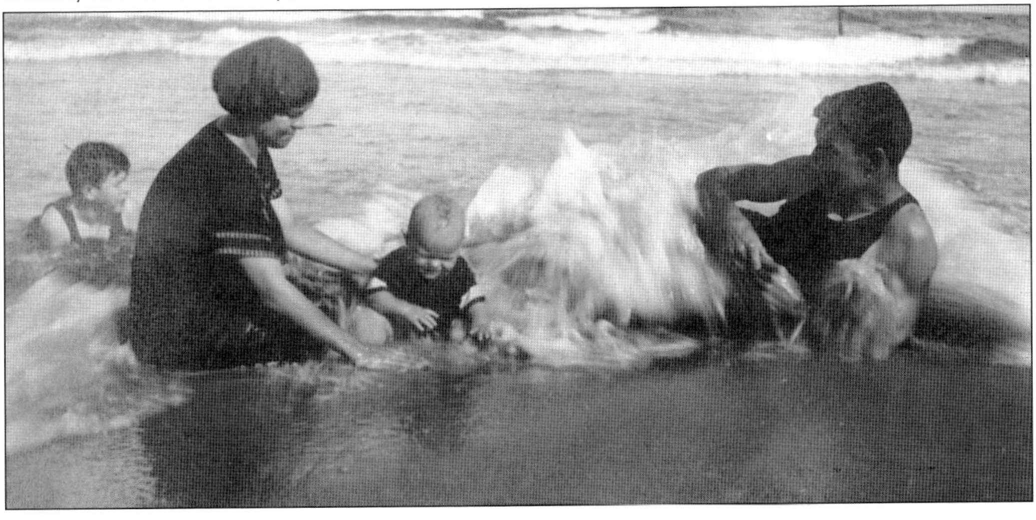

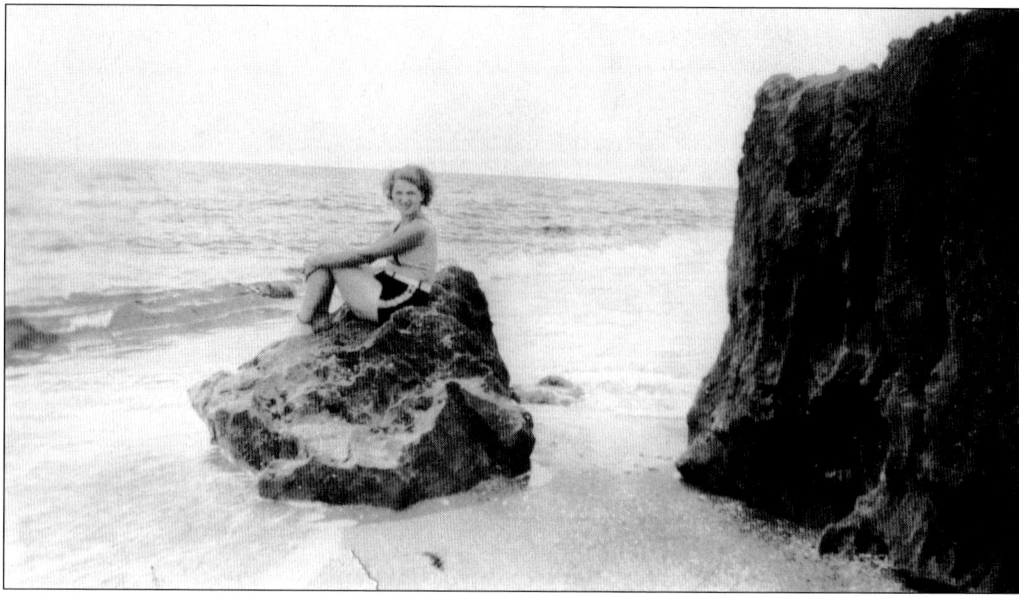

Stretching more than a mile along Jupiter Island is a tall limestone terrace that dominates the meeting of sand and sea. It is the longest and most dramatic stretch of rocky shoreline in Florida. Blowing Rocks gets its name from what the waves and rocks do during rough seas at high tide—water spurts out of holes in the limestone, at times spouting 50 feet into the air. These conditions are most common in winter. Often, this limestone is called coquina, and it has been a building material for 400 years. In fact, the Spanish used it to build Castillo de San Marcos in Saint Augustine in 1672. It is composed of the remains of ancient coral reefs, sand ridges, and shells. It crops up in several places along the coast, but the biggest is at Blowing Rocks Preserve. Above is Hobe Sound resident Vee Chambers posing in the 1920s. Below is a group of friends. (Above, courtesy of Sandra Thurlow; below, courtesy of the Martin County Historical Society.)

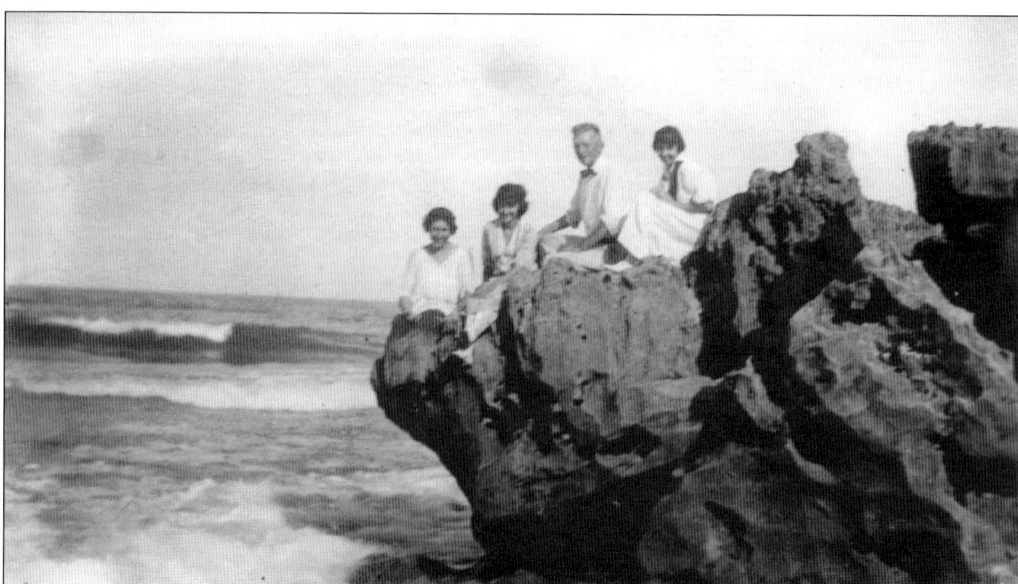

Sea turtles are among the oldest creatures on earth and have remained essentially unchanged for 110 million years. There are indications that ancient Florida tribes had eaten sea turtles and then placed the skulls in burial mounds. Sea turtle meat and eggs were also important foods for the early settlers. Pictured is a young local resident holding up a sea turtle for a photo. (Courtesy of the Martin County Historical Society.)

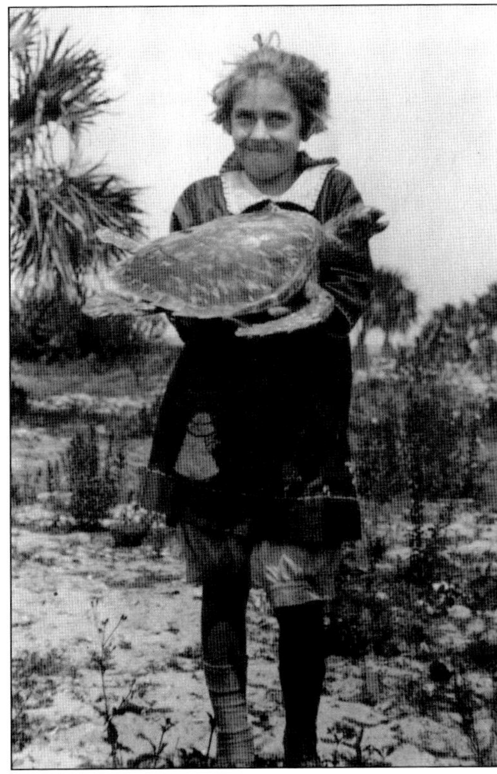

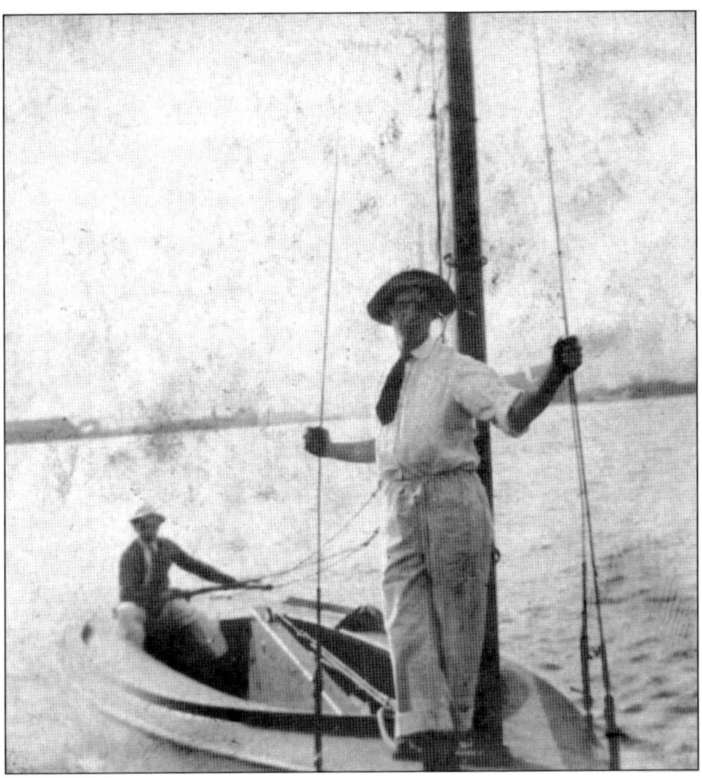

Since prehistoric times, sailboats have been used for travel, fishing, and recreation. Just like any other sport, sailors would gather in one place and discuss future and past competitions, yachts, and any social aspect of their time. Hobe Sound had its first yacht club in 1892. Seen here are sailors on the Indian River Lagoon. (Courtesy of the Martin County Historical Society.)

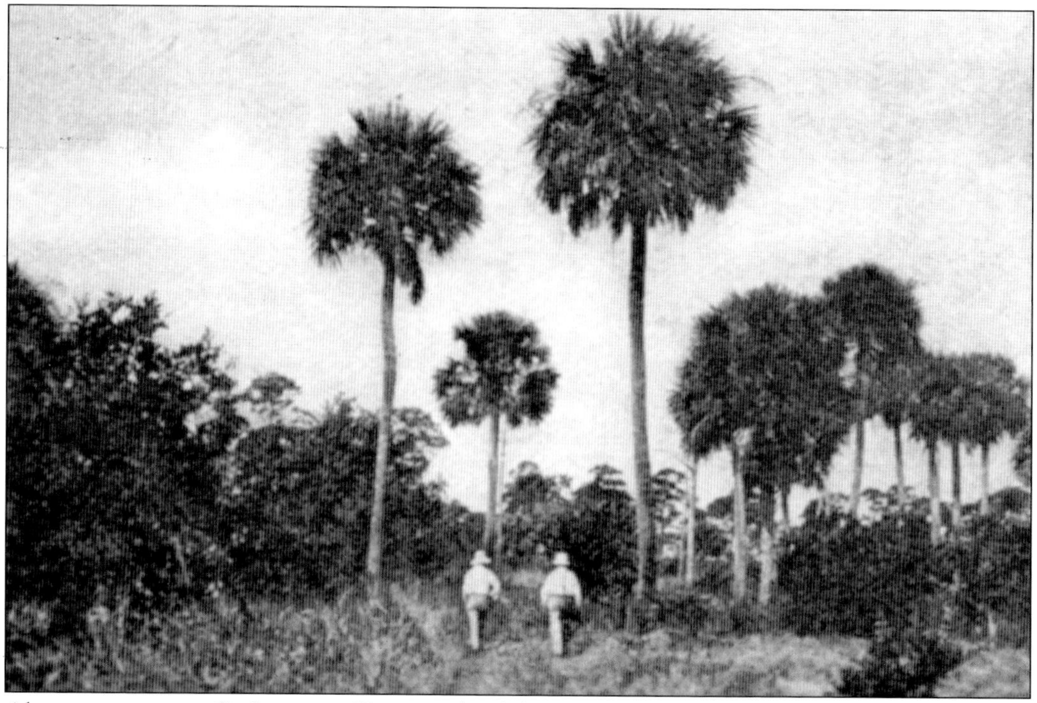

Above, two men walk the area of Jupiter Island that would become the Jupiter Island Golf Club. Golf has a long history on the island. As early as the 1890s, the Scottish Pineapple Plantation owners played golf on the sand hills that are now part of the current golf club. The more modern nine-hole course was built in 1922. The second nine holes were designed by landscape architect Dick Webel and completed in 1957. Below is the Jupiter Island Golf Club logo on a bag tag. (Above, courtesy of the P.K. Yonge Library of Florida History, Special and Area Studies Collections, George A. Smathers Libraries, University of Florida; below, author's collection.)

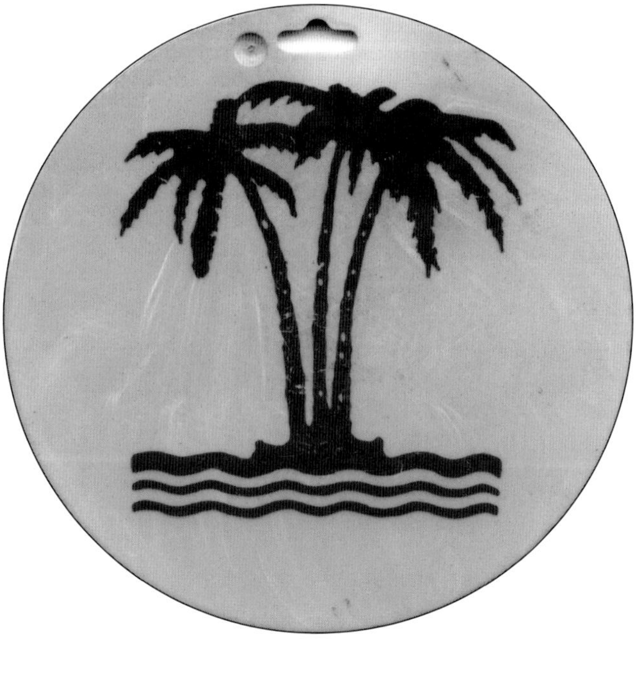

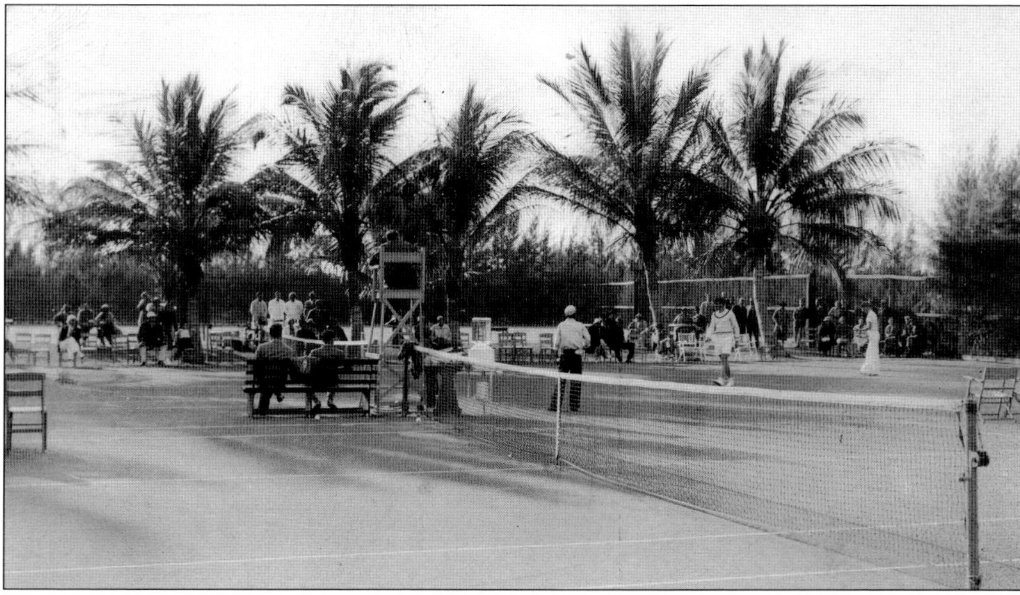

Tennis was developed out of a 12th-century French handball game called *paume* (palm). The first racquet was developed in Italy in 1583, and by 1873, lawn tennis was created by Maj. Walter Wingfield in Wales. By 1874, the game had made it to America, and tennis clubs were established by the wealthy. Jupiter Island was no exception. Seen above in a c. 1938 postcard are the Jupiter Island tennis courts. Below is the note on the back of the card. (Both, author's collection.)

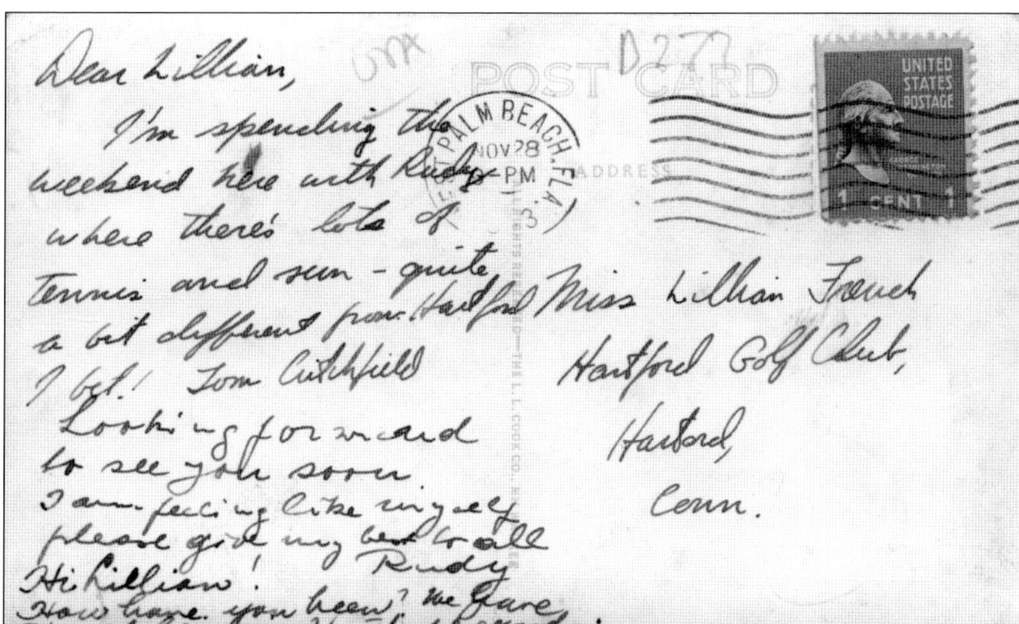
POST CARD

UNITED STATES POSTAGE 1 CENT 1

PALM BEACH, FLA. NOV 28 PM

Dear Lillian,
I'm spending the weekend here with Rudy where there's lots of tennis and sun - quite a bit different from Hartford I bet! Tom Critchfield
Looking forward to see you soon.
I am feeling like myself please give my best to all
Rudy
Hi Lillian! How have you been? We have missed tennis in Hartford Regards

Miss Lillian French
Hartford Golf Club,
Hartford,
Conn.

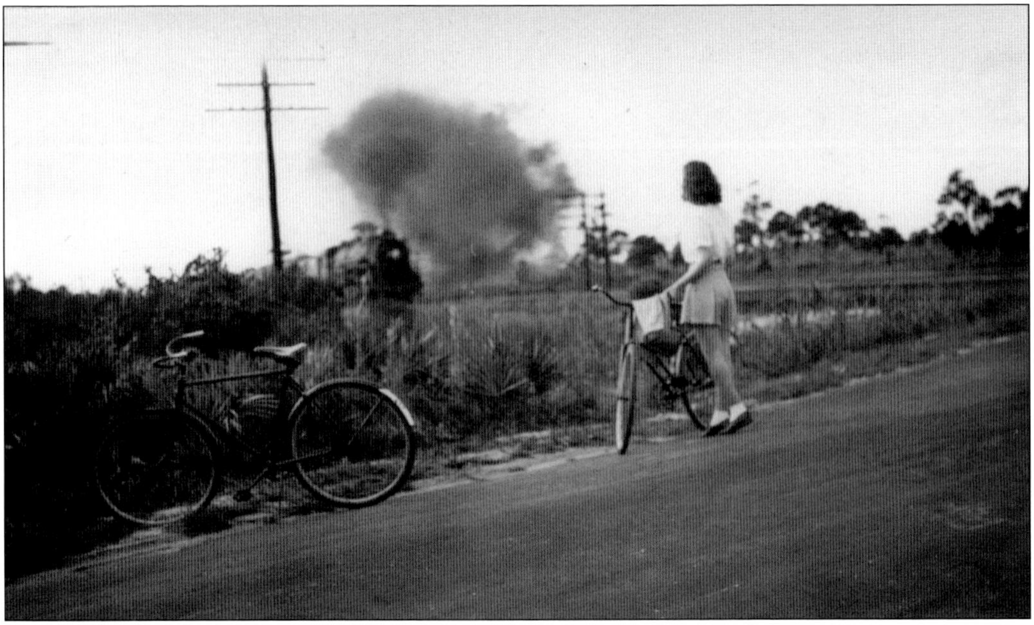

Pictured is Ione (Jensch) Maertz biking to Jenkins Beach in 1943 from Camp Murphy. This photograph is believed to have been taken by Ione's finance, Pfc. Robert J. Maertz, who was stationed at Camp Murphy (currently Jonathan Dickinson State Park). (Courtesy of the Martin County Historical Society.)

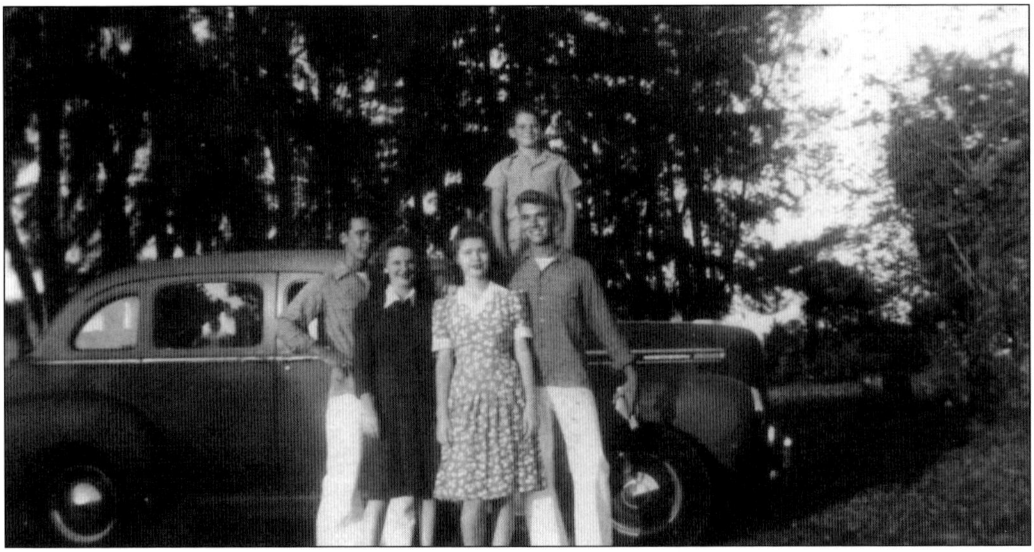

Pictured under the oaks at Camp Murphy are, from left to right, "Buddy," unidentified, Lillian Rudd, and Wayne Wells. The young man on the hood is unidentified. Many friendships were made during the war years between the local girls and young soldiers stationed at Camp Murphy. (Courtesy of the Martin County Historical Society.)

At right is a personal letter to Lillian Rudd from Donald Anthony Burroughs asking about parties, dancing, and friends. Lillian worked at Camp Murphy, which opened in 1942. It was the home of the Southern Signal Corps School during World War II and served as a US Army base for instruction in radar operation in the early part of the war. Below is an image from Lillian's photograph collection taken at a dance on base in 1944. (Both, courtesy of the Martin County Historical Society.)

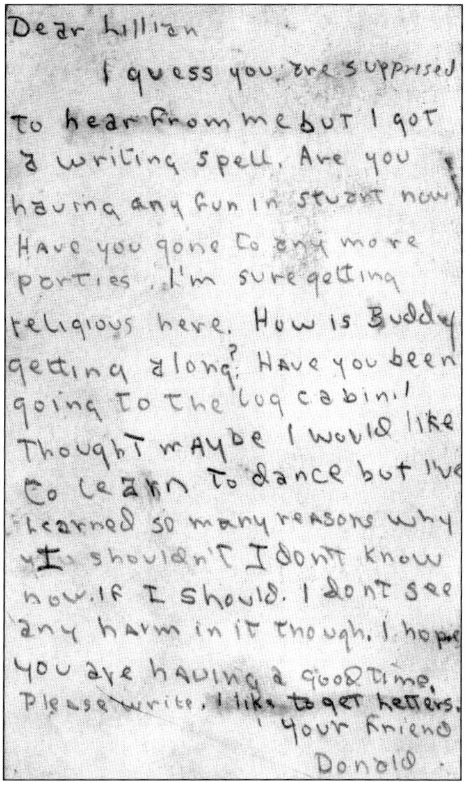

Dear Lillian

I guess you are supprised to hear from me but I got a writing spell. Are you having any fun in stuart now Have you gone to any more parties. I'm sure getting religious here. How is Buddy getting along? Have you been going to the log cabin. Thought maybe I would like to learn to dance but I've learned so many reasons why I shouldn't I dont know now if I should. I dont see any harm in it though. I hope you are having a good time. Please write, I like to get letters.

Your friend
Donald

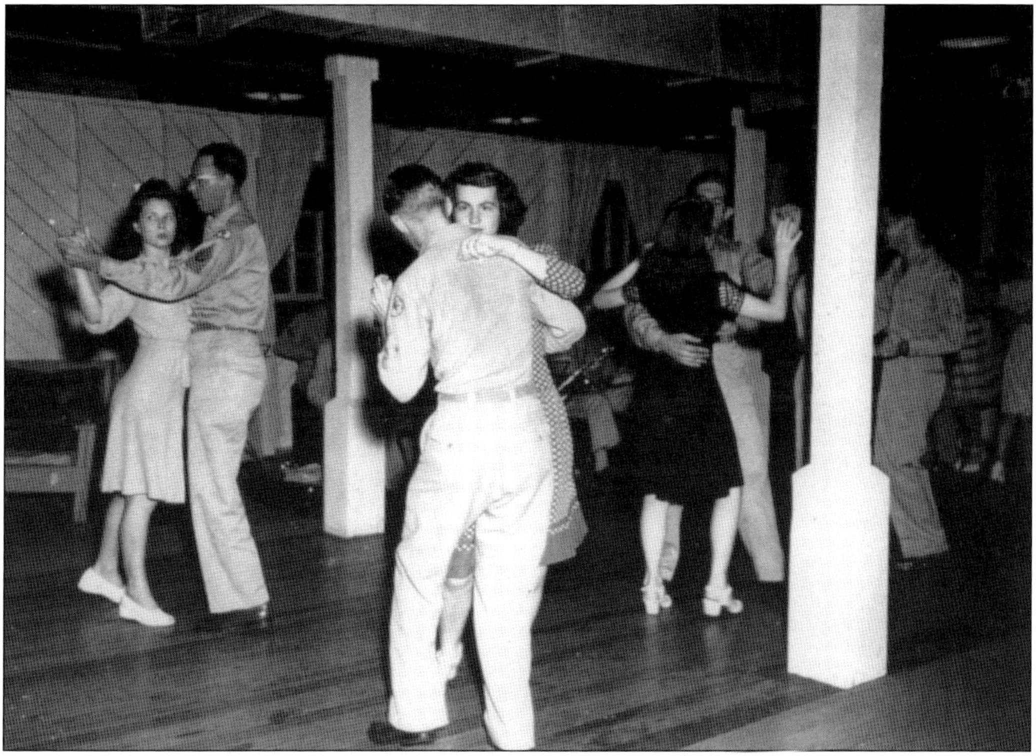

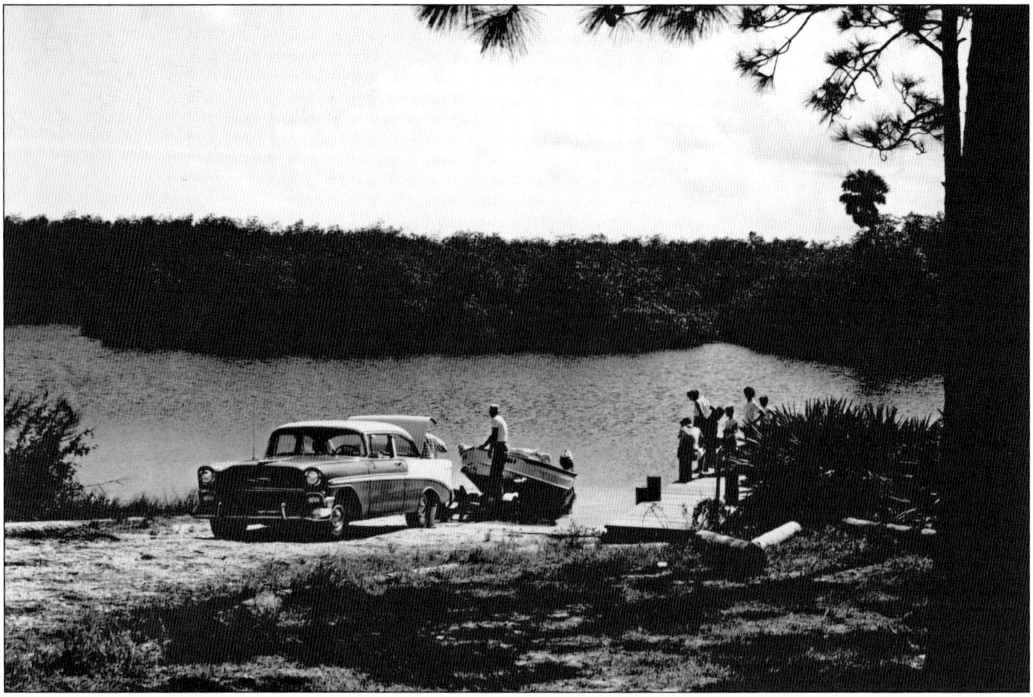

Camp Murphy was decommissioned in 1944 after only two years. The land was transferred to the State of Florida in 1947 and opened as Jonathan Dickinson State Park in 1950. The park offers many opportunities for boating and recreational swimming. Above is a photograph from 1960 showing the boat ramp. Below are children swimming in the Indian River Lagoon as part of the beach area in the park around 1970. (Both, courtesy of the State Archives of Florida.)

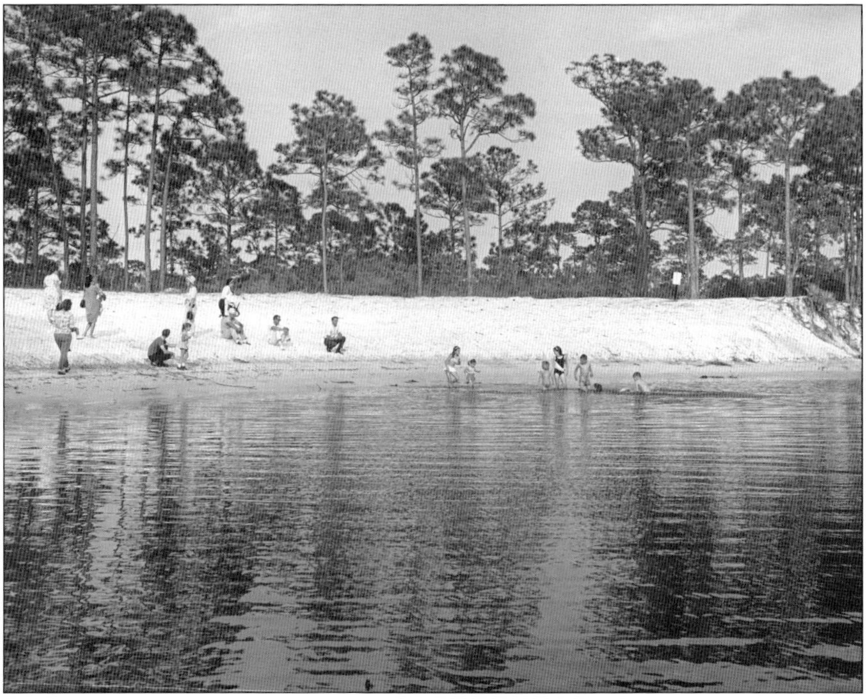

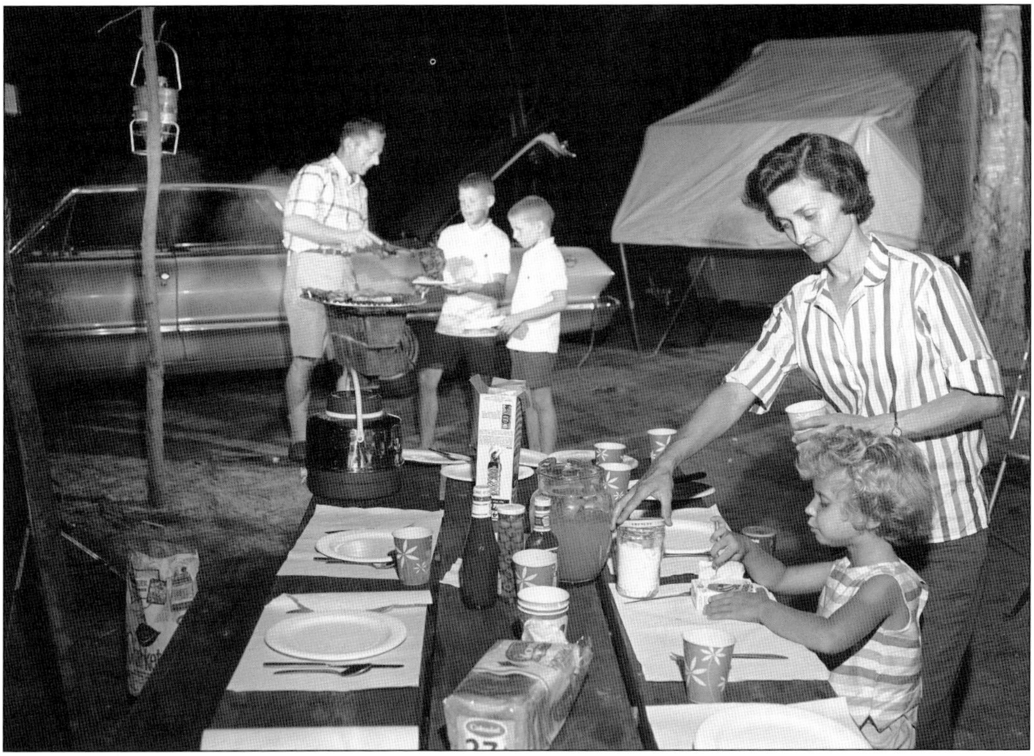

Camping is one of the most popular activities in the state park. Above is the Hackett family in the early 1960s preparing dinner at their campsite. Below is a group of park visitors enjoying a horseback ride through the park in 1970. (Both, courtesy of State Archives of Florida.)

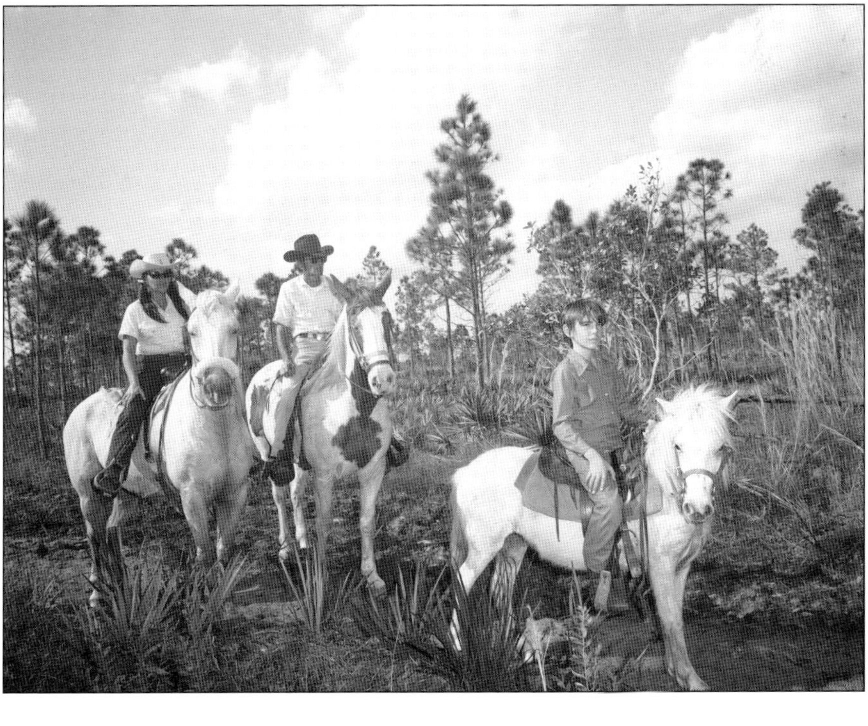

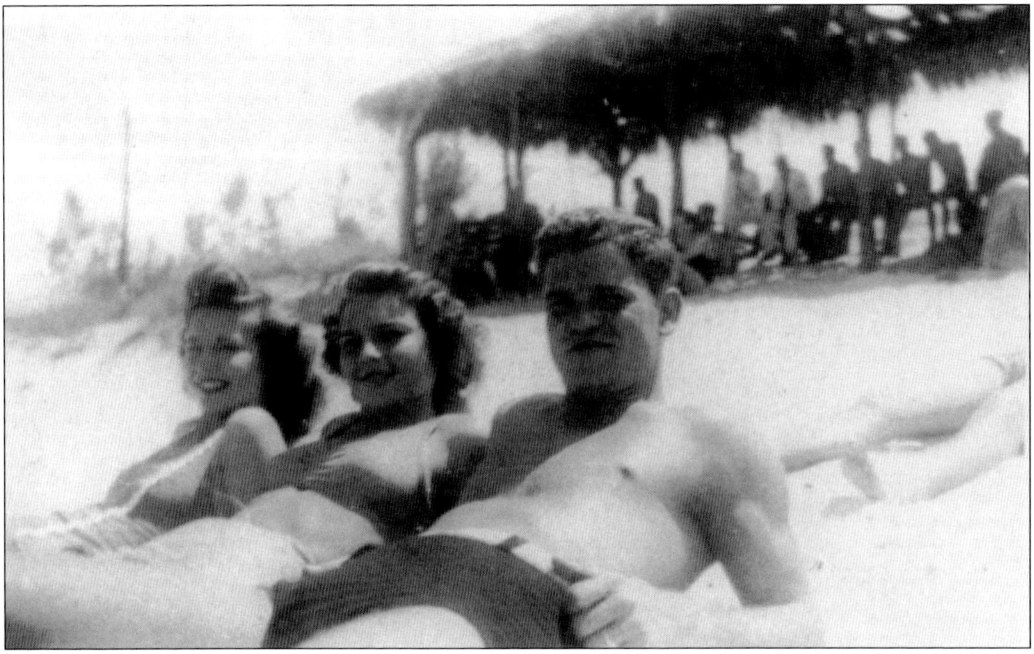

The beach continues to be a popular destination for residents and visitors alike. During the 1940s, many GIs, along with local residents, spent their free afternoons sunbathing. From left to right are Lillian Rudd, Emily, and a friend at Hobe Sound Beach in the 1940s. Below is an aerial view of Hobe Sound Beach in the late 1950s or early 1960s. The shelter roof is shingled rather than thatched. (Both, courtesy of the Martin County Historical Society.)

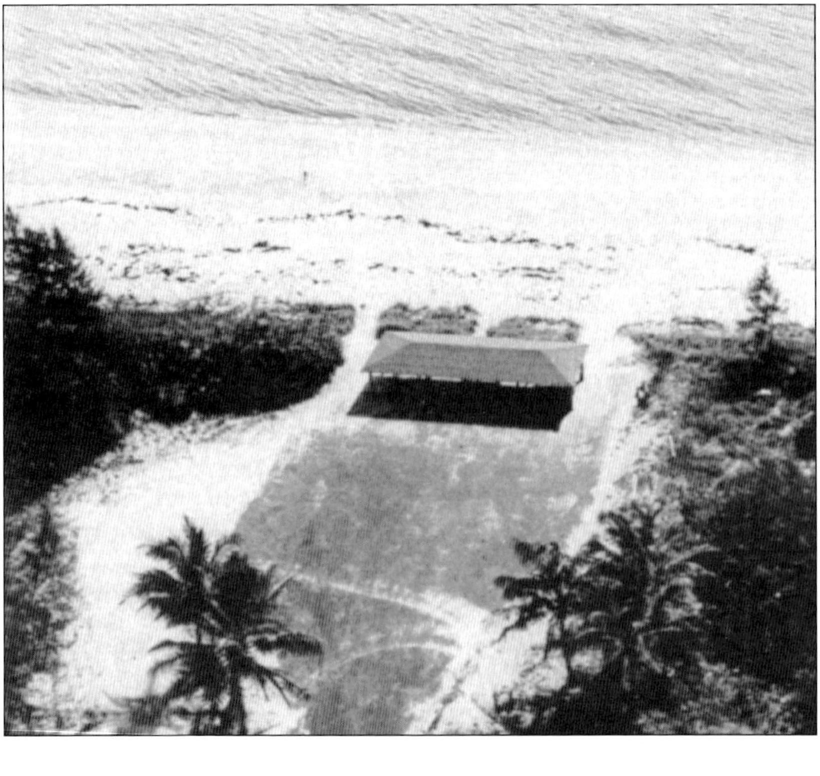

Six

Newsworthy and Notable

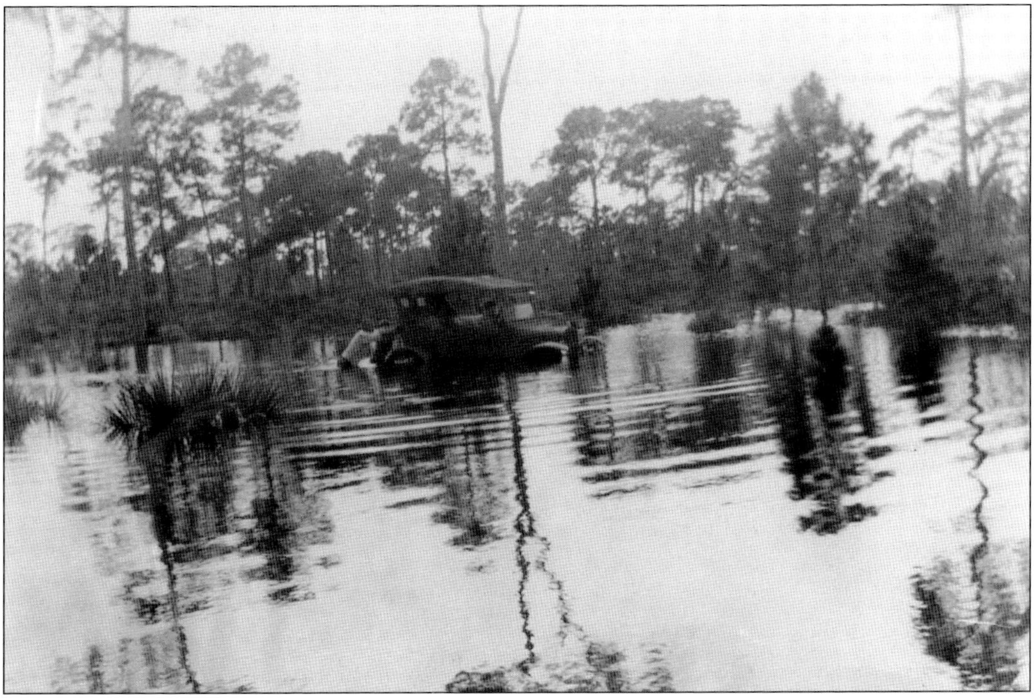

Throughout the history of Hobe Sound, there have seen several momentous occasions. These are just a few of the notable events. This photograph, taken after the hurricane of 1928, shows a car stranded in standing water. The Okeechobee hurricane is considered to be one of the most devastating events of its time, and Hobe Sound was not spared. (Courtesy of the Martin County Historical Society.)

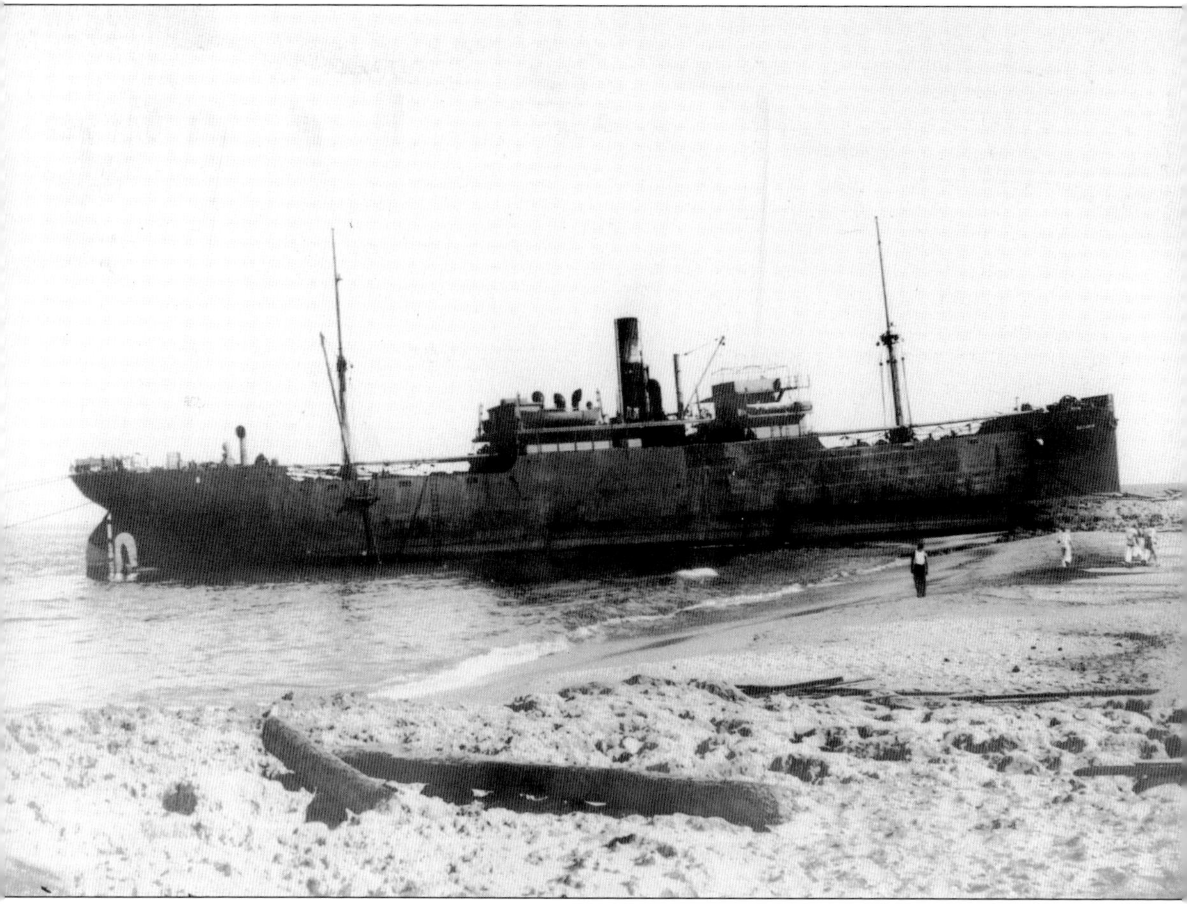

Hurricanes continue to be notable events in South Florida and Hobe Sound. Pictured is the tanker *Elizabeth*, which was driven to shore and beached in the 1928 hurricane. (Courtesy of the Library of Congress.)

On May 18, 1917, the Selective Service Act was passed, authorizing the president to temporarily increase the military of the United States. Approximately 24 million men registered for the draft (about 23 percent of the population in 1918). This is the registration card filled out by Malcolm Meacham, vice president of the First National Bank of Palm Beach and president of the Olympia Improvement Company. (Courtesy of the US Military Department, Malcolm Meacham, Library of Congress.)

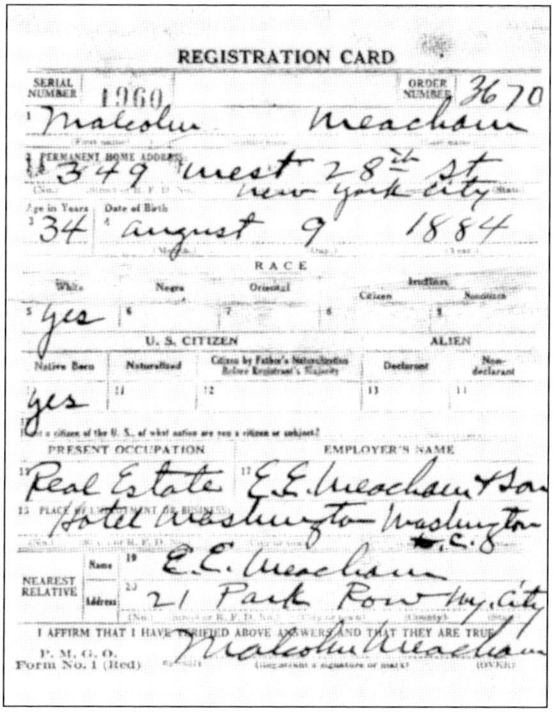

REGISTRATION CARD

SERIAL NUMBER 1960 ORDER NUMBER 3670

1 Malcolm Meacham

PERMANENT HOME ADDRESS
2 349 west 28th st new york city

Age in Years 3 34 Date of Birth 4 august 9 1884

RACE
White 5 yes | Negro 6 | Oriental 7 | Indian: Citizen 8 | Noncitizen 9

U. S. CITIZEN
Native Born 10 yes | Naturalized 11 | Citizen by Father's Naturalization Before Registrant's Majority 12

ALIEN
Declarant 13 | Non-declarant 14

15 If not a citizen of the U. S., of what nation are you a citizen or subject?

PRESENT OCCUPATION
16 Real Estate

EMPLOYER'S NAME
17 E.E. Meacham & Son

18 PLACE OF EMPLOYMENT OR BUSINESS
Hotel Washington Washington D.C.

NEAREST RELATIVE
Name 19 E.E. Meacham
Address 20 21 Park Row N.Y. City

I AFFIRM THAT I HAVE VERIFIED ABOVE ANSWERS AND THAT THEY ARE TRUE

Malcolm Meacham

P. M. G. O.
Form No. 1 (Red)

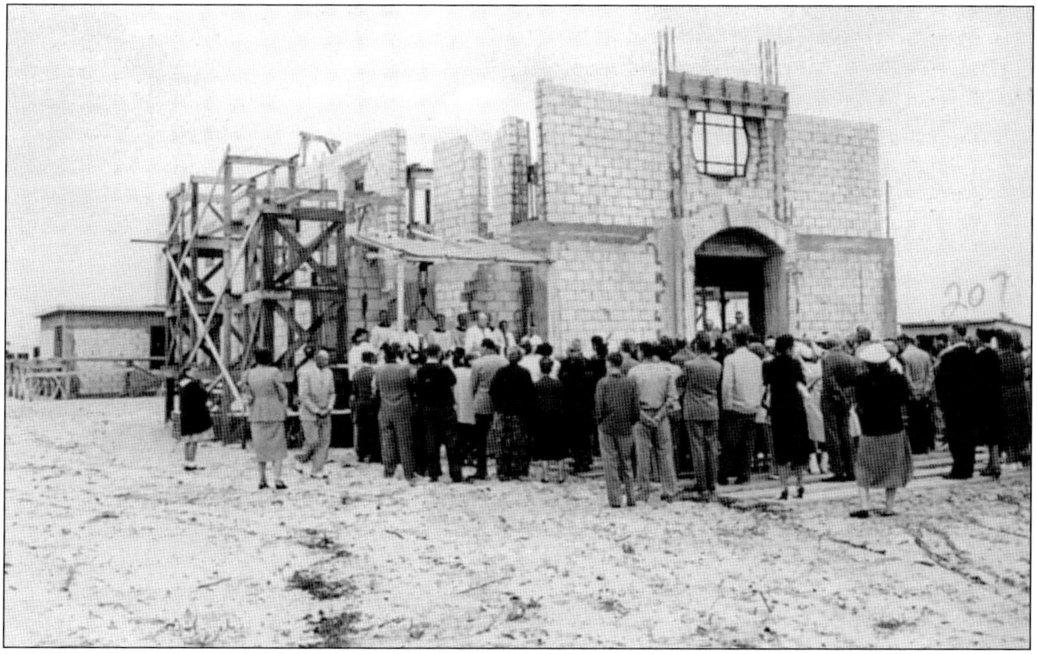

In the late 1940s and early 1950s, while most of the people wintering on Jupiter Island were Protestant, there was a contingent of Catholic families, including Mr. and Mrs. Christopher Devine. They envisioned the growth to come and offered to build a church to serve the few Catholics in the area and those yet to move to Hobe Sound. The ground breaking took place in 1952, and the attractive Spanish Revival St. Christopher Parish, with its impressive bell tower, became an instant landmark along US Route 1. (Courtesy of the Martin County Historical Society.)

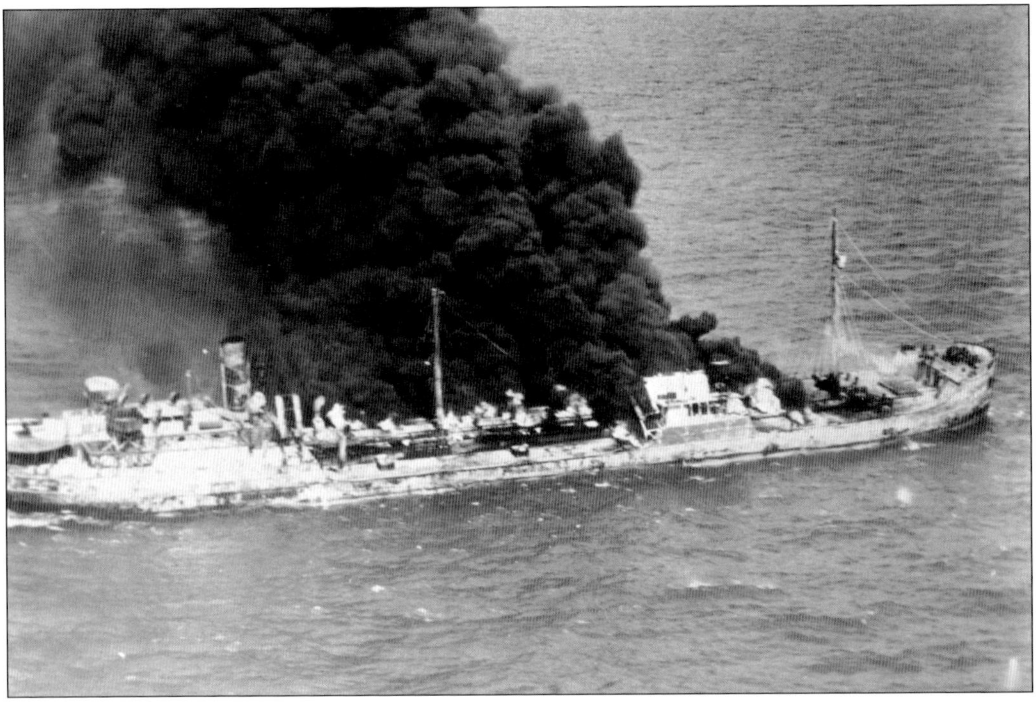

The tanker *Gulfland* burned off Hobe Sound for 53 days after colliding with the tanker *Gulf Belle* on October 21, 1943. Both were traveling without lights to avoid German submarines that hunted ships along the Florida coast. Eighty-eight men perished. Below is a photograph of the salvage operation. (Both, courtesy of State Archives of Florida.)

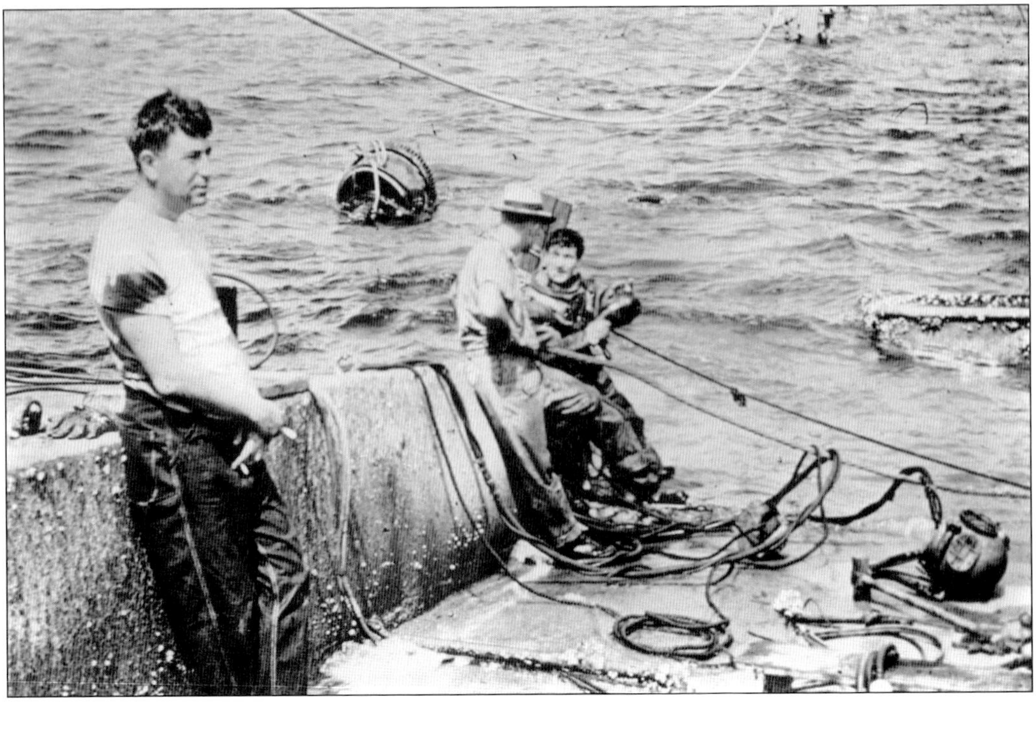

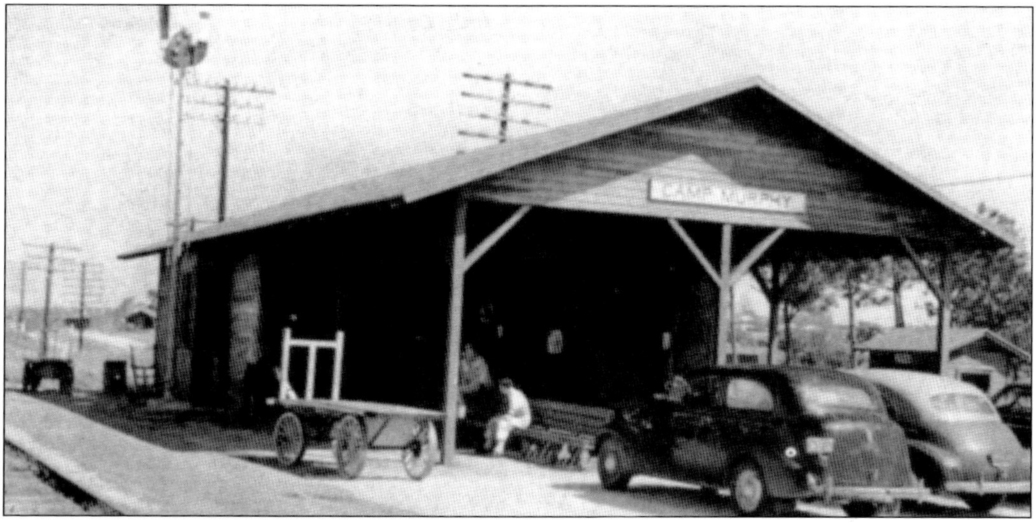

During the years of 1942–1944, Camp Murphy had its own train depot to streamline arrivals and departures of GIs and supplies to the base. Below is an access pass given to Ione Jensch to visit her fiancé, Robert J. Maertz, on January 6, 1944. (Both, courtesy of the Martin County Historical Society.)

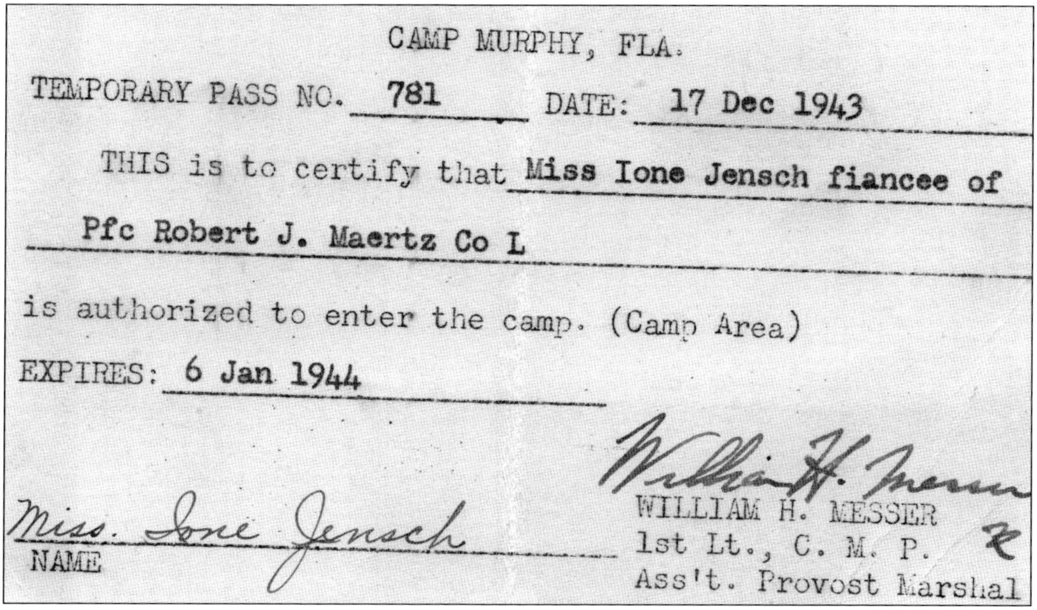

CAMP MURPHY, FLA.

TEMPORARY PASS NO. 781 DATE: 17 Dec 1943

THIS is to certify that Miss Ione Jensch fiancee of

Pfc Robert J. Maertz Co L

is authorized to enter the camp. (Camp Area)

EXPIRES: 6 Jan 1944

William H. Messer

Miss. Ione Jensch

NAME

WILLIAM H. MESSER
1st Lt., C. M. P.
Ass't. Provost Marshal

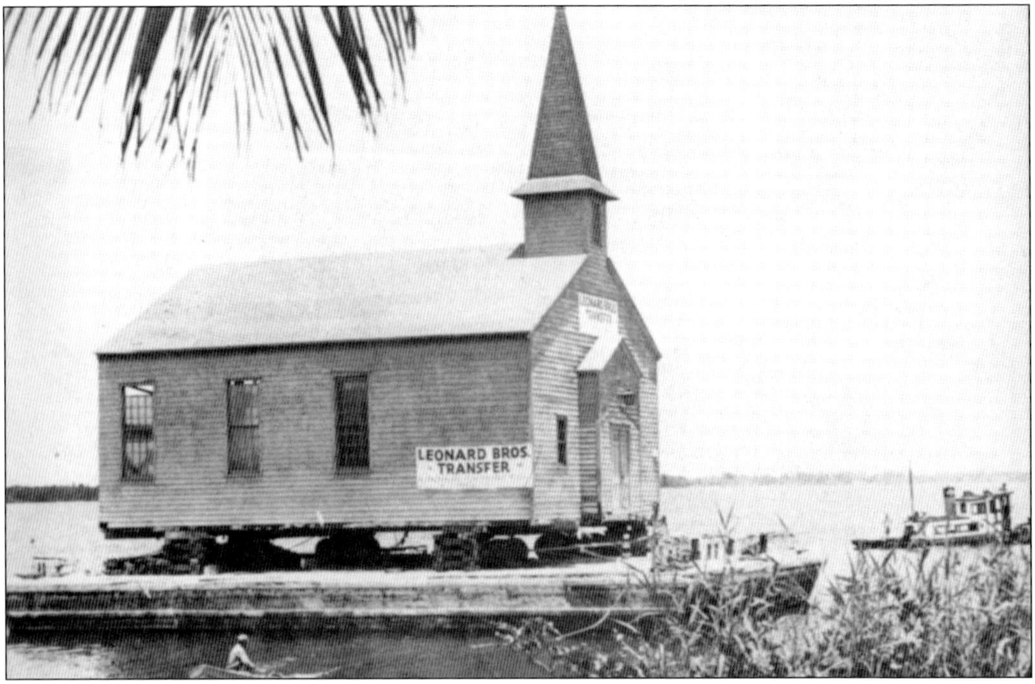

Camp Murphy and the Southern Signal School were closed by November 30, 1944. By 1946, the War Assets Administration authorized the disposal of property at the camp. One of the camp's two chapels was taken by barge up the Intracoastal Waterway and placed on East Fourth Street (East Ocean Boulevard) across from Memorial Park as a new home for St. Joseph's Catholic Church, dedicated in February 1948. (Unfortunately, a fire on February 2, 1960, caused by a faulty oil heater destroyed the church's interior.) (Courtesy of St. Joseph's Catholic Church.)

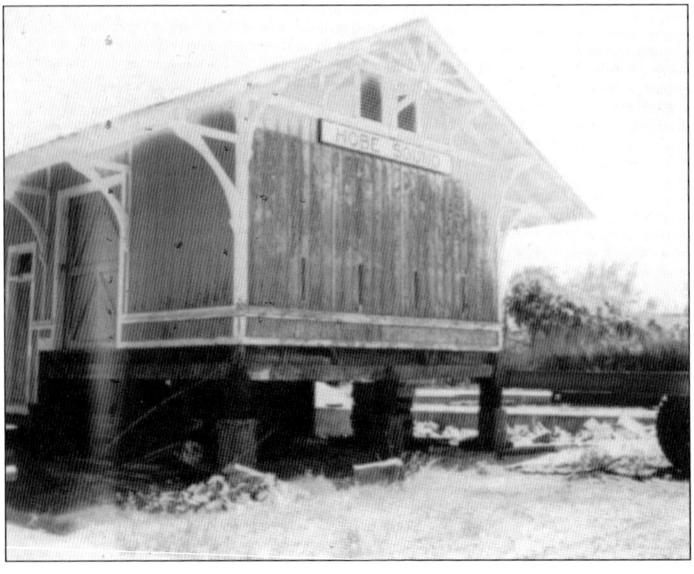

Most of the train depots in Martin County were constructed between 1894 and 1935. The hurricanes of 1926 and 1928, coupled with the real estate crash of 1926, were a big part of the railroads' demise along the Eastern Seaboard. Pictured is the moving of the Hobe Sound depot west on Bridge Road to the Polo Fields around 1965. (Courtesy of State Archives of Florida.)

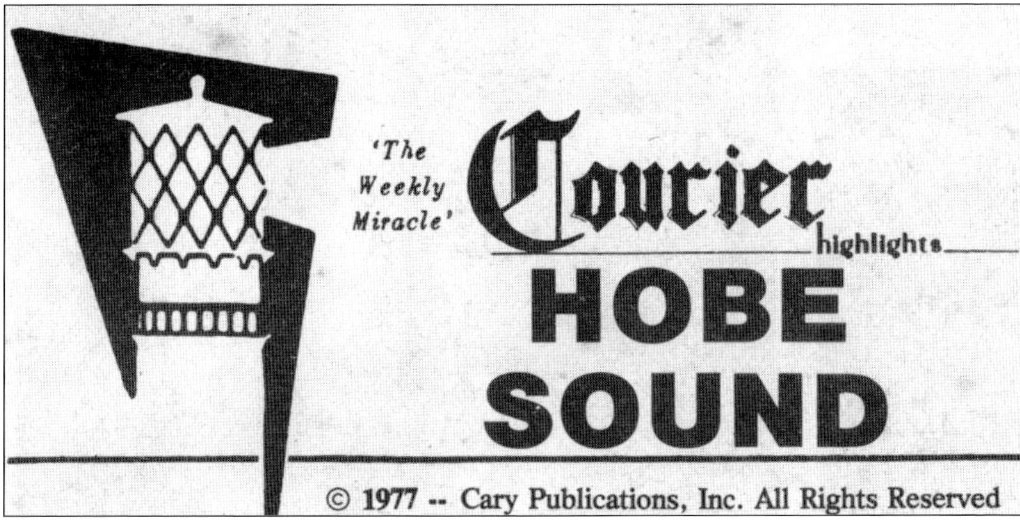

The local *Hobe Sound Courier* featured the goings-on around town each week. This is the masthead of an issue from 1977. (Courtesy of Sandra Thurlow.)

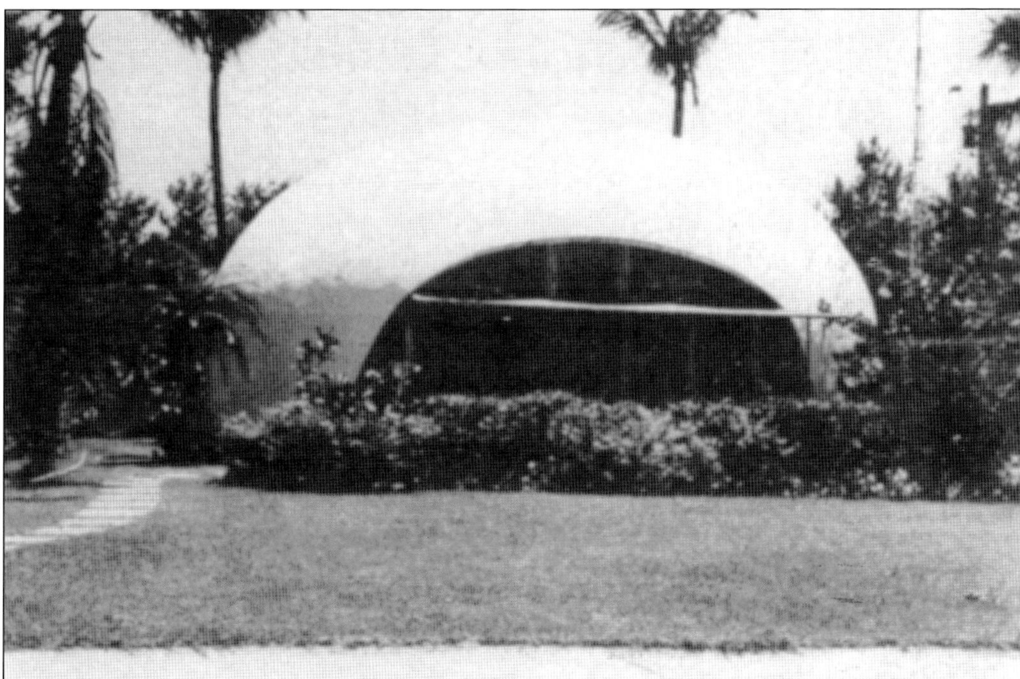

This is one of the famous bubble, or Airform, houses on Venus Street in the Zeus Park Neighborhood. Completed in 1954 by Airform, the bubble houses were designed by Eliot Noyes using the monolithic dome system developed by Wallace Neff. The original interiors consisted of a bathroom and open concept living, dining, and kitchen area and were only 569 square feet with a loft-style, raised sleeping space above. They were built to sell for $6,500. Shortly after their completion, it was stated that more than 3,000 people had toured the newly constructed bubble houses. The nearby Olympia School even closed early one afternoon so that its students could tour them. (Courtesy of Sandra Thurlow.)

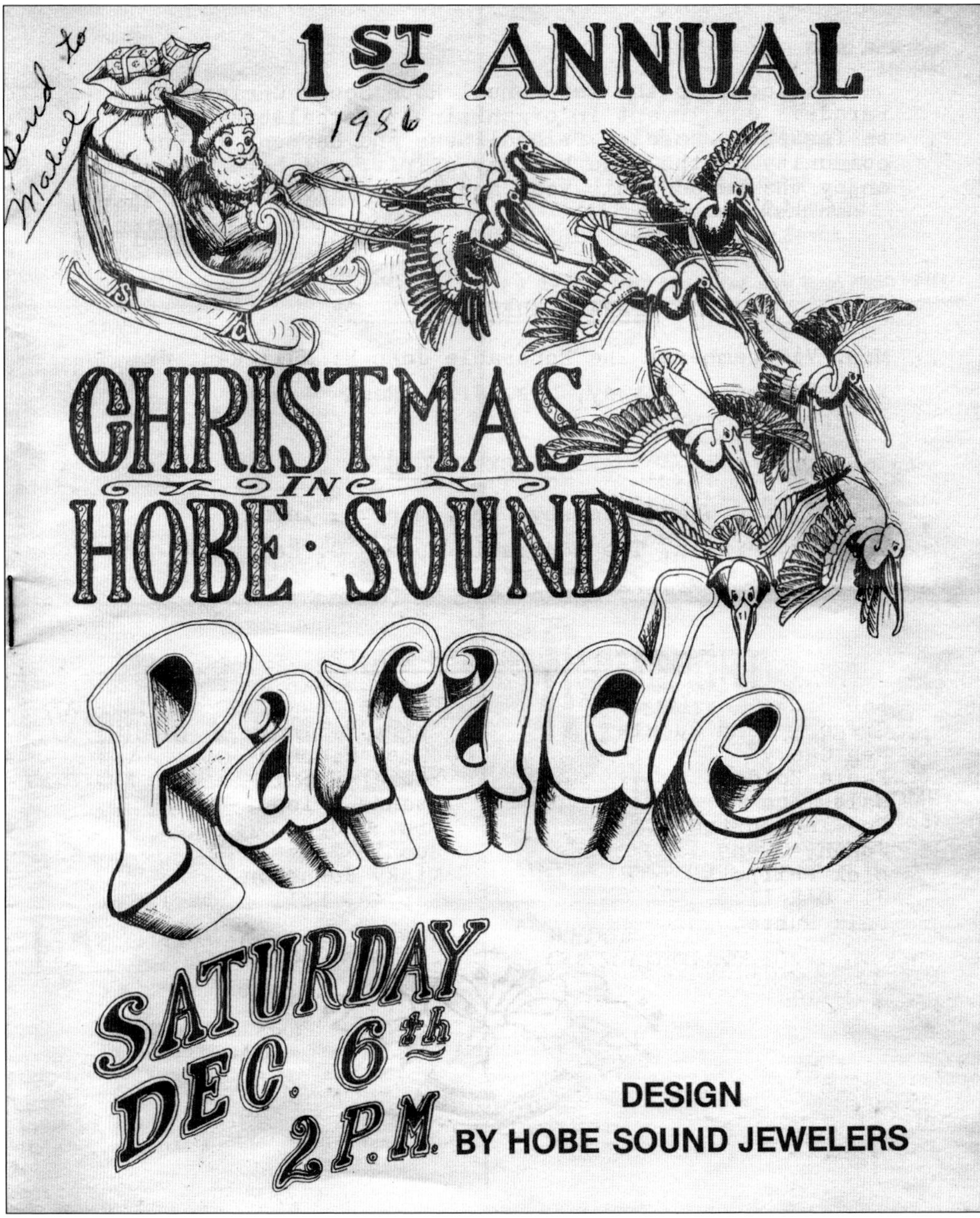

The Hobe Sound Christmas parade is a treasured event that generally happens on the first Saturday of December. It began in 1986. Pictured is the original bulletin announcing the parade to the community. It is attended by residents and visitors alike to usher in the holiday season. (Courtesy of Sandra Thurlow.)

Joseph Verner Reed (1902–1973) and Permelia Pryor Reed (1906–1994) were responsible in part for the Hobe Sound National Wildlife Refuge, the Hobe Sound Nature Center, the Blowing Rocks Preserve, Sand Hill Preserve, Harbor Island, and Ficus Alley, a 60-year-old stand of towering ficus trees. They were instrumental in founding the Hobe Sound Community Chest, which provides support to civic and charitable organizations. The Reeds donated land for a community center, churches, and schools. Their son Nathanial Reed wrote the history book *A Different Vision, The History of The Hobe Sound Company and The Jupiter Island Club*, published in January 2010. The story of Jupiter Island and Hobe Sound would be incomplete without mentioning the importance of the Reed family to this community. (Courtesy of M&K Publishing.)

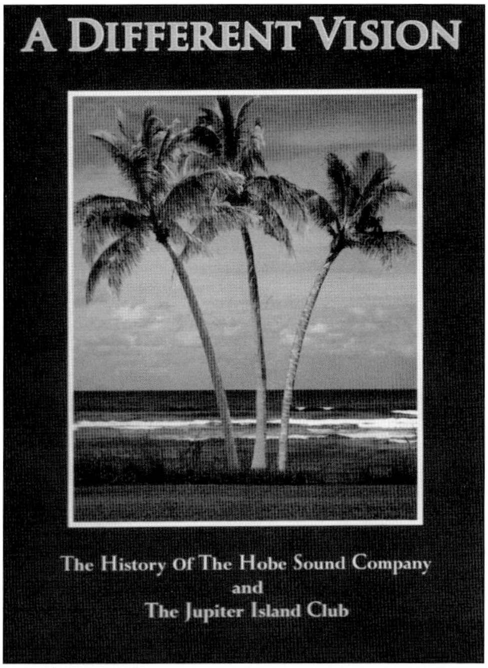

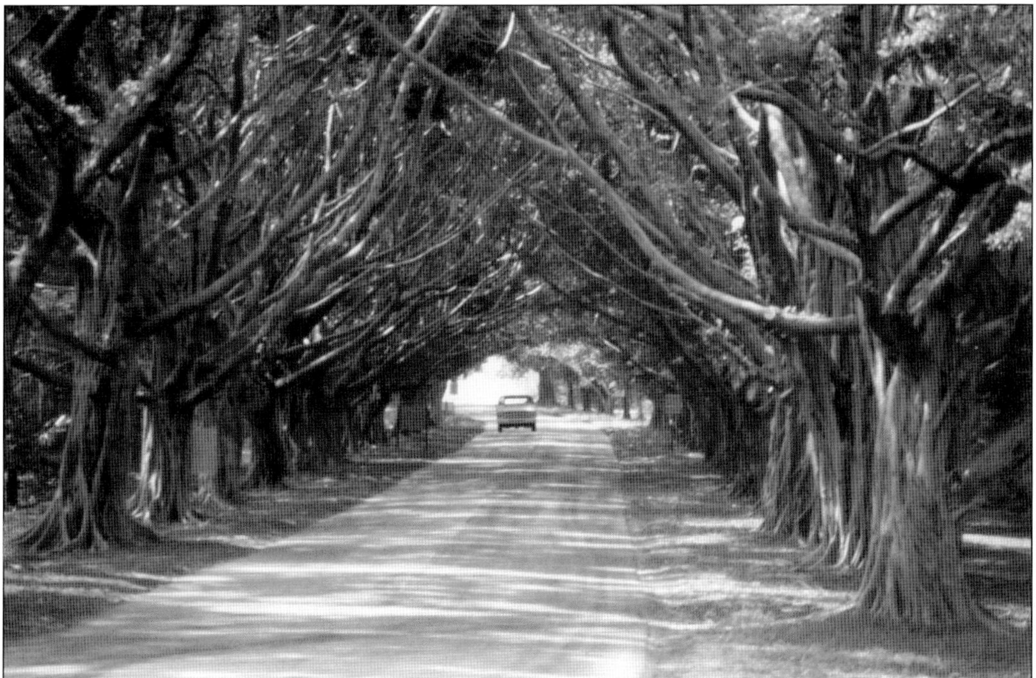

Bridge Road on Jupiter Island is also dubbed "the Tunnel of Trees," and driving through this natural tunnel is about as magical as it sounds. While it is not an extremely long drive by any means, it is a beautiful road to drive, bike ride, or walk along the path. Light filters in through the banyons, and it is a perfect backdrop for photographs. It is quite famous and loved by visitors and locals alike. The Tunnel of Trees was a vision of Permilia Reed, and it is to her that Hobe Sound residents owe thanks for this treasured gem. (Courtesy of Florida State Archives.)

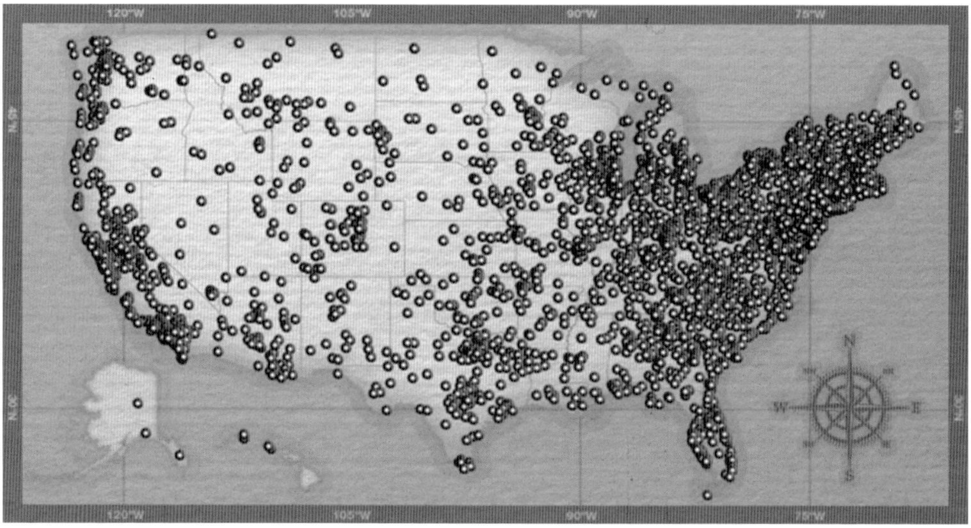